Greater Milwaukee's Growing Pains, 1950 – 2000: An Insider's View

T0164330

© 2001

ISBN Number 0-938076-16-7

Library of Congress Card Catalog Number 2001135458

Milwaukee County Historical Society
910 North Old World Third Street
Milwaukee, WI 53203

Printed in the United States of America
Burton & Mayer, Inc.
Brookfield, WI

Greater Milwaukee's Growing Pains, 1950 – 2000: An Insider's View

By
Richard W. Cutler

Published by
The Milwaukee County Historical Society

Sponsored by
**The Lynde and Harry Bradley Foundation
The Leslie T. Bruhnke Fund,
Greater Milwaukee Foundation**

2001

Table of Contents

Foreword

From a number of different perspectives, that of a political scientist, historian, educator, or citizen, one can only express great appreciation when a key figure in public affairs chooses to share his experiences. Too often the complex elements of decisions central to community life are shrouded in mystery and misinformation. It is indeed rare when a participant in such decisions has both the ability and inclination to write a compelling blend of local political history and autobiographical memoir: *Greater Milwaukee's Growing Pains, 1950-2000: An Insider's View* is a noteworthy example.

Richard Cutler's active role in a broad spectrum of areas allows us to see very clearly the interconnectedness of local issues and that what occurs in one issue area has repercussions in others. Similarly, events in the past can have considerable impact on current concerns. It is this historical context that I wish to briefly amplify for the events that are the focus of this book.

Milwaukee area citizens have long had the general expectation that the functions of local government will be carried out in an honest and effective manner. While some might argue that stability and what appear to be interminable delays in rendering policy decisions also characterize the execution of such functions, few would accuse the system of being corrupt and riddled with rampant criminality. In fact, past local government operations were characterized by corruption and criminality and to such a degree that it provided the impetus for critical changes in how public affairs were to be accomplished in Milwaukee.

By the end of the Nineteenth Century conditions were so bad that "throwing the rascals out" became the order of the day. As a rule, one political party became the villain of the day; not so here during this period. Republicans controlled the county and Democrats the central city, with both refusing second billing in bad government. In the case of Milwaukee the alternative became the local Socialist Party and its emphasis on efficient and effective government rather than the vaguer concepts of socialist dogma. The narrowly drawn focus on day-to-day governmental activities resonated with those seeking reforms and was embraced with great enthusiasm by them.

Coupled with these monumental changes was a gradual decline in economic conditions that enhanced the ability of Milwaukee governments to attract and retain outstanding public administrators to establish and maintain what became a long standing reputation for "good government." Throughout this book such individuals will make their appearance – and one applauds Mr. Cutler for giving them much deserved recognition. Consequently, *Greater Milwaukee's Growing Pains, 1950-2000: An Insider's View* can focus on how honest alternative courses of action were reconciled and how public affairs allowed talented and hardworking private citizens to willingly become involved in a most worthwhile experience. Without such involvement the Milwaukee area would have been deprived of much of the talent that has provided a positive foundation for our future.

> Donald B. Vogel
> Professor Emeritus
> University of Wisconsin Milwaukee

Preface

Writing this book was not originally my idea. A friend suggested it. Many times. He was John Dahlberg of Brookfield, a Harvard MBA, convivial skiing companion, theater lover, and veteran of Normandy and the Battle of the Bulge. John served Milwaukee in many civic roles, such as president of the Friends of the Museum, but he is most remembered for encouraging others to lift their efforts to a higher level and accomplish more than they thought they could. He was a born mentor. Between 1993 and 1997, when he died, he patiently edited over six hundred pages of two memoirs of mine. One described growing up during the Depression; the other, my work in espionage during the last year of the hot war and first of the cold war. In that editing role, John amazed me – for he was a businessman by occupation – by helpfully quoting rules for better writing by the legendary editor of the *New Yorker,* Harold Ross.

When the second memoir was nearly completed in 1997, John told me that I must write this book, which, as he put it, would complete a trilogy of memoirs: growing up, war service, civic career. He reasoned that I had participated in many Milwaukee area events containing tales to be told. He spoke of numerous civic happenings in which I had been involved. One led to another, or to a legal assignment in the same field. And then back again. It was as if a magic carpet whisked me off to a new place each time I started to settle down.

My community roles started with membership on the Village of Fox Point Planning Commission in 1952. That propelled me into a battle between four municipalities to annex land bordering Fox Point. Repeated newspaper stories about the annexation war caused Town of Brookfield residents twenty-five miles away to ask me to incorporate their area as a new city. I did, becoming City Attorney for six years – which gave me an early learning experience. The city was new and growing. It faced the classic problems of rapid growth.

To learn more about how a growing city should, and could, cope with land use problems, I wrote several articles for the *Wisconsin Law Review*. Two bore descriptive titles that caught the attention of the State Legislature, the Wisconsin Supreme Court, and the top appellate court in New York. They were: *Characteristics of Land Required for the Incorporation or Expansion of Municipalities* (1958) and *Legal and Illegal Methods of Controlling Community Growth on the Urban Fringe* (1961). In 1967, the University of Wisconsin Press published my first book, *Zoning Law and Practice in Wisconsin.*

Shaping municipal boundaries and advising municipalities and citizens on how to control growth rapidly became my specialty. Over many years I represented governments or residents in annexation, incorporation, zoning, and environmental disputes in about half of Wisconsin's seventy-one counties.

Several times I was asked to serve on study committees appointed by the Governor or Legislature to seek better remedies for land use problems. Legislative committee efforts in 1959 and 1969 sought drastically to improve municipal incorporation and annexation laws. As early as 1957, Governor Vernon Thompson appointed me to the Metropolitan Study Commission, which the Legislature had asked to recommend how to make local governments within Milwaukee County more effective and, above all, how to lessen the inter-municipal fighting of the 1950s. I served as chairman of its Land Use and Zoning Committee, which recommended the creation of the Southeastern Wisconsin Regional Planning Commission (SEWRPC).

A second governor, Gaylord Nelson, and three later governors appointed me to serve continuously on SEWRPC from 1960 through 1984. In turn, SEWRPC appointed me to chair six advisory committees, two of these in the 1990s after my formal role as a commissioner had ended. Advisory committees were a key to developing SEWRPC recommendations that the public and private sectors would carry out. Committees consisted of knowledgeable persons who represented the diverse, often conflicting interests concerned with a specific problem. They included those causing a problem, its victims, and those with the power and potential desire to contribute to solutions. One committee addressed the deadlock over further freeway construction (1977); another, flooding, pollution, and other growing problems in the Milwaukee River Watershed (1964-1971). In the early 1990s, two advisory committees tried to push Governor Tommy Thompson's administration into creating a regional transportation authority and another to use state power to reduce, or at least not encourage, further urban sprawl.

Serving on the Milwaukee River Watershed Committee enabled me to work with several distinguished public officials. Later their recommendations indirectly led me and my law firm to serve as outside lawyers for the Milwaukee Metropolitan Sewerage District. I became its lead counsel in the Lake Michigan Water Pollution lawsuit started by the State of Illinois. A very able legal team and I were asked to undo a drastic judgment by a lower federal court in Chicago which had ordered Milwaukee to build sewer improvements costing a billion dollars more than those already required by a Wisconsin state court. We persuaded the United States Supreme Court in 1981 to review and reverse the draconian order. That wasn't easy. The Carter administration joined Illinois and Michigan in opposing us.

While most of my civic activities led to another role in the same field, at least two quite different but significant consequences resulted for me. One arose out of my experience as Brookfield City Attorney. I watched developers propose a rash of subdivisions. Subdividing looked easy, so I thought I would try my hand at actual land development. I did and still do.

The other resulted from my energetic service on the Metropolitan Study Commission, which caught the eye of a banker. He recommended me to one of his customers, Bud Selig, for legal help in creating the Milwaukee Brewers and acquiring a baseball franchise. I served the Brewers nine exciting years, 1964 to 1973. Highlights of those years included battles that succeeded in overcoming both American League resistance and court orders prohibiting the transfer of the Seattle Pilots to Milwaukee.

John Dahlberg was thinking of my Brewer and sewer activities when he repeatedly urged me to describe them in this book. After he died in 1997, Kurt W. Bauer became the gadfly constantly prodding me. Before his retirement, Bauer had been a land-use planner and civil engineer who served as executive director of the seven county South-eastern Wisconsin Regional Planning Commission for thirty-five years. A scholarly man, Bauer is also an all-consuming history buff. He contended that I, as a participant, should extract facts and opinions from players on both sides of the complex freeway and water pollution battles, who are aging as rapidly as I am. Otherwise, he said, three quarters of the facts would be lost. He backed up his request by providing me with invaluable research and by extensively correcting and enlarging multiple drafts of chapters on the freeways and water pollution.

Writing brought unexpected concerns and pleasures. One disappointment came when I gradually recognized that recounting the very recent past would necessarily lack historical perspective; it would read more like current events. Still, a writer has to start recording even the most recent past. My pleasantest surprise was finding that unearthing previously unknown facts, on deeper reflection, sometimes modified or reversed my earlier opinions. Perhaps a favorite maxim of Wisconsin's greatest naturalist, Aldo Leopold, who quotes a sage from 2000 years ago, explains best why that happened. Leopold wrote:

> It is doubted whether a man ever brings his faculties to bear with their full force on a subject until he has written on it.

CICERO

Richard Cutler, Fox Point Village Hall, 1993.
(*Photograph courtesy of* CNI Newspapers)

Part One

Milwaukee in Mid-Century:
The Starting Point

Chapter 1

Coming to Milwaukee in 1949

Poor eyesight kept me out of military service – at least for more than a year after Pearl Harbor. Instead, I moved to Washington in 1942 to perform economic intelligence for the Board of Economic Warfare. In 1943 the Army Air Force inducted and trained me to be a Combat Intelligence Officer for the B-29 bombing of Japan. On the hour of my departure for the Pacific in July 1944, the Joint Chiefs of Staff, by a fluke, transferred me to America's new espionage agency, the Office of Strategic Services (OSS). OSS had requested the Air Force to release to OSS eleven Pacific-bound lieutenants who spoke European languages for service in Europe. I was one of them. I spoke French and Spanish. The Air Force refused my release but the Joint Chiefs overruled them.

I worked for OSS, and its successor which merged into the CIA, from 1944 to late 1946, first in counter-espionage in London against Hitler and then in Wiesbaden and Berlin against Stalin. Berlin quickly became the spy capital of the world. I was lucky to serve there as chief of counter-espionage operations against the Soviet intelligence services. My successive bosses in Berlin were Allen Dulles and Richard Helms, who later became the most famous and ablest of the Directors of the Central Intelligence Agency.

My Berlin job was more than cloak and dagger. I read with fascination secret reports on the actions of all powers affecting occupied Germany, Europe, and – above all – the rapidly escalating Cold War. My greatest fortune in Berlin was meeting my future wife, Elizabeth

2

Fitzgerald of Milwaukee. She was then on the American prosecution staff at the Nuremberg trial of the top twenty-three Nazis, including Hermann Goering. She flew to Berlin to obtain evidence from a British Admiral against a top Nazi. Through a friend she borrowed my jeep to travel around the bombed-out city.

Returning to the States in late 1946, I resumed practicing law in New York. I had grown up in Westport, Connecticut, a New York suburb forty-two miles from Times Square. After graduating from Yale College in 1938 and Yale Law School in 1941, I worked briefly for General "Wild Bill" Donovan's Wall Street law firm. In 1946 I became an attorney for the Criminal Branch of the Legal Aid Society in order to obtain cross-examination training. I represented defendants, including members of Manhattan's West Side gangs, the sort who were glamorized in the musical *West Side Story*. Then I became a trial attorney for RCA Communications, Inc., the international wireless subsidiary of the Radio Corporation of America. In 1947 Elizabeth and I were married and lived in New York City. Somewhat later I turned down an offer to head the newly created Central Intelligence Agency operations for all of Scandinavia. The assignment included sending spies across the Baltic into the Soviet Union. That our spies were all captured and executed, I learned forty years later. Instead of Stockholm, Liz and I moved in 1949 to more tranquil Milwaukee, her home town.

Milwaukee attracted us as a fine community in which to raise a family. It was large enough to offer me stimulating legal cases, yet small enough to permit both of us to engage in civic activities that could have an impact on our community and our lives.

I joined a small law firm, James D. Porter and Associates, whose major client, A. O. Smith Corporation, generated significant challenges. One of these came along during the Korean War when A. O. Smith could not obtain enough steel to fill Chevrolet's orders for automotive frames. An enterprising Texas scrap dealer dug up unexploded American Air Force bomb shells in Manila, removed their explosive contents, and shipped them by freighter to Seattle for conversion to scrap in a blast furnace. The scrap was then to go by rail to Milwaukee for shaping into automobile frames – a sort of return trip, because the shell casings, we believed, had probably been manufactured originally by A. O. Smith for the Air Force in World War II. Unfortunately,

3

traces of TNT remained in a few shells. The blast furnace's owner prudently refused to accept any shells for fear one might explode in the 2,200-degree heat. Litigation followed while the freighter, filled with its controversial cargo, hugged the dock. A. O. Smith asked several of us to go to Seattle to resolve the problem, and, if possible, save the desperately needed steel. We hired a retired Navy ordnance captain who said he knew a way to eliminate the TNT by carefully blow-torching it out, shell by shell. An explosion would not occur, he assured us, provided the worker inserted the blow torch into the shell in such a way as to leave a wide space for air to enter the shell while he slowly burned out the dynamite traces. No confinement, no explosion, he said. That laborious process cleansed many shells and reclaimed much steel until – after we had returned to Milwaukee – one shell did blow up. Three workmen were killed. The Mayor of Seattle immediately ordered the freighter out of the harbor. That tragedy shocked us all and made our wives even more apprehensive about the danger to which we had been exposed. Naturally, the souvenir artillery shell I brought into our home did not stay there long.

Having settled in Milwaukee, I promptly undertook a crash course to learn all I could about my new home town. Of course Elizabeth's help was invaluable. She had numerous friends, rose quickly to leadership positions in several organizations, and knew many business and civic leaders in her own right as well as through her father, Edmund Fitzgerald, a warm, indefatigable, effective community leader. He was also president of Northwestern Mutual Life Insurance Company.

As challenging as the law work was in my new home city, finding useful civic activities was easier than in giant New York City. Milwaukee in 1949 offered many possible outlets for my extracurricular interests. Foreign affairs was my passion. I promptly joined the Milwaukee branch of the New York-based Foreign Policy Association and rose to become its chairman within two years. The association sought to educate the public about foreign affairs through lectures and radio broadcasts by domestic and foreign leaders. One guest speaker, Hector McNeil, a rising star in the British Labor party with reputed aspirations to become Prime Minister, detected my dormant fantasy about pursuing a political career. While visiting my home, he suggested that I should run for Congress before age forty.

However, seeking political office was not in the cards. I was too independent.

The glamour of rubbing shoulders with prominent political leaders such as a potential Prime Minister faded as I gradually became aware that I could never hope to influence foreign policy through a mere discussion group. However, in another field, land-use planning, I could have more impact. My interest in this topic was shaped by my having grown up as the son of a architect who was very active in civic affairs. Westport, Connecticut was a New York suburb on the north shore of Long Island Sound. It included Wall Street lawyers and Madison Avenue advertising executives, for some of whom my architect-father designed impressive homes. Westport was also well known for its colony of prominent artists and writers. A *New Yorker* magazine article in 1997 suggested that Westport in the 1920s was the setting for F. Scott Fitzgerald's *Great Gatsby* because the book's landscapes resembled what Fitzgerald could have seen from his nearby summer home. Moreover, many wild parties occurred in Westport in the roaring twenties, which my father and mother only heard about. Their interests were more civic than social. Both took part in Westport's community affairs, he as its best known architect and long-time chairman of the Town Zoning and Planning Commission. My parents were role models. Mother served for many years as president of both the local garden club and the New England Wildflower Society. Mother also wrote a newspaper column, "Lost Landmarks," delving deep into local history all the way back to the first settlers arriving in 1635. She sometimes received research help from Samuel Morison, a famous Harvard professor of history. My father drafted Westport's first zoning ordinance seeking to preserve its residential character and prevent building in unsuitable places, such as seemingly dry stream beds. He fought vigorously against developers' frequent efforts to weaken zoning.

In 1951, Edmund B. Shea, a distinguished lawyer and former president of the Village of Fox Point, where Liz and I made our home, asked me to record the minutes of the Fox Point Planning commission, a favorite of his. Within two years I became a voting member and ended up serving on the commission for the next forty-one years. Membership on the Fox Point Planning Commission unexpectedly became the springboard for my energetic participation in the turbulent municipal boundary wars of the l950s. By one of those strange quirks of fate, these disputes projected me rapidly into high level efforts in Milwaukee and Madison to curb the resulting balkanization of metropolitan Milwaukee.

As a newcomer from New York, I was surprised to see babushkas covering the heads of women shoppers on Wisconsin Avenue and was immediately impressed by Milwaukee's warmth, informality, and multi-ethnic heritage. New acquaintances quickly greeted each other on a first-name basis. Milwaukee papers diagrammed Green Bay Packers plays on the front page, an inconceivable layout in the staid *New York Times*. Welcome to the Midwest! Prominent manufacturing companies carried German names, like Harnischfeger, Heil, and Falk; German pronunciation and phrases lingered in the local language; Burleigh Street was pronounced "Burl I" as if written in German, not "Burl – EE" as in England where the name originated; shoppers went not "to," but "by" Schuster's (from the German "bei"), Milwaukee's popular old-time department store on North 3rd Street. The red brick mansions of the Uihlein and Pabst beer barons on West Wisconsin Avenue and North Lake Drive could have stood in the prewar suburbs of Berlin or Hamburg. Milwaukee's tallest building, the graceful 330 foot city hall, loomed like the Rathaus in Munich, though its true model was Flemish.

Milwaukee's image has always varied according to the viewer. To outsiders, Milwaukee was America's beer city in the 1950s. It boasted five breweries, Schlitz ("the beer that made Milwaukee famous"), until 1953 the largest in the nation, plus Pabst, Miller, Blatz, and Gettleman. (Only Miller survived in 2000.) Business executives more correctly, as I soon learned from daily professional and social contact with them, knew Milwaukee as a strong capital goods center. It employed 43 percent of its highly skilled labor force in manufacturing, the second highest figure in the country. Politicians and sociologists described the city as well managed, and blessed with a sound mixture of largely compatible ethnic groups. Approximately 30 percent of the population traced their ancestors to Germany and a like number to Poland, according to the 1950 Census.

Fundamentally, Milwaukee was a giant machine shop. The city and its key industrial suburbs, Cudahy, South Milwaukee, and West Allis, were proud of being the corporate headquarters for leaders in their fields or, like Allis Chalmers, just plain large. Allis Chalmers in 1951 employed 16,700. It manufactured turbines for the Hoover Dam on the Colorado River and also produced farm tractors, and many other product lines in its attempt to compete with front-running John Deere, International Harvester, General Electric, and Westinghouse. A. O. Smith, employing 9,300, turned out large diameter pipe, automobile frames, water heaters, and, in World War II, struts to brace the landing gear of the B-17 (Flying Fortress) bomber. Bucyrus-Erie built 90 percent of the power shovels used to dig the Panama Canal. Ladish, with its narrow mile-long plant in Cudahy, specialized in high precision giant forgings. Briggs and Stratton was the premier manufacturer of small horsepower engines. (For larger employers see Appendix A.)

Milwaukeeans affectionately referred to their city's primary occupation as metal bending. Approximately 79 percent of the companies having over 500 employees manufactured heavy machinery, engines, heavy pipe, or electrical controls (Allen-Bradley, Cutler-Hammer, and Square D). In sharp contrast, Milwaukee's famous beer industry employed only 9.4 percent of the total employed in Milwaukee County in 1951.[1] There were, of course, countless enterprises with fewer than 500 people on the payroll. They were the hundreds of tool and die or job shops, often family-owned. They supplied the larger manufacturers with parts, usually of metal, thus reinforcing Milwaukee's image as a metal-bending city.

Milwaukee was also home to several strong and distinctive institutions, primarily Northwestern Mutual Life, then America's seventh largest insurance company, and the highly profitable and influential *Milwaukee Journal.* The paper, reaching virtually every home, was one of the most respected American newspapers. The *Journal's* great prosperity, before television drained off much of its advertising revenues, enabled it to attract astute reporters whose penetrating articles kept Milwaukee on its toes.

Milwaukee had grown and prospered at its location because, in early years, its harbor was one of the finest and most heavily used in the Great Lakes. First-rate railroads connected Milwaukee with Chicago, the nation's transportation hub, and the West Coast through the Twin Cities. In the 1950s, the heart of downtown Milwaukee centered on Wisconsin Avenue where it crossed the Milwaukee River. A white five-story Gimbels department store looked down on pedestrians scurrying across the bridge. Milwaukee was conservative – even staid – clean, law-abiding, and reliable. Milwaukee was also a closely-knit series of communities, tightly bound together by traditions of hard work, a fine public school system, a well-managed fiscally conservative local government, and a nationally recognized county park system, museum, and zoo. The parks had been started long ago by early German settlers who brought with them a love for city parks. Along the way, Charles B. Whitnall, the father of the county park system, wisely located many parks along the rivers.

Milwaukee's municipal honesty was legendary. State Street's self-appointed mistress of civic morals, the *Milwaukee Journal*, hounded one Krause, a lowly alderman, out of office in the early l950s through repeated headlines. The unfortunate Krause had accepted a $1,000 contribution from an automobile dealer in apparent exchange for city approval of an extra entrance to his sales lot from the street.

In 1950 metropolitan Milwaukee included Milwaukee County and the growing four eastern townships of Waukesha County, the Village of Menomonee Falls, and the southern part of the Town of Mequon. Although the city had 637,332 residents in 1950, ranking it twelfth among American cities, it occupied only 23 percent of Milwaukee County's 241 square miles. Seven unincorporated townships governed 61 percent of the county.

The townships were about to disappear. Milwaukee would undergo many changes during the 1950s and beyond. To my surprise, I was to participate actively. Before describing the disappearance of townships in Chapter 3 and a chain of ensuing events in many later chapters, I turn briefly in the next chapter to what may be more important to some readers, the comings – and – goings of major league baseball between 1953 and 1970. There, too, luck put me on center stage.

Chapter 2

The Braves and Brewers Come to Milwaukee

In 1953 the seventh place Boston Braves National League baseball team transferred to Milwaukee and shot up to second place, putting sleepy Milwaukee on the national map. The origins of this unexpected achievement went back many years. Milwaukee had long been proud of its Brewers baseball team in the old American Association AAA minor league. The Brewers performed at a rickety Borchert Field which occupied a city block between North 7th and 8th Streets and West Chambers and Burleigh Streets, now buried under the I-43 Freeway. Borchert's 14,000 seats were the bane of loyal fans who had long hoped Milwaukee might attract a major league team but realized the city's chances depended on first building a larger stadium.

After sputtering for sixteen years, the prospects of building a new baseball stadium suddenly picked up speed in late 1946 when Lou Perini, a Boston contractor, acquired the Boston Braves of the National League and its farm clubs, including the Milwaukee Brewers. For years, county officials had envisioned building a structure adaptable to the needs of both minor league baseball and professional football but which could be converted to major league standards if the need arose. At the same time they realized that attracting a major league team could not occur until the community had a better ball park than Borchert Field.[2] On January 17, 1950, Perini told the Milwaukee County Park Commission that if they would build a new stadium he would like to lease it for $30,000 a year for his Milwaukee Brewers. Perini's offer speeded up the process. By June the county board voted 19 to 1 to proceed toward building a new stadium at the Story quarry, a location that had first been recommended to the city land commission for a stadium in 1909 by Charles B. Whitnall, the legendary father of the Milwaukee Park System. In July 1950 the county authorized borrowing $3.5 million to build the stadium. The new 35,000 seat facility was completed in early 1953 after construction was delayed by a labor strike and steel shortages attributable to the intervening Korean War.

The completion of the new Milwaukee County Stadium success-fully acted as the intended lure to a major league franchise. Although the newspapers in 1953 featured the self-described efforts of Frederick Miller, the freewheeling, sports-fan president of the Miller Brewing Company, to acquire and transfer to Milwaukee one of various major league teams, including the St. Louis Browns[3], it was Perini who brought the Braves here.[4] By March 18, 1953 he quickly obtained permission from the National League to move his Boston Braves and quietly moved his minor league Brewers to Toledo from which, providentially, the Toledo Mud Hens of the same American Association, had just departed.

The new Milwaukee Braves opened in Milwaukee on April 9, 1953, and were an instant hit with 34,357 fans. I was one of them when they jammed the baseball park to see the Braves edge out the St. Louis Cardinals by 3 to 2 on Billy Bruton's tenth inning home run, his only one of the year. In the first season the Braves attracted 281,278 fans in their first thirteen home games, more than attended games in Boston during the entire 1952 season. The Braves responded by climbing in their first season from seventh place to second in the standings. Warren Spahn, a left-handed future Hall of Fame pitcher, Lew Burdette, and Bob Buhl pitched superbly, while Eddie Matthews, and Joe Adcock (reinforced in 1954 by the seventeen-year-old rookie sensation, Henry Aaron) supplied the batting punch. In their first year in Milwaukee, the Braves attracted 1,826,397 fans, a new National League record. After the stadium was enlarged to hold 44,000 in 1954, attendance in the fifties exceeded two million for four successive years, reaching 2,215,404 in 1957 when the Braves won the World Series, vanquishing the hated New York Yankees in seven games. Milwaukee was delirious and proud to be finally recognized nationally as an up-and-coming city.

After the World Series Championship, the Braves' competitive standing slowly declined, as did attendance. When the Braves finished sixth in 1963, attendance slipped to 773,018. In 1962, Lou Perini sold his team to a Chicago syndicate headed by William C. Bartholomay, who rather quickly decided that more money could be made owning a team in Atlanta because its television market included far more viewers. Bartholomay obtained permission from the National League to transfer the franchise to Atlanta in 1964. However, in his hurry to move after the 1964 season, Bartholomay overlooked the fact that his lease from Milwaukee County had one more year to run. The county sued for breach of lease, won, and forced the Braves to play here in 1965. Fan support evaporated for the lame-duck team, declining to 555,584. Bartholomay bad-mouthed Milwaukee as a weak major league city. Milwaukee County Board Chairman Eugene Grobschmidt of South Milwaukee rashly accused the Braves of deliberately throwing games in order to persuade the county to agree to a quicker, mid-1965-season exit for the team.

What happened next turned out to be a colossal mistake of judgment, which was to cost Milwaukee dearly. Milwaukee County sued the National League baseball owners, claiming that they had violated the federal anti-trust laws by conspiring to move the Braves and depriving Milwaukee of the opportunity to compete in baseball. The Wisconsin Supreme Court on July 27, 1966, threw out the case by a 4 to 3 vote, holding that baseball was exempt from the anti-trust laws because Justice Oliver Wendell Holmes, in a U.S. Supreme Court case in 1922, had ruled that baseball is not a business. On December 12, 1966, the U.S. Supreme Court let the Wisconsin decision stand by refusing to hear an appeal.

The departure of the Braves for Atlanta in 1965 left Milwaukee smarting like an abandoned bride. Luckily, an ardent baseball fan vowed he would obtain a replacement team. He was Allen H. ("Bud") Selig. His relatively young age, thirty-one years, seemed no obstacle to him. As a teenager Bud had attended fifty to sixty Milwaukee Brewers games a year in the old AAA American Association together with his rabid baseball-enthusiast mother, Marie. Each rooted for the home team while absorbing the finer points of the sport. Bud even dreamed a child's maximum fantasy – that he would one day own a major league baseball team. He seemed an unlikely candidate for the role; he was young, largely unknown in the business community, and did not possess the typical baseball owner's fortune. However, Selig's lean figure, crew haircut, and soft-spoken modesty concealed an exceptional intelligence and passionate zeal – even obsession – to succeed in a task most considered hopeless. His first move was smart and doubled his slim chances.

Selig teamed up with my brother-in-law, Edmund B. Fitzgerald, a baseball fan whose executive background brought many advantages to the task. Fitzgerald, at thirty-eight, was president of the well-established electrical controls manufacturer, Cutler-Hammer, a company to which I bore no relationship except that it had been founded in the 1890s by his and my wife's maternal grandfather, Frank R. Bacon. (Bacon in 1906 bought Cutler-Hammer of Chicago, a competitor, and took its name for his Milwaukee company, American Rheostat.) Fitzgerald was also a director of Northwestern Mutual Life Insurance Company, the First Wisconsin National Bank (the city's largest bank) and the Milwaukee Braves. He had voted against the Braves' departure and stayed on their board during their ensuing fights with Milwaukee. He held on to learn what Bartholomay might divulge to his directors – after receiving supportive counsel from community leaders as to his ethics in doing so. Fitzgerald was well known, a born salesman, and, having served a stint as the youngest chairman of the United Way annual fund drive, knew where to locate the money needed to purchase a new baseball team.

Selig and Fitzgerald worked well together. Fitzgerald loved to wisecrack and jocularly called Selig "Abner," after Abner Doubleday, baseball's founder. In 1965, Selig invited me, on the recommendation of his banker, George Kasten, to incorporate the Milwaukee Brewers Baseball Club for the investors who would purchase a replacement baseball team. Selig and Fitzgerald and eight others pledged $200,000 each toward the equity portion of the purchase price, then innocently estimated to be only $2 million. Kasten had seen my civic work close up in 1959 when I reported to him on a crisis in the Metropolitan Milwaukee Study Commission. At that time I was its acting chairman and he the president of the Greater Milwaukee Committee, an influential group of 150 business and labor leaders. However, I believe Kasten recommended me for the role of the Brewers' lawyer mostly out of gratitude for my moving the law firm I had joined in 1954[5] into his bank building when a major tenant left unexpectedly.

The Brewers for a long time publicly vowed not to try to entice another existing team to transfer its franchise to Milwaukee. They said they would not duplicate the shameful act of the "carpetbaggers from Chicago" who had moved the Braves to Atlanta. By 1965 there was increasing talk that both major leagues would add to the original sixteen longstanding franchises and seek out new cities with substantial baseball fans. The flight of the Philadelphia Athletics in 1955 to Kansas City, the New York Giants and Brooklyn Dodgers in

1958 to San Francisco and Los Angeles, respectively, and the Washington Senators in 1960 to the Twin Cities foreshadowed both a national realignment and the creation of new baseball franchises. That expansion started with the awarding of franchises by the American League in 1961 to the Los Angeles (later California) Angels and to Washington and by the National League in 1962 to the Houston Astros and New York Mets. Selig, as president of a family-owned Ford dealership, could devote as much time as he liked to helping the Brewers seek a new baseball franchise after 1965. That was a big plus.

As part of their attempt to win a new baseball franchise, Selig and Fitzgerald took many steps to improve Milwaukee's case. They carefully studied all of Bartholomay's damaging statements to the National League about Milwaukee weaknesses. They rebutted some and, where feasible, corrected particular flaws cited by Bartholomay. For example, he had asserted that the Milwaukee County minimum lease payment of $250,000 was crippling in a year of poor attendance. Selig and Fitzgerald proposed to the county board that it share good times with the bad in the future by providing a sliding scale rent with no minimum. They persuaded the county board on November 14, 1967, to authorize a lease for a dollar a year plus parking fees plus a share in ticket and concession revenues if attendance exceeded one million.[6]

The Brewers, even without a team, made imaginative efforts to demonstrate Milwaukee's continuing love of baseball. In 1967 they arranged an exhibition game between the Chicago White Sox and the Minnesota Twins, drawing an all-time record of 51,144 fans (including 4,500 standing in the outfield – by special permission of the American League.) The White Sox played several regular season games in Milwaukee in 1968 and 1969, drawing many more fans per game than the White Sox did in Chicago. Through all this I acted as the Brewers' treasurer and secretary, being the only paid Brewers' officer. In 1969 the Brewers almost purchased the White Sox for $13 million when one 50 percent owner agreed to sell but the other declined. Most of all, from 1965 onward, Selig and Fitzgerald continuously applied to both the National League and American League for the grant of an expansion franchise whenever one was authorized. They presented Milwaukee's case to both leagues at frequent meetings but were turned down while other cities won. In 1968, each league granted two franchises to start operations in 1969: Kansas City (the peripatetic

Kansas City Athletics having moved in 1968 to Oakland) and Seattle in the American League; and San Diego and Montreal in the National League.

The Brewers' rejections were peremptory. As Selig recalled thirty years later, "Baseball didn't want to see Milwaukee again. Nobody would even talk to us. It was as if we had leprosy."[7]

Milwaukee was quarantined for a reason. Baseball owners had been incensed by Milwaukee's audacity in challenging baseball's sacred anti-trust laws exemption. That exemption, created by the U. S. Supreme Court in 1922, provided in 1965, among other things, the fundamental legal foundation for a team's compensation-depressing lifelong ownership of a player's contract after he initially signed one to play for them. (Much later, baseball decided under pressure from players to limit the length of players' contracts.) Baseball owners would be damned if Milwaukee would get a second chance. It did not matter that it was the Milwaukee County Board that had brought the unsuccessful anti-trust lawsuit, not Selig, Fitzgerald or me as their lawyer. Most observers in Milwaukee after several rebuffs came to believe their city would never get another team. Not Selig. Nothing extinguished his faith: just keep trying and eventually the leagues would see the light.

Finally a break occurred. In 1968, the American League, after rejecting Milwaukee's application one more time, had awarded a franchise to the Seattle Pilots, a weakly financed group headed by two brothers, Max and Dewey Soriano, and Bill Daley of Cleveland. Low Seattle attendance and inadequate revenues from other sources threatened to bankrupt the Pilots after their first season. In the fall of 1969 the Pilots sought American League permission to sell their franchise to the highest bidder in another city, knowing that at least Milwaukee was interested and possibly Dallas. In fact, the Brewers had offered in writing to purchase the Pilots in late September, 1969, and had "shaken hands" on a purchase in early October.[8] The American League repeatedly said "no," having been stung by criticism in the press and in the halls of Congress. Senators and members of Congress had earlier threatened to end baseball's prized anti-trust exemption for having allowed the Braves to abandon Milwaukee four years before. In addition, the two senators representing the State of Washington, alarmed that the Pilots might leave, renewed the threat. Never again, thought the American League. Repeatedly the Pilots appealed to the League, which as often urged them to find a well-financed Seattle purchaser. Various Seattle syndicates unsuccessfully tried to raise the money required to purchase and operate the Pilots.

Fortunately for Milwaukee, necessity forced the League's hand. The Pilots ran out of money. The American League lent them $650,000. It was not enough. The ghastly facts ultimately convinced the American League that the Pilots might not be able to meet their players' payroll in the spring of 1970. So the American League finally began, very reluctantly, to listen to the Brewers. However, the attorney general of the State of Washington, Slade Gordon, later a U.S. Senator, not only listened but acted. He obtained a state court injunction forbidding the transfer of the Pilots out of Seattle. King County, where Seattle is located, not to be outdone in any effort to curry local favor, also obtained a duplicate state court injunction.

Meanwhile, the Pilots secretly agreed to sell their franchise to the Milwaukee Brewers, subject to American League approval and a termination of the injunctions. The contract of sale for $10,800,000 was drafted on my typewriter and signed at our home on a snowy Sunday, March 8, 1970, barely a month before opening day. My wife graciously overlooked someone's spilling coffee on our white living room rug. Selig and my law partner, Elwin J. "Bud" Zarwell, flew to an American League meeting in Dade County, Florida, to request League approval of the Pilot's sale and transfer to Milwaukee. I chose Zarwell because his exceptional analytical skills had earned him a reputation as a superb problem solver. Not only was the American League stymied by two Washington state court injunctions, but also during the meeting in Dade County, a Florida court injunction against the transfer was served on the owners. The three injunctions stimulated discussion but inhibited action by the American League. At 3:15 A.M. Zarwell proposed a solution: the Pilots, he said, being technically insolvent, could petition for Chapter XI protection in bankruptcy. That would give the federal court jurisdiction over their assets, including the franchise, the players' contracts, and all baseballs and uniforms. The federal court, he added, under federal bankruptcy law, could vacate the state court injunctions if it chose. It would do so, he predicted, because the referee-in-bankruptcy would feel his duty was to liquidate perishable assets in a manner most likely to maximize some return for the unpaid creditors of the bankrupt party. The Pilots case was comparable to a bankrupt who owned carloads of perishable lettuce. The referee would sell it hurriedly to get cash while the lettuce had value; likewise he would sell the franchise and players' contracts for a reasonable cash bid immediately payable. The American League reply: it was "unthinkable" that one of its teams would be bankrupt, as if the wish could banish the fact.

Yet the League, acting contrary to its strongly stated rejection of Zarwell's solution, asked Max Soriano, representing the Pilots, and Zarwell to meet with an American League attorney summoned from Cleveland. He confirmed that Zarwell was indeed right. The League then asked Zarwell to go to Seattle for as long as it took to guide the bankruptcy proceedings – while staying discreetly in the background – until the federal court approved the sale, got the Brewers' cash for Pilots' creditors, and dissolved the three state court injunctions.

While Zarwell worked behind the scenes in Seattle, the owner of the Chicago White Sox publicly called the "Seattle situation a mess" and the exasperated president of the American League, Joe Cronin, explained why. If the Pilots folded, it would be "almost impossible to operate the League with 11 teams" because one club (of the twelve) would have to have a bye, that is, not be scheduled to play. The League, he added, had been hoping one purchaser would come up in Seattle and was not closing its eyes to the possibility of another purchaser "but our hands are tied just now [by the court injunctions]."[9] Zarwell's assignment was completed at 10:20 P.M. Milwaukee time on March 31, 1970, eight days before opening day.

Earlier, back in Milwaukee, Selig, Fitzgerald, I, and many others worked feverishly during March to get the purchase price financed by $5 million from investors plus loans. The Brewers negotiated to borrow from civic-minded Northwestern Mutual Life Insurance Company and Sports Service, the Brewers' future food concessionaire. While Selig toiled round the clock on an infinite number of baseball operational details, Fitzgerald and I rounded up investors. The Brewers now needed two and a half times the amount of equity the existing ten investors had agreed to invest. Two of the ten dropped out. The Brewers needed new investors in a hurry. Fitzgerald knew many prospects;

Selig, some; and I, others. Eventually, with the help of my partner who managed Ralph Evinrude's affairs, I raised 40 percent of the equity. Ralph Evinrude was a principal owner of Evinrude Motors, founded by his father, Ole Evinrude, inventor of the outboard motor.

One challenge we faced was that the Brewers required two investors with large sums in order to keep the average investor's contribution at well below $500,000. Brewers' investors were attracted by one or more of three motives: a fanatic love of baseball; substantial income tax deductions; and a civic-minded devotion to Milwaukee and Wisconsin. Eight investors came from Madison, the Fox River Valley, and La Crosse.[10]

Yet potential investors faced the risk, if the team failed financially (it nearly did), of losing their investment and possibly being liable for unpaid debts. These risks had to be faced and, if possible, contained within tolerable limits. That is what lawyers are for. We created a limited partnership, which assured the limited partners of freedom from personal liability while being eligible for potential handsome tax deductions for operating losses. Such tax losses were more or less assured by a team's legal ability to charge off or depreciate the value of players' contracts over the average playing life of a player (a mere five years). The contracts were appraised at $10.2 million,[11] or 94 percent of the team's purchase price. Depreciation of players' contracts could reduce the federal income taxes of a limited partner in what was then the top federal income tax bracket of 70 percent by an amount, over several years, equal to 140 percent of his investment.[12] Or so it seemed. Actually, the Internal Revenue Service unsuccessfully challenged the deductions as excessive, with the result that Brewers' limited partners did not realize their tax benefit for so many years that their investment was not handsome in the end.[13]

The Brewers' general partner, or partner with the authority to manage the team, was a corporation that shielded its shareholders from personal liability but gave them no tax deductions other than a 100 percent capital loss if the venture went under. Selig and Fitzgerald, highly respected by all investors, became stockholders and officers, the first as president and the other as chairman of the executive committee. In all, twenty-one men invested in the Brewers,[14] fifteen as limited partners, six as shareholders, and one, Evinrude, as both. Evinrude was the largest; he contributed 22 percent of the equity. One Cleveland shareholder in the Pilots, William R. Daley, held a 20 percent interest. In contrast, the other investors, including Robert Uihlein, president of the Joseph Schlitz Brewing Company, contributed, on the average, under $500,000. Later, Selig and the Brewers' partnership purchased substantial interests from many other Brewers' investors or their estates, enabling Selig to eventually become the largest single owner.

As opening day 1970 approached, another glitch threatened. In 1967 Milwaukee County had by resolution promised to enter into a twenty-five year lease with a one dollar annual minimum rent. Several county board supervisors shocked the Brewers by announcing a few days before opening day that the twenty-five year lease offer of the prior board in 1967 was not binding on them since they were not then in office. They proposed an amendment to the lease, permitting the rent to be renegotiated every five years.[15] Such a clause would violate the promised lease terms which the Brewers had cited to the American League, and to potential Brewers' investors and their lenders, such as Northwestern Mutual Life and Sports Service, as evidence that the Brewers would be financially viable – notwithstanding what Bartholomay had said about the softness of the Milwaukee market. The Greater Milwaukee Committee's executive director, Rudolph Schoenecker, worked around the clock to lobby the county board to honor its 1967 resolution and turn down the proposed disastrous five-year renegotiation amendment to the lease. The board did, by a 13 to 9 vote on April 7, 1970, opening day.

Further illustrating the tight schedule under which the Brewers were operating, it was not until eleven o'clock on the same day that the City of Milwaukee approved a license for the Brewers to sell beer in the stadium. Imagine a Milwaukee opening day without beer!

Baseball was back. The Brewers drew 37,237 fans on opening day and 933,690 for their opening season. However, large cash deficits in the first two years required the owners by the end of 1971 to contribute an additional $2 million in equity or 39 percent of their initial investment. The Brewers became financially stronger only when the team improved many years later and admission and TV revenues increased. In 1982, the Brewers participated in the World Series, losing to the St. Louis Cardinals in seven games, notwithstanding sterling performances by Robin Yount and Paul Molitor. If Rollie Fingers, the injured record-breaking relief pitcher, had been able to play, Brewers' president Wendy Selig-Prieb says, the Brewers would have won the World Series. Yount and Fingers were elected to baseball's Hall of Fame at Cooperstown and Molitor will be elected in 2003 when first eligible.

The Milwaukee County Stadium was built in 1953 to attract the Braves from Boston. They departed in 1965. Major league baseball returned in 1970 when Bud Selig's Brewers bought the Seattle Pilots.

(*Copyrighted Photograph,* Milwaukee Journal Sentinel)

The Town of Granville, still largely rural in the 1950s, was the object of a prolonged dispute between the City of Milwaukee and the Village of Brown Deer. This view looks southeast from North 43rd Street and West Good Hope Road.

(Photo courtesy of the Historical Photo Collection of the Milwaukee Public Library)

Part Two

Geographic Fragmentation

Chapter 3

Boundary Wars, 1950-1957

Milwaukee by 1950 was growing again. War-time shortages of virtually everything had ceased. Factories hummed. Fully-loaded trolleys clanked up and down Wisconsin Avenue. After the war-time slowdown, the city's population increased. Before the war, Milwaukee had been a highly compact, densely populated city, well served by public sewer, water, good roads, and an excellent privately owned streetcar system. Too, electric inter-urban railway lines extended north to Sheboygan, west to Waukesha and Watertown, southwest to East Troy and Burlington, and south to Racine, Kenosha, and Chicago. The expanding population could, as before, have been housed in newer apartments or city subdivisions reached by streetcar lines. However, several economic forces combined to disperse much of the new growth into outlying open lands near or beyond the old city limits. Urban sprawl had started.

Veterans returning from World War II quickly married and started families. As was true nationwide, a friendly government offered easy credit for new homes, especially for veterans. Builders sought to accommodate them by building less-expensive single story ranch homes in outlying townships where land was open and cheap. Population soared in Granville to the northwest, Wauwatosa to the west, and Greenfield to the southwest. Frank Zeidler, mayor from 1948 to 1960, together with the Milwaukee Common Council, quickly reacted to this migration to areas outside the city. They sought to annex town land so as to protect Milwaukee's tax base and political power.

The city's Department of Annexation campaigned to persuade residents of neighboring towns to sign petitions seeking annexation by the city. However, many long-time town residents and officials vigorously opposed annexation. They feared Milwaukee's property taxes which were often 33 percent higher than what they paid. Towns charged little for fewer local services. The city attracted two highly effective annexation allies: subdividers and builders.

To construct houses as inexpensively as possible, builders wanted to crowd more homes – up to three times as many – on their newly purchased farmland than the towns permitted. So builders went to extremes to annex. They gerrymandered. Annexation required the written consent of over one-half of the to-be-annexed area's resident voters and property owners (measured by area or assessed valuation.) In one case, the subdivider, with the help of the city annexation department, drew the annexation petition's boundaries so as to include 287 acres and two sympathetic voters while zigzagging around twenty-seven opposing electors.

The city hastily adopted shortsighted policies favoring developers by permitting lots with 50 foot frontages and as small as 6,000 square feet. That contrasted with much higher frontage and square footage requirements under county zoning ordinances in towns. The city also offered water and sewer (mains) which were installed at less than cost.[16]

In contrast, thrifty towns required subdividers to construct their own roads and rely on private wells and septic tanks. The threat of discharges from septic tanks seeping into private wells dictated substantial minimum lot sizes, such as the half acre (approximately 20,000 square feet) prevalent in Granville.

Milwaukee's aggressive annexation policy and successful alliance with builders as annexation agents alarmed many town residents. They feared they would be swallowed up by undesired annexations. They could assure their independence only by incorporating new cities or villages. Incorporated municipalities were legally immune from unilateral absorption by the city. Incorporation campaigns in the 1950s were fueled by widespread concerns. Both sincere and demagogic suburban residents warned that annexation to Milwaukee would bring

23

high taxes and smaller residential lots (with possibly less affluent neighbors). Residents would also lose their ability to persuade officials to zone for large minimum lot sizes. Some critics disparagingly labeled zoning for large lots "snob zoning." It was not that simple. Public health alone necessitated larger lots because then prevalent septic tanks on small lots could contaminate drinking water drawn from wells.

Between 1950 and 1957 interminable boundary wars flared up among the City of Milwaukee, many bordering suburbs, and the would-be organizers of new suburbs. The prize: seizing township lands comprising two-thirds of Milwaukee County's 241 square miles. (Map 1) When the dust settled, Milwaukee's area almost doubled, rising from 51.8 to 91.7 square miles; the City of Wauwatosa tripled; the City of West Allis more than doubled; and eight new suburban villages and cities sprang up. The territorial and population changes between 1950 and 1960 were staggering. (Appendix B shows the changes by each town and municipality, new and old, and Appendix C by totals in each classification.)

Cold statistics measure only the drastic changes in municipal boundaries. They do not reveal two major features of the boundary wars which shocked the legislature into reforming the statutes that permitted them to happen. Unfortunately, reform came only after all town lands in Milwaukee County were gobbled up. First, newspaper headlines dramatized annexation and incorporation campaigns, counter moves and accusations, name calling, and exaggerations. Such publicity focused the legislature's attention on the problem. Second, many new municipal boundaries proved to be grossly illogical. They frequently hopscotched back and forth across contested streets or sliced through neighborhoods. Residents as well as police and fire fighters couldn't be certain which municipality was supposed to respond to emergencies at a particular address. New boundaries seldom followed natural service boundaries, such as a river, railway, or major highway.

More important, some suburbs turned out to be too small, at least in the opinion of academicians who had not been consulted on their creation. An exceedingly small suburb could not provide municipal services as efficiently as a larger municipality whose area presumably, though not invariably, enclosed an adequate tax base. The first five suburbs to be incorporated between 1950 and 1954 averaged less than two square miles in size: City of Glendale, 1950; City of St. Francis,

1951; Village of Hales Corners, 1952; Village of Bayside, 1952; Village of Brown Deer, 1954.[17] That minuscule size, as to villages, stemmed in part from a Wisconsin statute requiring new villages to contain 400 residents per square mile. Incorporators after l955 universally opted for city status. Why? The shamefully disjointed state statutes contained no similar explicit density requirement for new cities. Furthermore, petitions for new cities did not have to go before a court for approval whereas petitions for villages did. Strange. A mandatory court proceeding on a proposed village incorporation[18] presented objectors with an easy opportunity to show up and question its legality.

Two particularly bitter annexation-incorporation battles in the mid-fifties provoked the legislature to reform Wisconsin's outmoded incorporation and annexation laws. For decades the legislature had been paralyzed by the equal strength of both the proponents and opponents of legislative intervention. One fight concerned the piece-meal dissolution of the Town of Granville in the northwest corner of Milwaukee County, and the other was the incorporation of the Town of Oak Creek in the south beyond the Milwaukee airport. The Town of Granville had been originally bounded on the west by Waukesha County, on the north by Ozaukee County, on the east by North 27th Street, and on the south by West Hampton Avenue. By 1955 successive annexations to Milwaukee had shrunk Granville from its original thirty-six square miles to twenty-two-and-a-half square miles. Granville encompassed many farms, some subdivisions, scattered small businesses, and a few manufacturing plants such as Evinrude Motors' new one on North 64th Street near West Mill Road.

Granville residents needed help to remain independent of Milwaukee. In 1955 they turned to me because I had been very busy in that field of law. Here is what led up to my involvement in the battle over Granville.

In 1953, as a thirty-six-year-old with no prior experience in municipal law, I got my baptism under fire in a four-municipality battle to devour the old Town of Milwaukee in northeastern Milwaukee County. In 1950 the town's administration had sponsored the incorpo-ration of its southern industrial half just north of Capitol Drive as the City of Glendale. They did not plan to abandon their residents in the

25

northern five square miles along Port Washington and Brown Deer Roads but to follow up by annexing this remnant to the new city as well. However, the Villages of Fox Point and Bayside, joined by a trustee from River Hills, John Allis, hired me to defeat the new City of Glendale's impending effort to annex that town remnant. The three predominantly residential villages believed Glendale might permit incompatible commercial and industrial development in areas adjoining them. Rumor said a popular but noisy nightclub, Jimmy Fazio's, was about to move to a vacant corner of Bradley and Port Washington Roads.

My role as an insider started when the Plan Commissions of River Hills and Fox Point (of which I was a member) held a rare joint meeting. Members recommended their villages beat Glendale to the gun by annexing all town land lying between them. They drew up a map – with later input from Bayside – establishing the proposed future boundaries between the three villages. River Hills and Fox Point were supposed to bottle up Glendale to the south within three weeks by circulating petitions to annex the land between them. Fox Point did so. River Hills did not. The president of River Hills, A. J. Kieckhefer, consulted the village attorney, Cornelius ("Con") Dineen, who just happened also to be Glendale's attorney. Kieckhefer told his trustees that Dineen assured him Glendale posed no threat, so he then vetoed River Hills' circulation effort. Glendale quickly annexed a mile on the west side of Port Washington Road up to Bradley Road, creating the "Glendale thumb" between the two villages. The thumb comprised a mile long, thin strip of Glendale territory between Fox Point and River Hills. John Allis, a River Hills trustee, would be damned if Kieckhefer could block the will of all the other six trustees. He, joined by Russell van Brunt, a friend living in the Town of Milwaukee adjacent to River Hills, then hired me to prepare the legal papers and political explanations needed for the annexation to River Hills of the remaining town land supposedly "earmarked" for it. By the end of a furious battle, the three villages obtained 90 percent of the land they sought. Van Brunt later became president of River Hills.

As a novice, working alone, but with crucial support of the influ-ential *Milwaukee Journal,*[19] I had managed to defeat Con Dineen, the respected dean of suburban lawyers and architect of Glendale's incorporation-followed-by-annexation plan. A Fox Point trustee jokingly asked me "When are you going to run for governor?"

My highly-publicized role in the Town of Milwaukee war caused the Town of Brookfield residents in eastern Waukesha County in 1954 to ask me to incorporate as much as possible of the eastern part of their town. They feared annexation by Milwaukee, which had provocatively attempted – by a narrow several-mile-long "shoestring" annexation – to annex nearby railroad yards. The annexation was defeated in the courts. (See Map 1.) Earlier seven successive attorneys had told the Brookfield residents that incorporating the entire town would fail in court. It lacked the population density required by court decisions.

I counseled they could win if they adopted a two-pronged strategy. First, they must incorporate only the seventeen-square-mile more populous eastern area. Later the new city could annex the sparser western part. That strategy resembled Dineen's Glendale plan to start by incorporating small, then annexing to become big. Second, they must avoid litigation testing the incorporation by going political. The most likely challenger was the town board whose powerful chairman lived in the less-populated western part of the town that would be left out. The incorporators, I said, should obtain the signatures of sixty percent of the town's voters on the incorporation petition – many times the small number required by the state's outmoded statutes. In this way the town supervisors would understand that if they sued and won, they would be ousted at the next town election. No one sued. Brookfield was born August 5, 1954, and I became its city attorney, serving for the next six years.

The beleaguered Granville residents had observed that Brookfield got incorporated. When they retained me in 1955 they immediately asked: how do we avoid annexation by Milwaukee? I advised that they must first temporarily freeze Granville's rapidly changing boundaries by slowing down the completion of Milwaukee annexations for a short time, then seek to incorporate as much as possible of the town as a new City of Granville. The town board was not sympathetic to our proposed incorporation. Its members would probably lose their positions if we incorporated. Perhaps they were thinking of selling their land at a premium to subdividers seeking annexation to Milwaukee. I suggested that the residents file a mandatory petition for a town meeting to be held on July 5, 1955 to act on *their* agenda.

The evening was hot and humid. Hundreds attended, jamming the town hall on West Good Hope Road to capacity. Many stood outside, listening through open windows. Naturally the town board did not enjoy this citizens' revolt against their seemingly passive attitude toward Milwaukee annexations. Likewise, its venerable counsel, Cornelius (Con) Dineen, did not relish my appearance, for the second time, as an upstart invading his turf. But several hundred aroused Granville electors could not be ignored. They ordered their reluctant town board to litigate each and every Milwaukee attempt at annexation. Suits would achieve our objective: temporarily freeze town boundaries.

Newspaper stories about a possible future City of Granville understandably stimulated Milwaukee's Mayor Frank Zeidler and several subdividers to speed up annexation efforts. It became clear that the city would be able to find some Granville landowner to contest a proposed incorporation. He could be a resident who would profit by selling his land to a subdivider if it were annexed. The outcome of a legal challenge of a possible incorporation could be risky and certainly very expensive. The would-be incorporators had limited funds, even though I worked for a mere fifteen dollars an hour. I kept the rate low because I enjoyed quasi-political work and the clients could not pay more. The Granville Town Board stayed financially aloof.

Noting the fierce opposition of the City of Milwaukee, and the prospective lawsuit contesting a possible incorporation, I advised my clients on a seemingly safer stratagem, since they appeared to have the political support of a majority of residents. They should seek annexation to the brand new, nearby 1.8-square-mile Village of Brown Deer, knowing that if successful, their comparatively large population addition would assure them future political control of the village. It was risky. Insular, tiny Brown Deer might say no. Its trustees might fear losing their positions.

The residents and I presented to Brown Deer trustees the alluring prospect of their controlling the land-rich northwest corner of Milwaukee County. They were persuaded. In late 1955, five annexation petitions embracing sixteen square miles, or 73 percent of the remaining town, obtained the statutorily required signatures of a majority of the resident electors and property owners. Brown Deer annexed over sixteen square miles early in 1956.

Milwaukee had no standing to bring its challenge. Oak Creek, unlike Granville, survived as an independent community.

During the 1950s new municipalities were sometimes created on the incorrect or true-for-a-short-time-only assumption that future tax revenues available to the incorporated area would support services on acceptable levels. For example, tax-conscious residents of the former Town of Lake on Lake Michigan chose to incorporate part of the area as the City of St. Francis. They included an electric power plant within the new boundaries. Wisconsin at that time remitted a substantial share of the taxes the utility paid to the state to be distributed to the municipality within which it was located. That largesse was intended as an incentive to put up with soot and ash. A later legislature substantially reduced that local share, deflating an important underlying fiscal assumption.

Most, or possibly all, petitions for incorporations were undertaken without a professional analysis of whether the proposed new municipal boundaries would be reasonably cost effective in raising revenues and providing proper municipal services. Boundaries were often shaped by how much land and how many voters could – rather than should – be included. In fact, the state at that time interposed no guiding hand or standards in controlling new incorporations or the expansion of old ones.

The boundary wars spilled over into adjacent Waukesha and Ozaukee Counties. In addition to incorporating the City of Brookfield in 1954, I handled Mequon's incorporation in 1957 and the City of Muskego's in 1964. The Village of Elm Grove was created in 1955 and New Berlin shortly thereafter. By 1970, all but a sliver of the six former townships bordering Milwaukee County on the west and north had been incorporated. (Map 2.)

While the incorporation boundary wars raged, Milwaukee abruptly adopted another method of warfare. It changed its prior policy of selling its Lake Michigan water to suburbs willing to pay the price. Suburbs away from the lake relied on wells for water, but steadily declining water tables made their residents anxious. On November 4, 1956 the City of Wauwatosa asked Milwaukee to sell it water for all its needs. Earlier Milwaukee had contracted to sell water only to that part of Wauwatosa where Milwaukee County's buildings and grounds were located. The City of Milwaukee refused. It told Wauwatosa it could purchase more water only if it consolidated with Milwaukee. Wauwatosa asked the Wisconsin Public Service Commission (PSC) to compel Milwaukee to sell water to it at such price as the PSC determined to be reasonable. Meanwhile Milwaukee had foolishly put off expanding the capacity of its water treatment plant. Yet demand for water grew steadily as new customers were added both by the city's natural growth and by its large expansion in territory. Water shortages followed, causing water rationing and frequent loud protests by taxpayers whose lawns turned brown. By 1957 the water crisis, years of city-suburban boundary squabbling, and city-suburban boundary wars led the legislature to consider new remedies. Earlier it had hesitated to act, both because the problems were seen as too complex and also because opposing political forces were evenly balanced. The water controversy shifted the balance toward action.

Chapter 4

The Governor and Legislature Respond

The legislature had watched while the city-suburban wars got worse. An organization of 150 Milwaukee civic leaders, the Greater Milwaukee Committee (GMC), acted. GMC had been formed in 1948 to encourage needed civic projects, such as building the War Memorial next to Lake Michigan. By 1955 the GMC had become deeply distressed by continuing city-suburban fighting. First, the GMC tried to cajole suburban and city officials to form a committee of twenty-one officials to study and settle their differences. The committee formed, but its members did no more than continue fighting. Then, in 1956, the GMC called on Governor Walter J. Kohler. They quietly persuaded him to appoint a committee of private citizens with a high-powered chairman. He was Robert E. Dineen, then vice president, and later president, of Northwestern Mutual Life Insurance Co. (and no relation of Con Dineen). Dineen was politically astute, having previously dealt extensively with the New York Legislature as superintendent of insurance for the State of New York. The Dineen committee was asked to study and make constructive suggestions concerning Milwaukee County's water supply, storm water disposal, and "many other municipal service problems which affect...the Milwaukee metropolitan area." At the same time Wauwatosa was continuing its suit to compel Milwaukee to sell it water.

While Dineen was no bull in a China shop, he did like prompt results. He became exasperated by the ongoing deadlock. In 1956 he issued an unusually blunt report urging Milwaukee to expand and modernize its water plant and to drop its policy of "economic coercion" by refusing to sell water to suburbs unless they agreed to absorption by Milwaukee. If Milwaukee would not do so, then the legislature should create a metropolitan water utility that would. To improve inter-community relations, Dineen recommended that the legislature authorize a committee of fifteen private citizens to study and make recommendations on urban problems in Milwaukee County.

The GMC vigorously backed Dineen's report by lobbying the legislature to create a Metropolitan Study Commission (Metro), which it did in 1957. The legislature solemnly directed the commission to investigate and recommend within four years solutions to multiple concerns regarding governmental efficiency in Milwaukee County. Specifically, the commission was to examine "the character, extent, adequacy, cost, and efficiency of principal services provided by governmental units" in Milwaukee County.

At the time Metro was formed, I was a member of the Fox Point Planning Commission, city attorney for Brookfield, and a newly elected member of the Greater Milwaukee Committee – presumably because the GMC assigned some weight to my annexation-incorporation assignments. At the same time I was initiating negotiations to strengthen my firm, Wood, Warner, Tyrrell and Bruce by merging with Olwell and Brady, counsel to Briggs and Stratton, Ladish Co., and many other major corporations. The merger brought me Bud Zarwell, later my closest partner in the law. (He performed spectacularly, as we saw in Chapter 2, by finding a way to transform the Seattle Pilots into the Milwaukee Brewers in the face of three court injunctions.)

Governor Vernon Thompson in 1957 appointed fifteen Metro commissioners. I was surprised to be one. Of course I was honored, but cannot remember the governor's words. I recall only my young secretary, excited by receiving a call from a real governor, yelling loudly enough for the entire office to hear: "Mr. Cutler, GOV-ER-NOR THOMPSON wants you on the phone." Most public officials and the press commented favorably on the commission's assignment and the appointed commissioners.

In contrast, Mayor Frank Zeidler, a conscientious and normally moderate leader who loved Milwaukee to his bones, publicly blasted my selection. He called me "one of the leading opponents of the City of Milwaukee."[22] He obviously assumed my recently concluded professional effort to help Town of Granville residents avoid annexation to Milwaukee proved that I would be biased against the city on the many different subjects about to be studied. Although I did not respond, and neither did any Metropolitan Commission (Metro) spokesman respond (it takes two to fight), Zeidler's repeated personal attacks upset me. When I developed symptoms of ulcers, Herbert Pohle, one of Milwaukee's most admired and beloved internists, sensed that I did not understand that an aroused politician tends to pop off as automatically as a guard dog barks. As my doctor, he gave me classically wise counsel in addition to a baby food diet for months: "Dick, whenever the mayor attacks you, say to yourself: 'I won't let Zeidler hurt my stomach.'" I followed the good doctor's advice; the symptoms gradually disappeared, never to return.

Politicians live by venting feelings, real or calculated. Zeidler could have quietly called the governor and gotten assurances that I was a closet moderate and might actually help Milwaukee.

The new Metropolitan Study Commission statute called for only twelve of fifteen Metro commissioners to be business, professional, or civic leaders rather than all fifteen, as the GMC had recommended. The remaining three commissioners were to be elected or appointed municipal officials, one from the Milwaukee, one from a suburban city, and one from a suburban village. I fell into the last category, as I was on the Village of Fox Point Plan Commission. Commissioners' occupations and places of residence within the county complied with a prudent political guideline: an investigating commission should not only be balanced but appear balanced. That composition of Metro was no accident. All members but me appeared on a list of possible members suggested to the governor by the Greater Milwaukee Committee. Why I was omitted will be explained shortly.

Metro appointments included a few highly intelligent workaholics who would carry the work of the commission, like John C. Lobb, executive vice president of the Marine National Exchange Bank (today Bank One). Lobb had come to the bank from the Wisconsin Investment Board, where he was noted for his political acumen. He exuded charm and self-confidence, entering any room with a take-charge air. I liked him immediately. He seemed a born leader, but unfortunately, in this job at least, soon showed severe shortcomings, especially a lack of patience when sorely needed.

Other top-flight hard-working appointees included Robert Foote, Robert E. Jensen, and Willis Scholl, each the executive vice presidents of, respectively, Red Star Yeast (later Universal Foods, now Salient), American Appraisal, and Allis-Chalmers. Foote was a smooth, born kingmaker, who relished behind-the-scenes maneuvers to get things

35

done by forging consensus; and soft-spoken Jensen shone as an extraordinarily diligent, precise, financial analyst. Incidentally, Metro soon found that the City of West Allis unfairly assessed Allis-Chalmers' sprawling plant at twice the rate applied to residences. (The legislature later transferred the assessment of manufacturing property to the state.)

The GMC had reasons to omit me from its deliberately cautious nominations to the governor. To be sure, I had recently been elected to the Greater Milwaukee Committee as its youngest member and had won name recognition through daily newspaper accounts of various municipal annexation and incorporation battles. That was not enough. In fact, just the opposite; it was disabling to the politically correct GMC. My appointment displeased its perceptive chairman, Howard Tobin. He was more than president of the Wisconsin Gas Company. He served many civic causes as a steady, witty, conscientious leader. He felt my appointment risked vital public, or at least city, acceptance of the commission as impartial. In fact, Tobin, was so upset with my appointment that he called me and demanded to know whether I had asked the governor for a place on the commission. I calmly replied "No".

My unknown sponsor, I later learned, was the Waukesha city attorney, William G. (Rusty) Callow, later to become a Wisconsin Supreme Court Justice. Callow knew me through my current work as the Brookfield city attorney, and participation in the monthly meetings of the League of Suburban Municipalities. Milwaukee mayors scathingly referred to the League as the "iron ring," meaning it existed, in the city's opinion, to block Milwaukee's natural outward growth. It discussed legislation to propose or oppose in Madison, often affecting the central city with which it rarely agreed. Callow regarded me as a rare moderate who believed that the fortunes of the central city and suburbs were interdependent rather than separate. He was right. Callow, who was close to the governor, also recommended me for my knowledge of the inter-municipal disputes that the commission was supposed to analyze and somehow lessen.

Whether the Metro appointments, including my controversial one, were wise or not can best be judged by Metro's ups, downs, and net accomplishments in the next four years.

Chapter 5

Metro – 1957-1961 – Success or Failure?

The public yearned for an end to city-suburban bickering. Encouraged, Metro started work at a rapid pace. It elected as its vice chairman George A. Parkinson, a respected, independent, energetic director and retired head of what was then called the Milwaukee Vocational and Adult School, and is now known as the Milwaukee Adult Technical College (MATC). Chairman John Lobb assigned all fifteen commissioners to three committees. (Their names and occupations appear in Appendix D.) Each committee was to study a major problem area: Revenue Sources and Distribution (Milwaukee felt its share of state revenues failed to match its deserved needs); Metropolitan Functions (many believed water and sewer service would be more efficient on an area-wide basis), and Land Use and Zoning.

Lobb appointed workaholic professionals to chair two of the committees, Robert E. Jensen for Revenue Sources and Distribution and me for Land Use and Zoning. Choosing us was fiscally fortunate because underfunded Metro could afford only one staff researcher[23] and commissioners served without pay. Jensen and I labored nights and weekends researching and writing our committees' recommendations. Later Metro beefed up its research by asking Marquette University to conduct research studies for Jensen's committee[24] and by adding many outstanding community volunteers to unpaid Metro research committees. Two were Norman Gill, executive director of the highly respected Citizens' Governmental Research Bureau (now Public Policy Forum), and Henry J. Schmandt, Assistant Professor of Political Science at the University of Wisconsin-Milwaukee (UWM). By 1965 Schmandt published the definitive book on Metro.[25]

Metro submitted twenty-five recommendations in four years. I shall sketch the major ones after this brief overview puts them in perspective. Three were major recommendations to transfer local governmental power that the city or legislature accepted. Five of ten revenue recommendations were enacted by the legislature. Two suggestions for transfer of local governmental powers were rejected. The commission itself nearly foundered from a backlash caused by its chairman's publicly advocating metropolitan government without support by the public or commission.

Here are Metro's more significant recommendations, why we made them, what happened to them then, and how they fare today, forty-odd years later. Metro, in my opinion, was primarily created to find a way to overcome Milwaukee's long-standing refusal to sell water to landlocked suburbs – even at a profit. Suburbs away from Lake Michigan needed lake water to replace their ever-deeper but inadequate wells. While Metro debated a solution to the water service problem, the Wisconsin Public Service Commission (PSC) provided an answer on April 2, 1958, by ordering Milwaukee to sell water to Wauwatosa. The PSC ruled that Milwaukee, by serving some suburbs within the county, had assumed a legal obligation to serve all so requesting. *Milwaukee, with a sitting Metropolitan Study Commission watching its every move, announced it would not appeal the PSC decision and offered to serve the suburbs.*

The city's prudent acceptance of the PSC decision substantially solved the water service problem. Eventually Metro formally suggested that the legislature require the City of Milwaukee water utility to sell water wholesale to any suburb within Milwaukee County other than the five then operating their own Lake Michigan water systems, namely, Fox Point, Whitefish Bay, Glendale, Cudahy, and South Milwaukee.[26] The legislature saw no need to act on Metro's water-service recommendation.

By 1998, forty years later, Milwaukee was selling water, wholesale or retail, to ten Milwaukee County suburbs and, in 1999, added part of Menomonee Falls in Waukesha County, and Mequon in Ozaukee County. Only Bayside, River Hills, and Franklin relied primarily on wells for water, while Fox Point, Whitefish Bay, Glendale, Cudahy, Oak Creek, and South Milwaukee obtained their water from Lake Michigan through their own or jointly owned utilities.

In 1958 Metro proposed that the legislature authorize the Metropolitan Milwaukee Sewerage District (MMSD) to extend its service to the 31 percent of Milwaukee County not served and also to the territory outside Milwaukee County lying within the Milwaukee watershed. The out-of-county communities comprised Mequon,

Thiensville, Germantown, Menomonee Falls, Butler, Brookfield, Elm Grove, New Berlin, and Muskego. Furthermore, Metro suggested that the sewer charges and taxes in the newly served areas should be the same as those prevailing in the existing areas being served.

Metro explained why MMSD's service area should be expanded.

> A grave threat to public health exists because septic tanks in unsewered areas in Milwaukee County discharge raw or partially diluted sewage to roadside ditches, watercourses, and fields.... A similar problem exists in suburban areas adjacent to Milwaukee County in Ozaukee, Washington, and Waukesha counties.[27]

The legislature in 1959 partly carried out the recommendation. It enlarged MMSD's service area to include all Milwaukee County except the City of South Milwaukee which already operated its own sewerage system. However, the legislature did not extend the MMSD's service boundaries to include communities outside the county. Rather, the legislature authorized those suburbs to be served only by voluntary contract. The outlying suburbs quickly signed contracts but by 1982 disputes over MMSD's charges led to the notorious fourteen-year "sewer wars." Possibly, the legislature could have prevented those wars by requiring outlying suburbs, as Metro recommended, to join the MMSD in return for sewer service.

Metro was most effective on regional planning. By 1958, Metro recommended the creation of an advisory regional planning commission. A 1955 statute had authorized counties to petition the governor to create one, but Milwaukee area counties hesitated. They did not like the statute's requiring a governing body of 151 members, one for each municipality in the seven-county region. Metro recommended slicing that cumbersome body to eighteen and the immediate creation of the advisory regional commission.

Metro explained:

> Many governmental programs require attention to regional, rather than county or municipal, require-ments. In planning watershed development, whole drainage areas must be treated. Transportation

planning requires attention to traffic movement through a natural, social and economic area. Land use development demands that the requirements for space by each competing activity within the region be balanced against available supplies and against other needs of the regional community.[28]

The Wisconsin Legislative Council in 1959 (with substantial help from me as described in the next chapter) drafted a bill amending the awkward 1955 law. There would be only twenty-one commissioners, three from each county. Metro then supported that bill which passed the Wisconsin Senate 33-0 in July 1959, but barely squeaked through the Assembly by 48-45. Mayor Zeidler (1948-1960) unsuccessfully opposed the bill, stating that the city, with over one-half of the region's population, should have majority representation. Governor Gaylord Nelson (1959-1963) championed the statute, realistically stating that outlying counties would never voluntarily join a regional commission if the central city had a majority vote. Further, he predicted that commissioners from outlying counties would probably become imbued with a regional perspective and vote for many improvements desired by city residents. He cited parks in outlying counties as an example. History proved Nelson right.

Henry Maier (1960-1988) became a strong supporter of the ensuing Southeastern Wisconsin Regional Planning Commission or SEWRPC (pronounced SEWER-PACK). Later, to be sure, Maier's successor, John Norquist, from his 1988 election to public office at age twenty-five, publicly attacked SEWRPC for violating, he said, the one-man-one-vote-principle.[29] He ignored a 1973 opinion by the Wisconsin Attorney General that SEWRPC did not violate the one-man-one-vote principle. Nor did Norquist's argument impress Milwaukee County, or any of the other six counties, the legislature, or any recent governor. They all regard SEWRPC as a useful regional data and planning resource, and, being practical, note that its continued existence is a prerequisite to eligibility for substantial federal grants, particularly for transportation.

Metro suggested two major transfers of local governmental powers which were rejected. One was that Milwaukee County take over the collection and disposal of garbage from local municipalities. Metro believed county-wide service would be more economical and efficient. The county promptly refused. Metro also proposed that the legislature authorize Milwaukee County to assess all property in the county. Metro said county assessment would lead to better and more uniform assessments than achieved by nineteen local municipal assessors. The legislature voted down a bill which would have transferred property assessment from municipalities to the county.

Metro advanced ten recommendations raising state revenues and enhancing the equity of their distribution to Milwaukee County municipalities, particularly the central city. Five ultimately passed the legislature and remain intact today. They included pioneering, controversial, big ticket items, such as: instituting both a 3 percent sales tax and withholding tax on payrolls, and abolishing the personal property tax on manufacturers' inventory. To be fair, the enactment of the lucrative sales tax in 1961 stemmed mostly from a politically skillful pro-tax campaign by Governor Gaylord Nelson. As a liberal Democrat, he sought new state revenues to sustain or increase governmental expenditures. For example, he appointed a prestigious Governor's Advisory Committee on Tax Policy in 1959, ostensibly to investigate, but in reality to build, public support for a sales tax especially among the majority of Democrats previously opposed to it.

Unfortunately, Metro's most interesting actions led up to a public explosion that nearly ended Metro's existence half-way through its four-year term. This is how it came about. In late 1957 or early 1958, the ever-restless Lobb appointed an executive committee consisting of the three committee chairmen and Robert Foote, with himself as chairman.[30] That committee met privately, and, until I objected, had no written agenda and kept no minutes. At first it seemed to justify itself as a sounding board for the brilliant but undisciplined chairman who once came to a breakfast meeting at the University Club and enthusiastically reviewed an article in *Economist*[31] which only he had seen. We barely got to the commission's business. Believing that the committee was drifting – some meetings aimlessly repeated earlier discussions – I volunteered to prepare an agenda, subject to Lobb's approval, and keep minutes. Lobb accepted.

Soon Lobb put metropolitan government – a bug-a-boo to the suburbs – at the top of Metro's agenda. We studied examples of combined city-county governments (Indianapolis), strong county

41

governments (Dade County, Florida), federated governments without a county (Toronto), and a recently failed effort to combine Cleveland, Ohio, with surrounding Cuyahoga County. I flew to Cleveland to learn the reason, which turned out to be quite simple: it would be voted down, surprisingly, by the City of Cleveland – its large block of black voters feeling they would lose political power if predominantly white suburbs were added.

By the end of its first year, Metro seemed on the verge of recommending a transfer of some powers from local government, noting in its annual report:

> Milwaukee area citizens feel...the frustrations of traffic congestion, low water pressure, overflowing septic tanks...[and] political acrimony between the central city and its suburban communities....

and, omnisciently:

> Twentieth Century civilization requires that certain metropolitan governmental services and functions "cannot be done at all...or, as well" by individual municipalities. Our metropolitan system of sewers, expressways and parks are existing recognitions of this fact.[32]

At this point our full-speed-ahead chairman became visibly impatient with the slow pace of his fellow commissioners in recommending a major centralization of municipal powers. He started to get ahead of his troops.

In October 1958, Lobb told Marquette University students that the commission would ask the legislature to expand its jurisdiction to include Waukesha, Washington, and Ozaukee Counties – but he had not yet submitted this proposal to the commission. Two months later the executive committee of the commission issued a report listing five alternatives for improving governmental service through structural change. The Metro report prematurely asked all municipalities in Milwaukee County *and* adjoining it in Waukesha and Ozaukee Counties to indicate the alternative type of government they considered to be best suited for discharging area-wide functions. The alternatives, ranging from the most extreme to least radical, were:

1. Consolidate all municipalities (merger with Milwaukee)
2. Create a federation of local governments something like Toronto where major functions, like police, are handled by the federated government)
3. Create a multi-purpose area-wide agency (water, sewer, and mass transit)
4. Create independent area-wide service agencies for individual functions (such as water)
5. Modernize county government

Although Metro's report raised the question of consolidation, it lobbied against that alternative by baldly stating that it "was a political impossibility" and that "bigness would have considerable disadvantages." Submitting the alternatives for a vote was "a major blunder," according to an informed observer, Henry Schmandt, later a UWM Professor of Urban Affairs and first chairman of SEWRPC. I fully agree with Schmandt, who scorched the commission for taking this major step "without first carefully preparing its case and formulating its strategy."[33] Haste makes waste.

At a jammed public hearing on February 25, 1959, responses of the municipalities became public. Mayor Zeidler unsurprisingly nominated consolidation as his first choice and federation as his second; Parkinson, the multi-function agency but with nine functions; the League of Suburban Municipalities (the iron ring), the multi-purpose agency with three functions (water, sewer, and mass transit.) Most significantly, seventeen suburbs of eighteen responding rejected federation. The next day, the ever hard-charging Lobb asked the full commission, without benefit of a supporting committee report, to recommend the creation of an area-wide "interim joint utility" for water and sewer services. I opposed Lobb's haphazard proposal because study commissions are supposed to study and document advisory recommendations but he was recklessly winging it. Metro turned Lobb's suggestion down, unanimously agreeing only to reaffirm its September 1958 recommendation that the jurisdiction of the Metropolitan Milwaukee Sewerage District be substantially expanded. That was politically safe: MMSD and the City Sewerage Commission were then preparing just such legislation.

The press said federation was dead and so was Lobb's leadership. On March 1, without first informing his fellow commissioners, Lobb resigned as chairman, effective April 1. He told reporters the chairmanship was taking too much of his time. Some commissioners questioned his real motive. They, according to Schmandt, speculated he was irked that the commission did not follow his lead toward metropolitan or federated government. Others guessed that Lobb had initially viewed the commission as a stepping stone to the governorship and that he had lost interest when it became apparent that no significant accomplishments would emerge from its work.[34]

Metro faced a crisis. Metro asked five of its members, including Foote, the born tactician, Parkinson, the vice chairman and City of Milwaukee representative, and me, to recommend a successor chairman to the governor. Foote acted quickly to forge a consensus while I went on a pre-planned vacation with my family. Foote called me in Arizona to say Governor Nelson had asked me to become chairman. I could hardly believe the offer and for a few hours was inclined to accept. Then, with help from my clear-headed wife, I came to my senses. If I was such a tense individual that Mayor Zeidler's earlier unjustified attacks could cause near ulcers when I was a mere appointee, what would happen if I were chairman when controversial proposals incited further personal attacks. I declined but did not wholly escape partisan fire. Although unaware of the governor's undisclosed offer Schmandt agreed I should not have served as chairman. Six years later he wrote:

> Cutler, at the age of forty-two, was regarded as one of the top municipal lawyers of the area. A brilliant and indefatigable worker, he at times antagonized others with his drive and initiative and his impatience with mediocrity. Cutler, to city officials, had become the symbol of the suburban "iron ring" which was wholly unwarranted, since his outlook on metropolitan affairs was far broader than the provincialism represented by the League of Suburban Municipalities, an organization which at no time looked to him as its spokesman. His municipal law practice, however, had occasionally placed him in opposition to the city in annexation and incorporation proceedings and his aggressiveness in

44

handling these matters had given rise to the "Cutler myth." At the time of the MSC appointment, for example, Zeidler had singled out Cutler as "one of the leading opponents of the City of Milwaukee."[35]

In Lobb's place Governor Nelson appointed Albert Houghton Jr., an affable, politically ambitious thirty-eight-year-old attorney who was a close friend of the governor. Houghton never became active, however. He soon suffered a massive manic-depressive nervous breakdown, resigned in August, the same year he received the appointment, and, unhappily, committed suicide in February 1960. When Houghton was appointed chairman in April, George Parkinson, the industrious, creative vice chairman resigned because the statute authorizing Metro provided there could be only one commissioner who was an elected or appointed official of the City of Milwaukee. Houghton was on the Harbor Commission; Parkinson held some other city post. He declined to quit that post and so, legally, had to leave Metro, and the commission elected me vice chairman. With Houghton unable to work, I became acting chairman, only to be summoned before Milwaukee's Common Council to answer hostile questions arising out of the resignation of Metro's second staff director. The director accused Metro of not letting him prepare its research agenda and me, as acting chairman, of bias against the city. He sent the letter to the press and city for good measure. On July 23, twelve of Milwaukee's twenty alderman asked the governor to abolish Metro. Tobin must have nearly died, his worst fears having been proven right.

In August when Houghton resigned, Nelson sought to patch up Metro's damaged image. He appointed as a new chairman the stable, politically tested Dr. J. Martin (Joe) Klotsche, Chancellor of the University of Wisconsin-Milwaukee (UWM) whose appointment the press hailed as a fine choice. Klotsche promptly told me that my continuing as vice chairman was a red flag to city officials and, although their criticisms were baseless, the commission's best interests would be served if I resigned as vice chairman. Though pained, I did. Klotsche did not suggest I quit chairing the Land Use and Zoning Committee which had already obtained Metro's unanimous approval of its recommendation that a regional planning commission be created.

Lobb's and Houghton's resignations nearly wrecked the commission and contributed to damaging turnover of personnel.

Parkinson had left; next Scholl and Foote resigned, probably because they believed Metro had abruptly lost any chance of being effective. Three other commissioners died or moved out of town; only four of the six were replaced, leaving the commission with thirteen members during its final two years. Klotsche's leadership of Metro was diametrically opposite to Lobb's. Whereas to Lobb bolder was better, to Klotsche caution was wiser. Some thought him timid. However, given the shambles he inherited after Lobb's pyrotechnical exit and the public controversy during Houghton's four-month nominal chairmanship, caution was probably the only course available.

Klotsche must have welcomed the quiet noncontroversial input from Norman Gill's careful research on less confrontational subjects. Gill was invaluable. A man of enormous intellect, he headed the Citizens' Governmental Research Bureau (now Public Policy Forum) for thirty-nine years (1945-1984). His sound research, unfailing courtesy, and shrewd advice endeared him to public and private leaders. He guided by asking penetrating questions rather than suggesting specific answers. He was called "Mr. Research" and "Milwaukee's Number One Civic Watchdog." He crafted two farsighted, deeply researched papers. They provided the basis for later-to-be-implemented Metro recommendations. One was for improving area-wide library service, leading to one library card throughout Milwaukee County, permitting a holder to withdraw books from any of seven library systems. The other facilitated inter-governmental cooperation which was then much needed but seldom practiced. A monument to that reform is the North Shore Fire Department, which since January 1, 1995 has ably served seven suburbs in northeastern Milwaukee County: Bayside, Brown Deer, Fox Point, Glendale, River Hills, Shorewood, and Whitefish Bay.

Predictably, the ever-conciliatory University Chancellor Klotsche indicated that the commission should not recommend any new form of government. Metropolitan government was dead. If governmental functions had to be transferred somewhere for reasons of public health, or efficiency, or effectiveness, they should go to a modernized county government. Metro warned in 1961 that spreading urbanization might outgrow the county's borders. It sketched alternative solutions to be considered then. I will discuss them in the Chapter 25, which looks to Milwaukee's future after 2000.

What did Metro accomplish? Quite a lot. All twenty-five Metro recommendations, major and minor, are listed in Appendix E. They are arranged by objective, and whether they were adopted. In a nutshell, Metro in its first twelve or eighteen months produced significant recommendations on water, sewer, and regional planning before nearly collapsing during a disastrous second year. In its two final years it completed comprehensive revenue recommendations from Jensen's committee, half of which the legislature accepted. I did not recognize until later a fundamental reason why Jensen's committee produced effective work over four years while Metro's accomplishments in the fields allotted to Scholl and me virtually ended after eighteen months. By then, Metro had published the only three transfer-of-governmental-functions recommendations which public opinion supported. Later, when Metro tried other transfers such as garbage collection and property assessment, Metro's legislative supporters were routed by local governments' fierce opposition. In contrast, Jensen's committee sought to create new revenue sources for the state, which was popular locally, and to suggest how the Milwaukee area might more equitably share in the larger state pie, which was less popular but not explosive.

In my judgment, Metro was worthwhile but could have accomplished more if it had been differently constituted and better led. That would have enabled it to be more sharply focused, and to devote more of its energies to explaining and lobbying for its recommendations. Probably one-third of its members should have been elected or appointed officials from both local government and the Wisconsin Legislature. Those officials best understand, on the one hand, the political forces and arguments favoring the status quo, and on the other, the need for change. Nominations of public officials would have to be undertaken by a neutral body such as the GMC. Hard work could identify the open-minded officials with the necessary courage and independence to review their own powers objectively. Henry Mixter, Whitefish Bay's wise and diplomatic president, would have been an excellent choice. Lobb, though bright and able (amply proven by his later becoming CEO of the giant Northern Telecom Co. [now Nortel]), was too impatient.

In 1958 the Wisconsin Legislative Council demonstrated a far more successful approach to finding legislative solutions to urban problems outside Milwaukee County and getting them enacted by the legislature.

Chapter 6

Legislative Reform At Last, 1958-1960

In 1958 the legislature requested the Wisconsin Legislative Council to study and recommend solutions to urban problems in Wisconsin outside Milwaukee County. To do so, the council established a fifteen-person Urban Problems Committee. Unlike the Metropolitan Study Commission, it deliberately narrowed its investigation to manageable proportions. It selected only three problems for study: incorporations, annexations, and regional planning. It developed legislative proposals on each and got all enacted in short order. The committee's intentionally narrow focus was probably suggested by its highly respected and legislatively-wise executive secretary, Earle Sachse. Metro sorely needed such high-quality experienced staff.

Sachse's committee minutes tellingly describe prior legislative failures to solve excessive balkanizing incorporations around major Wisconsin cities. Two years earlier, the Legislative Council had drafted a bill which failed to pass the legislature. That bill, 1957 Senate Bill 5 (5-S), required the local circuit court judge to review any proposed incorporation and determine whether its territory possessed "the requisite urban characteristics."

By coincidence three months before the Urban Problems Committee met I had authored an article right on their target. Entitled "Characteristics of Land Required for Incorporation or Expansion of a Municipality", it appeared in the *Wisconsin Law Review*.[36] It suggested 5-S was unconstitutional. Sachse apparently agreed. He deftly urged all committee members to read my article, doubtless hoping they would reach the same conclusion. They did. Moreover, the committee's ultimate report to the 1959 legislature – written by Sachse – included five key excerpts from my article verbatim. The only thing missing was quotation marks and source's name. The report even endorsed one of my opinions as that of an unnamed "expert." The five excerpts led the committee to conclude two things: (1) Bill 5-S's approach of authorizing a judge to determine whether a proposed incorporation met a vague standard was unwise, and (2) many recent uncontested incorporations were apparently illegal.

About this time I wrote the committee as chairman of Metro's Land Use and Zoning Committee, suggesting it consider legislation that would avoid Milwaukee County's recent municipal fragmentation. The committee asked me to draft an outline of proposed legislative standards for future incorporations. I did so, closely tracking my law review article. On June 2, the Urban Problems Committee appointed me and two professors as a subcommittee to outline remedial legislation, based on my memo as a starter. The professors were Jacob Beuscher of the University of Wisconsin Law School, and James Donohue of the University of Wisconsin Extension Service.

We finished the outline by July 8, after first refining my standards. Professor Beuscher, who was considered the Number 1 expert on land use law in Wisconsin (and who jokingly told me I was "Number 2"), then drafted a specific bill, while I returned to my law practice in Milwaukee. Earning a living required me to make up for the many unpaid hours spent weekly for Metro and the Urban Problems Committee.

Our subcommittee's bill was radical. Each proposed incorporation would be required to meet two sets of standards. The first consisted of clean-cut measures which could be applied by the circuit court. These included the minimum area required (in metropolitan areas, two square miles for villages; three, for cities), population (2,500 for such villages and 5,000 for such cities), and population density. The second set of standards were discretionary guidelines to be applied by a state administrative official.

An administrator was needed for two reasons. The first was to provide consistency statewide in applying the standards. Circuit judges around the state had given substantially different opinions as to the characteristics land must possess to be constitutionally eligible for incorporation. Second, the constitutional doctrine of separation of powers meant that only the legislature or its delegate, an administrator, could determine whether a proposed incorporation complied with discretionary standards.

The bill gave the administrator, to be called the Wisconsin Director of Planning, several extensive standards to apply. The land had to be reasonably homogeneous and compact. Its territory beyond the urban core must have a potential for substantial urban development within three years (one must not incorporate farm land). Finally, the administrator was required to find that the proposed incorporation was "in the public interest." To come to that conclusion he or she must first weigh complex legislative standards. They were: sufficiency of the tax base; the level of services needed; and – most devilish of all – the impact of the incorporation on (a) the remaining unincorporated area of the town and (b) on the orderly development of the entire metropolitan community. In plain English, the standards meant: (a) the incorporation must not impoverish a town's remnant by siphoning off the richer part of its tax base, and (b) must not excessively fragment the community or deprive the central city of areas into which it might more logically expand.

I explained to the full committee that the subcommittee's bill, if it had been enacted before 1950, would have prohibited most of the eight incorporations that occurred in Milwaukee County between 1950 and 1957. Five would have flunked the minimum area or population requirements: Bayside, Brown Deer, Hales Corners, Glendale, and St. Francis. Two of the other three incorporations, Oak Creek and Franklin were large, respectively, 28.4 and 34.4 square miles. That large size combined with low population density meant they possibly would not have passed all the discretionary standards to be applied by the proposed new director of planning. I added that the five too-small municipalities could conceivably have been enlarged enough at incorporation to pass our subcommittee's minimum size and population tests, but some might still have failed the "public interest" tests as to fiscal viability, ability to render adequate public services, and so on.

The Urban Problems Committee debated whether its massive reform of the basic incorporation law should repeal the special "Oak Creek Law" discussed at page 30 above. Logic said "Yes" because Oak Creek was the result of special legislation wholly inconsistent with the principles of the committee's proposed revision. Politics said "No." The Oak Creek Law's supporters might oppose and endanger passage of the reform bill, 1959 Assembly Bill 226 (226-A). Further, the Oak Creek Law was already a largely useless appendage. Virtually all territory contiguous to the City of Milwaukee to which it might apply had already been incorporated.

The committee discussed and fine-tuned the bill at length and approved it, knowing that future incorporations would be drastically reduced. I warned them of a danger: some people might seek to evade the strict new incorporation standards by submitting the same land for *non-state-controlled* annexation to a neighboring municipality. I had done just that with the sixteen-square-mile annexations to Brown Deer in 1956. I suggested in my June 2 memorandum that the bill also require state approval for annexations larger than one square mile. For unrecorded reasons, probably fear of extra administrative expense, the annexation provision did not appear in Beuscher's draft.

I then suggested that over-one-square-mile annexations at least be reviewed by a court. The committee agreed, specifying that the circuit court must find that any such annexation "was not against the public interest." The committee defined "public interest" in terms of three factors: governmental services to be supplied to the annexed territory, its shape, and its homogeneity with the annexing municipality. Unfortunately, everyone else and I underestimated the likelihood that a court, in determining whether an annexation complied with the legislative definition of the "public interest," would be violating the state constitution's prohibition against a court's exercising a legislative function. Within nine years of 226-A's becoming law, the Wisconsin Supreme Court, for just that reason, voided the statute's provision for court review of large annexations. The case, ironically, was one in which I was asked to defend the statute. I did and properly lost.[37]

The committee also examined why regional planning commissions were not being created as expected. It asked a second subcommittee, consisting of Beushcer, Robert Sundby, and me, to come up with an answer. Sundby was then counsel to the Wisconsin League of Municipalities and later an appellate judge. Our solution was 1959 Assembly Bill 227 (227-A) authorizing twenty-one commissioners, three from each of the seven counties in the Milwaukee area. The bill also sought to ensure that regional commissioners would bring a regional perspective to their work. It authorized the governor to appoint two-thirds of the commissioners, a provision which remains in effect today, though later modified to require that one-half of his appointments come from a panel of nominees nominated by each local county board. The bill passed the legislature easily in 1960, as did the accompanying municipal incorporation bill, 226-A.

In retrospect the Urban Problems Committee's achievement in rapidly enacting two reform bills can be both praised and criticized. The committee achieved overdue comprehensive legislation on a controversial subject after prior incorporation-annexation revisions had failed to pass the legislature. Regional planning commission authorization had passed but was never implemented because sufficient counties had not petitioned the governor to create such a commission. The 1960 twin acts were a major accomplishment. However, the committee's delegating the drafting of the incorporation-annexation bill virtually carte blanche to two very busy activists, Professor Beuscher and me, had a price. It would be paid later.

Chapter 7

Unintended Consequences, 1959-2000

While I had early cautioned the Urban Problems Committee that the new municipal incorporation-annexation law should reduce but not eliminate the creation of new suburbs, in practice it virtually halted new incorporations. What a contrast! Under the old law, incorporations were easy and frequent. Between 1954 and 1959, for example, the small Village of Elm Grove and four large suburbs (Brookfield, New Berlin, Mequon, and a greatly enlarged Village of Menomonee Falls) were created on Milwaukee County's western and northern borders.

In the next thirty-five years (1960-1995) incorporations in eastern Waukesha County dried up. That area was the most rapidly growing in Wisconsin. Yet the director of Regional Planning approved only one petition for incorporation out of eight submitted to him. Muskego, which I handled in 1964, was the sole exception. In the same thirty-five years he vetoed three out of three petitions in eastern Kenosha County.

Efforts to incorporate the Town of Pewaukee became a laboratory case. They failed three times. The fourth succeeded on February 15, 1999. Pewaukee lies just north of the legislatively-favored "central city" of Waukesha and west of Brookfield. The town board asked me to incorporate it in their first effort in 1977. The statute was so tough I advised the town supervisors they had only a 3 percent chance of success. They replied "Go ahead." By the time of the third unsuccessful effort in 1991, the town's population had grown substantially to 9,672. By then the town also provided both city-like sewer and water services.

By early 1998, the town's population reached nearly 12,000. Its assessed valuation, boosted by the presence of a giant QuadGraphics printing plant, had risen to fifteenth highest in the metropolitan area. Milwaukee was naturally first, followed by Brookfield and then Wauwatosa. Pewaukee finally became a city in 1999, but then only on a sensible condition imposed by the director of planning. Pewaukee must first, he ruled, negotiate a mutually acceptable boundary with its old antagonist, Waukesha. It did.

The virtual shutdown of new incorporations in metropolitan areas of Wisconsin stemmed primarily from hasty drafting, by Beuscher and me, of the criteria defining whether an incorporation would be "in the public interest." Beuscher later somewhat defensively explained to me – after the statute had demonstrated its stultifying effect – that he had delegated the drafting of certain provisions of the new law to a graduate student without field experience. However, I believe the fault lay primarily with Beuscher and me, especially me. We had not noted its inclusion of so many strict pro-central-city criteria that the administrator might well believe the legislature was commissioning him to turn down virtually all incorporations near central cities. Minutes show I advised the Urban Problems Committee early on that the bill should not prohibit all incorporations. However, I later failed to test the bill's evolving criteria against recent incorporations with which I was generally familiar to determine whether a desirable few would have passed – especially if their boundaries were drawn differently.

Perhaps it was too big a job to expect a volunteer to undertake. Perhaps the committee desired to err on the side of possible overkill. They were aware of my statement to them that most of the eight incorporations in Milwaukee County between 1950 and 1957 would not meet the new standards. However, the over-toughness had an unintended effect of its own – as we see next.

In 1969, yet another state study committee was appointed, the Tarr Task Force. It was named after Curtis W. Tarr, its vigorous, politically aspiring chairman, who was president of Lawrence University. It looked again at "urban problems" and criticized the 1959 statute as too "stringent" and unsuccessfully sought to modify it. The Tarr Task Force ("Tarr") declared the 1959 statute to be:

> an effort to reduce the tendency to inhibit metropolitan development with a tight ring of too small or otherwise ill-conceived incorporated units surrounding the central city.[38]

Tarr further reported:

> The 1959 law had the effect of virtually forbidding new incorporations anywhere in the vicinity of large cities.[39]

By 1983 the Wisconsin Supreme Court agreed with Tarr that the statute was that strict. It rejected an argument by an attorney, Robert Sundby, that the denial of his client's incorporation stemmed from an erroneously strict interpretation of the statute by the administrator (department):

> [It] is apparent from a mere reading of the procedures for the incorporation of villages and cities that the legislature, not the department, has placed substantial obstacles in the path of incorporation of a city or village which falls in the metropolitan area.[40]

On the other hand, the Tarr Task Force reported that Wisconsin's many central cities (defined in the 1959 Act as those of 25,000 in population) were often unable to annex nearby unincorporated land. Annexation had long required the consent of the majority of both the annexed territory's resident voters and the owners of over one-half of the land. Conditioning annexation on obtaining the consent of a majority of the electors is a democratic form of self-determination. However, asking also for the consent of a majority of the land owners (measured by assessed value or acreage) seems a throwback to an era when only property owners could vote. Moreover, requiring a double majority unfairly favored opponents of annexation. My field experience had taught me that. I so advised Tarr. Annexations realistically needed the support of approximately 55 percent of the electors and landowners to be able to garner the signatures of over 50 percent of them. Some potential signers were invariably traveling, on vacation, or congenitally opposed to signing a *public* petition of any kind even if they favored what it proposed.

The Tarr Task Force concluded that the double majority had this undesirable consequence:

> The veto over annexation held by fringe voters frequently blocks the orderly enlargement of the incorporated area to include the urban territory surrounding it.[41]

Finally, the Tarr Task Force with exceptional insight identified the unintended consequence of central cities not being able to expand *and* border areas not being able to incorporate:

> The inability of an area to incorporate under current legal standards, coupled with the unworkability of the

annexation laws, has produced a rash of unincorporated legal settlements served by a confusing proliferation of special purpose government agencies [like sewer districts]. Thus, proliferation of government units on the urban fringe has not been prevented; the State has merely limited the proliferation to one type of government – the suburban city or village. To thwart this disorder both annexation and incorporation procedures must be available, with control over the type of procedure firmly held by the [proposed] Boundary Review Board.[42]

The unincorporated legal settlements in southeastern Wisconsin in 1969 most conspicuously included the urban towns of Pewaukee (next to Waukesha), Mount Pleasant (next to Racine) and Pleasant Prairie (next to Kenosha). I was asked to incorporate all three and advised two, Pewaukee and Mount Pleasant, that incorporation was not feasible; the best way to protect their independence was to negotiate agreed boundaries with their city neighbor. Mount Pleasant did. Pewaukee and Waukesha could not agree for years. Pleasant Prairie was incorporated in 1989, by my successor in municipal law, James Baxter, and then only through legislation specially enacted for that purpose (with the essential support of the City of Kenosha) and two pre-existing statutes.

The Tarr Task Force sponsored remedial legislation that was even more complex than the problems it meant to solve. Perhaps that was partly my fault. They asked for my advice at many sessions. At the time I was disgusted with the stalemate over curbing feverish competition between cities and towns for land and had become infatuated with planning as an answer. Tarr accepted my heavily planning-oriented general solution. Tarr proposed a Boundary Review Board of three persons appointed by the governor. The board would review *all* municipal boundary changes – whether by annexation, incorporation, or consolidation. Cities could annex areas *without the vote of their resident voters* if the annexation complied with four concepts dear to planners. It must eliminate jagged municipal boundaries. It must be supported by a professionally drafted boundary expansion plan for the systematic and orderly expansion of the municipality. The city had to submit detailed plans for the extension of sewer, water, and storm sewer services into the area to be annexed. The board must find them practical, needed, and not just empty promises. Eau Claire had abandoned service promises after a large annexation.

The Tarr Task Force proposed legislation that would also make municipal incorporations near cities feasible, though (still) difficult. The sole administrator would be replaced by three gubernatorial appointees. Three appointees of the governor would not be as susceptible to a pro-central-city bias as a solitary lower level civil servant. A bill (S 364) incorporating these changes passed the senate in 1969 but failed in the assembly. In 1971, the Legislative Council, convinced that the senate's bill needed improvement, introduced a modified proposal, Assembly Bill 84. The bill was narrowly defeated in the assembly. With these two unsuccessful efforts, serious reform of the incorporation and annexation laws remained stalled until today. The stalemate reflects the underlying fact that each of the opposing forces has customarily had sufficient clout with the legislature to defeat any proposal not acceptable to it.

However, the 1959 incorporation law's shutdown of new incorporations near central cities, plus the Tarr Task Force's inability to achieve its complex reforms, did, in one sense, stop further fragmentation around central cities. The urban towns, though frustrated by their inability to become cities or villages, did largely remain intact. Too, they continued, for the most part, to administer large areas where economies of scale might assist in providing good governmental services.

Slowly after 1960 central cities like Waukesha, Racine, Kenosha and their bordering towns realized that the legislature would not come to the aid of either side. The cities and bordering towns gradually learned to negotiate their differences through boundary agreements. Agreements were achieved only by cobbling together various elements of statutory authority and pushing the envelop of that authority. One originated with the Metropolitan Study Commission's 1959 bill aimed at settling the six-year Brown Deer-Milwaukee litigation of 1956-1962. It said: if two municipalities have litigated a boundary dispute for two years, they can agree on a common boundary with the court's approval. Racine and Waukesha entered into such agreements with their respective principal urban town rivals – Mount Pleasant (early) and Pewaukee (late). In the 1990s Pleasant Prairie next to Kenosha concluded a far-reaching agreement with the Town of Bristol, west of north-south I-94, establishing a timetable for annexations and the extension of sewer and water services.

These negotiated settlements responded better to the parties' special needs than anything the far-distant legislature could have formulated. The legislature tends to over-correct one problem while ignoring others. In 1959 it corrected excessive incorporations on the urban fringe while doing nothing about improving the annexation law or providing a mechanism for extending sewer and water services to areas where their presence would advance public health.

Nevertheless, the frustrating stalemate in boundary changes after 1959 was better than the rapid municipal fragmentation of 1950-1957 in Milwaukee and Waukesha Counties. The Beuscher-Cutler law did some good, though in an unintended way.

In April 1968 the Marquette Interchange – the hub of the Milwaukee freeway system – was nearing completion.

(*Copyrighted Photograph*, Milwaukee Journal Sentinel)

Part Three

Transportation Planning and Freeway Wars

Chapter 8

SEWRPC Plans Land Use and Freeway System

Clearer success was achieved by regional planning legislation drafted in 1959 by the Urban Problems Committee and enacted in 1960. The revised enabling act permitted Governor Nelson to create a regional planning commission only after all the potential member counties petitioned him to do so. A strong believer in planning, Nelson immediately started a campaign to persuade all seven counties in southeastern Wisconsin to sign the necessary petitions. They included Milwaukee, Waukesha, Racine, Kenosha, Walworth, Ozaukee, and Washington. The region was Wisconsin's most economically significant. It included 40 percent of the state's population and assessed property value within 5 percent of the state's area.

Nelson dispatched David Carley, secretary of the Department of Resource Development, to lobby each county board. Carley was a fan of planning and, at thirty-five, a tornado of energy who worked eighteen-hour days. Carley was not a lawyer. He took me along to appear before the county boards concerned, in part because the Metropolitan Study Commission's Committee on Land Use and Zoning, of which I was chairman, had initially recommended the simplification of a regional planning commission's governance. Carley wanted me to tell the seven counties' board members why the proposed commission would serve their counties' interests by binding the region together through advisory regional plans. Carley also asked me to describe SEWRPC's responsibilities and limited powers.

Probably because I had become such a red flag to Mayor Zeidler and the Milwaukee Common Council, Carley met alone with Mayor Zeidler and the common council. Later when Zeidler said that the commission could not be trusted to reflect the city's concerns unless a

60

majority of its governing body resided in Milwaukee, Carley told Zeidler in a private session that he was full of baloney (the actual word was more vulgar). Zeidler's opposition did not deter the Milwaukee County Board from joining six other counties in quickly petitioning Nelson to create the commission, whereupon Nelson convened a formal public hearing. Mostly supporters attended, such as the venerable Leo Tiefenthaler, secretary of the City Club, and Milwaukee City planner Elmer Krieger, both of whom had long championed regional planning.

Bill Bowman, an orator of the old school and attorney for the City of Franklin in southwest Milwaukee County, loudly warned that a re-gional commission – even though advisory – would become a dreaded metropolitan government stripping municipalities of their cherished home rule.

In August of the same year, 1960, Nelson signed the Executive Order creating the Southeastern Wisconsin Regional Planning Commission, (promptly dubbed SEWRPC and pronounced SEWER-PACK). He appointed fourteen of the twenty-one commissioners. He chose care-fully, after receiving suggestions from Carley, me, and others. He felt commissioners should reflect a regional viewpoint and be respected in their own communities. Accordingly, many of his appointments lived in one county while working or having substantial business in another. George Berteau, an attorney for American Motors, lived in Racine but worked in Kenosha; Maynard Meyer, an architect from Pewaukee, had offices in Milwaukee; James Egan from Mequon, who would later become its mayor, worked for a business in Milwaukee; Milton LaPour was a Racine mortgage banker with clients in several counties; I was from Fox Point and had my office in Milwaukee and land use assign-ments in many counties.

Nelson showed his pragmatic streak. He put the success of regional planning above party, choosing mostly Republicans. His reason? Smart politics. In the outlying counties Republicans dominated the local governments to whom SEWRPC would address many future suggestions for the wisest land use. Seven commissioners were selected by the seven county boards. All were county supervisors, and two of them were county board chairmen, signifying the importance attached to this new agency.

After two years of intensive effort helping create SEWRPC, I nourished the hope of becoming its first chairman, even making a bungled effort to run for the office. I wrote fellow new commissioners before our first meeting describing the history of the commission's creation and, doubtless, not concealing my role. That was too obvious and was judged by some to be overly aggressive or arrogant. As soon as the commission met and picked a nominating committee, I asked a Waukesha County member, who knew my recent six years of service as Brookfield city attorney, to put my name before the committee. He did, but also nominated himself and, unknown to me, campaigned for himself within the committee. I lost. So did he.

Henry Schmandt became the first chairman and served one year. This thoughtful, soft-spoken assistant professor at UWM was then writing his book on the Metropolitan Study Commission.[43] I played several roles within SEWRPC over the next twenty-four years. I was secretary for seventeen years and chaired six hard-working advisory committees of outside experts. I also counseled receptive governors on the comparative contributions of commissioners up for reappointment. One commissioner flunked reappointment because he had, over my protests, illegally and unwisely excluded the press from committee meetings he chaired. Once I went to Governor Patrick Lucey's office to persuade him to reappoint a very able SEWRPC chairman whose condescending attitude toward state officials had inclined Lucey, initially, toward dropping him.

We original commissioners knew that SEWRPC's success in the long run required it to create advisory plans so appealing they would be carried out by all levels of government (federal, state, county, and local) and by the private sector. SEWRPC's success in the short run depended on strong financing, good leadership, and a talented staff. SEWRPC was well-financed – provided counties or communities did not exercise their statutory right to withdraw from it.

The existence of that right of exit figured heavily in a county's willingness to join SEWRPC. Twelve small isolated communities – but no counties – did withdraw in early years. They were motivated either by a vague fear of metropolitan government or by a thrifty concern that SEWRPC would do nothing for their taxpayers. In any event, those that withdrew (all of which rejoined later) had departed before they could witness SEWRPC's benefits to them. Benefits included more than the advisory regional plans. Counties and communities increasingly used the regional data bank and contracted with SEWRPC for local planning services. SEWRPC's thriftiness reassured elected officials. SEWRPC could levy taxes up to three mills per $1,000 equalized assessed valuation, or up to $250,000 annually in 1961. The commission raised only $75,000, an act of self-restraint popular with county-appointed commissioners. They bore the responsibility of explaining the new agency's work to their county boards and defending its tax levy. SEWRPC also won large planning grants from the federal and state governments, who were then keen on regional planning. Between 1963 and 1965 grants totaled approximately two-and-a-half times the amount SEWRPC raised in local taxes.

SEWRPC fortunately acquired stable leadership and highly qualified staff. By 1962 a successful duo started a twenty-year run managing the agency: a hard-working, politically savvy George Berteau as chairman, who made the commission the central part of his life, and Kurt W. Bauer, a talented engineer-planner, as executive director. Bauer previously worked under Donald Webster, dean of municipal engineers in the Milwaukee area. Bauer, as a Ford Foundation scholar, helped create the long range planning division of the Wisconsin Highway Department. Bauer's encyclopedic knowledge earned him great respect with key advisors to two levels of government that SEWRPC would ask to implement its advice. They were engineers for local governments and the state Highway Department.

The widely respected Bauer served from 1962 to 1997, a remarkable thirty-five years. He steadily built a reputation for painstakingly objective research as a foundation for practical advisory plans. The plans addressed a long list of area-wide development problems: land use, transportation routes and design capacity, water and air pollution, the location of large parks and shopping centers, the preservation of woodlands and flood lands from urban development, flood control, and improved sanitation through well-designed sewerage and storm water systems. Bauer, ever insightful, also created a highly useful parcel-based computerized land-use information system at the county level.[44]

Bauer's objectivity, sound plans, and modesty won the respect of factions that often warred with each other such as suburbs and agricultural towns – and even crusty Henry A. Maier who had replaced Zeidler in 1960 as mayor of the City of Milwaukee. Maier's respect for SEWRPC was doubly significant. The city was an important political power. Too, Maier's almost daily verbal assaults on the suburbs and on *The Milwaukee Journal* (because it did not always agree with him) made many incorrectly believe the feisty Mayor could not appreciate any government or person. Maier supported SEWRPC's studies of the Milwaukee River and other watersheds and twice asked engineer-planner Bauer to accept a top-level executive post in his administration. Bauer declined. He liked to be his own boss. He appreciated that commissioners had consistently accorded him an independence from interference in planning that he could not expect when working for elected officials whose longest horizon was the next election. Bauer was well aware, as were the commissioners, that during this time a number of prominent civil servants quit their posts because some elected officials increasingly usurped their professional roles. In due course Bauer's growing national reputation for excellence led several states to ask him to head their highway departments.

The decisive measure of SEWRPC's long-term achievement is the extent to which its plans were carried out by the governments and private agencies to which they were addressed. From the start, SEWRPC, under Bauer's experienced counsel, extensively engaged professional and public leaders in the evolution of its advisory plans. One objective was to ensure input from and debate among all major interests likely to be affected by the prospective plan. The other, more subtle objective, was to pre-sell compliance with an evolving plan by drawing representatives of potential implementing agencies into its creation. Better to be there at the take-off than at the crash landing. This technique of involving potential implementors in plan creation helped achieve a nearly l00 percent implementation of park plans and early transportation plans.

In chapters that follow I examine the implementation of three of SEWRPC's plans, especially one dealing with flooding and pollution on the Milwaukee River and the highly strategic and politically controversial plan for Milwaukee area freeways. Later I analyze how the region responded to commission land use recommendations intended to lessen the scattered, often hodge-podge outward development from central cities. I am speaking of urban sprawl, one of the most enduring, misunderstood, and increasingly deplored trends of our times.

By 1965 SEWRPC had completed a monumental land use and transportation system plan for the seven-county region. One and one-half million dollars in federal and state grants helped SEWRPC staff to grow for a time to over three hundred engineers, planners, economists, demographers, natural resource conservationists, and cartographers. This small army built a plan that recommended the best land use for every neighborhood in the region and the transportation routes required to move people and goods within it. The plan presented its suggestions authoritatively through extensive text, many colored maps and charts. Colored charts depicted the recommended use by every broad category – residential, commercial, agricultural, industrial, recreational.

The quality of SEWRPC's work won national recognition. In 1972, the National Society of Professional Engineers named SEWRPC's plan for land use and transportation as one of ten outstanding engineering achievements in America. That award was the first ever given to a non-construction project. The basic plan and the library of statistical data underlying it (such as population projections, land use needs, employment projections, traffic patterns, soil conditions, air and water quality conditions) became the foundation for more detailed plans for specific functions. Two advisory plans in particular shaped the future. They planned the freeway system in greater Milwaukee, and the best way to eliminate growing flooding and water pollution on the Milwaukee River.

Chapter 9

Freeway Construction Moves into High Gear, 1953-1968

In the early 1950s increasing traffic overloaded Milwaukee's streets. Between 1945 and 1953 automobile and truck ownership expanded by 61 percent in the city and 66 percent in the county.[45] Drivers drove more miles as they moved from the inner rings of the city toward or to its outskirts. City traffic grew by 100 percent between 1945 and 1952.[46]

Heavy traffic and multiple traffic lights at busy intersections caused frequent stops and long delays. At rush hour major routes and their at-surface intersections were clogged with cars and lumbering trolley cars, delivery trucks, and buses whose sluggish movement and frequent stops slowed auto traffic and increased blood pressure. Travel to the North Shore suburbs along North 3rd Street took forty-five minutes in rush hour. Suburbanites taking West Wisconsin Avenue and Bluemound Road to the western border of Milwaukee County at North l24th Street used up twenty-five minutes. Traveling from downtown south to the airport required twenty minutes.

Milwaukee sensed a need for freeways to move increasing traffic more easily than could be done over arterial streets. In 1951 the city hired traffic consultants, Amman & Whitney, who in 1952 proposed a 20.4-mile expressway system within the city. The estimated cost of $158 million would be defrayed by a county-wide vehicle or property tax. Here is how the consultants described the need for expressways:

> Traffic congestion in Milwaukee is presently costing its citizens thousands of dollars in daily operating losses. With traffic increasing at a steady rate and little operating margin of unused vehicular capacity, the situation is becoming critical. If substantial additions to traffic ways are not provided within the next few years, motorists will experience rapidly increasing delays and accidents. Additional congestion would bring further economic losses, diffused throughout every segment of the local economy, and result in

noticeably accelerated depreciation in property values.[47]

The common council and Mayor Frank Zeidler approved the plan for expressways. By 1953, only a year later, 2,200 feet of freeway had already been constructed in the South 43rd Street corridor north from National Avenue. This was the start of what was later to be known as the Stadium Freeway South. It was intended to connect two sections of Milwaukee by going through the tiny industrial Village of West Milwaukee. That village, an independent tax haven boasting the lowest tax rate in Milwaukee County at the time, showed no interest in allowing the intended highway to pass through its area. Village officials possibly feared the freeway would displace manufacturing plants that were the source of its large tax revenues.

Milwaukee recognized the political futility of trying to develop freeway routes through potentially non-receptive neighboring communities and, in 1953, turned over its plans and most of its experienced expressway staff to Milwaukee County. The county then created the Expressway Commission to design and acquire the right-of-way for a freeway system throughout Milwaukee County. The state Highway Commission assumed responsibility for construction, operation, and maintenance. No dissenting municipality could unilaterally block an essential through route.

In the late 1950s and most of the 1960s freeway construction was very popular. Civic leaders such as Eliot G. Fitch, the well-respected president of the Marine National Exchange Bank, and Robert S. Stevenson, future president of Allis-Chalmers, gladly accepted long hours of unpaid toil as members of the Expressway Commission. When elected city and county officials spoke to the commission of freeways, it was to demand faster construction.

The *local* desire to build freeways fortuitously coincided with the *national* creation of the generously financed Interstate Highway System by Congress and President Dwight D. Eisenhower. "Ike" had, after World War II, observed Germany's astonishingly efficient, virtually level, multi-lane Autobahn. It spanned Germany in all directions, linking cities and leading to borders in a way Hitler had considered vital for modern warfare. Hitler had sought to move troops and arma- ments to any border with lightning speed. Ike, too, had experienced the inadequacy of the American highway system while conducting demonstration cross-country military convoys before World War II. One of Ike's goals when elected in 1952, early in the Cold War, was to create a modern national freeway system that would promote defense as well as economic development.

Ike summoned General Lucius Clay, the hero of the Berlin Airlift of 1948-49 and a superb administrator. He asked Clay to head a blue-ribbon committee that would develop detailed standards for a new national highway system and propose it to Congress. Clay in turn picked a top Bureau of Public Roads engineer to head the committee's staff, Francis (Frank) Cutler Turner. Turner's rich prior experience included constructing highways in Alaska during World War II and reconstructing the war-damaged highways of the Philippines after the war. The work of Clay and Turner was based in part on data assembled for an earlier 1944 feasibility study for a national highway system. Initially it had been suggested by Franklin Delano Roosevelt.[48]

Often, a new idea's success or failure depends on its details. The Clay committee's report began to establish design criteria for criss-crossing America with 42,000 miles of super-speed, super-safe highways. Question number one was, which cities to link by these new routes; question two, whether the freeways should enter cities or go around them. The Europeans kept their railway systems from crossing cities. Hitler did the same with the Autobahn. It circled cities in "ring" roads. London has eight railway stations; Paris, five; no railway crosses either city, even though they are their nation's economic hubs. Likewise, American railways did not cross Chicago, nor, with one small exception, New York City. Constructing major transportation facilities through cities can be disruptive and enormously expensive. The large cost of acquiring land and buildings might substantially reduce the number of inter-city miles which the nation could finance.

Nevertheless Frank Turner strongly believed that freeways should enter cities. The question of whether the freeways should penetrate cities, as advocated by Turner, was vigorously debated within the Eisenhower administration.[49] He and the Clay committee visualized a system which would serve commerce as well as defense, unlike the German Autobahn, that had primarily military objectives. Turner explained the Clay committee's decision to penetrate cities:

> We looked at the needs of most Americans. One of the major problems was in the city, not the country. This is where travel was difficult; congestion high. So we needed roads both between cities and to penetrate into cities because that is where most of the miles are driven. That is where the need was.
>
> So our concept was to go through – not around – cities.... We knew that cities would be hurt by being bypassed. That is one of the reasons we did not go around them, as the Autobahn did, but chose to penetrate into the city. And not just through the city, but to provide a route to specific points inside the city. That would aid commerce. You need to be able to get trucks into the cities – right up to the loading dock. You can't just have them go up to the city limits and dump their loads there. You have to build into the cities.[50]

Turner's views stimulated vociferous minority opposition. The remarkably clairvoyant U.S. Senator Daniel Patrick Moynihan from New York recalled forty years later his concern when the historic 1956 Interstate Highway Act was debated:

> It was possible to see that these roads were too big for our cities and that they were going to smash them to pieces....You could see it happening but you couldn't get anyone to hear you.[51]

Congress liberally funded the construction of the popular Interstate Highway System by levying a federal gasoline tax. States were reimbursed for 90 percent of the construction costs, the other 10 percent being provided by the states or, at their option, the local counties or municipalities concerned. The federal government made the final decision on the routes and the specifications for the highways. It also required that each state finance (with substantial federal assistance) the preparation of advisory metropolitan transportation system plans. Such plans would both nominate *federal* freeway routes and devise a *local* highway system to serve, or support, such freeway routes. The federal government recognized that maximum freeway utilization depends on efficient local access. The local highway planning requirement assured well-thought-out access roads.

SEWRPC with its 1961 three-year $1.5 million grant completed a regional land use and transportation system plan by 1965. I remember spending countless hours reading and critiquing drafts prepared by SEWRPC's expert technical staff. The advisory plan was then approved as the official blueprint for the construction of freeways – including interstate highways – in the Milwaukee area by the Milwaukee County Expressway Commission, the Wisconsin State Highway Commission, and the U.S. Bureau of Public Roads.

As already noted, freeways were planned and constructed by the city until 1953, and thereafter by the County Expressway Commission until the early 1960s. Then responsibility for planning and construction was split. SEWRPC took over the influential advisory planning, culminating in its 1965 plan for freeway routes. (See Map 3.) The Expressway Commission and state Highway Department shared responsibility for designing, financing, and constructing the freeways. SEWRPC's plan anticipated staged construction sufficient to accommodate traffic demand through 1990. SEWRPC after 1965 frequently updated its plan in response to subsequent demographic and political developments.

Though no one knew it then, the 1965 plan also represented the high point in freeway planning. It included many proposed segments of a system which, as it turned out, were never to be started in some cases nor finished in others. Meanwhile construction appropriations at federal and state levels flowed freely. Between 1962 and 1967 construction averaged 9.5 miles annually.

But, in 1969, vocal opposition to further freeways had replaced the prior steady demand for more rapid construction. The early popularity of freeway construction was declining. The county board cut future annual funds for expressways to one half the figure expended in 1968.[52] New freeway openings dropped abruptly to 1.9 miles. Why?

The short answer is: the freeways, while almost universally popular for the first fifteen years of construction, incurred rising opposition by the late '60s. Its roots lay in the sudden and totally unexpected emergence of young political activists who challenged the very need for freeways. Where they came from and how they developed great political power requires a look at the evolution of the Civil Rights Movement between 1965 and 1975.

Chapter 10

Activists Turn Milwaukee Upside Down

In the mid- and late-1960s growing social unrest in America and disrespect for civil authority escalated into outbursts of violence. There were many causes. Action on one cause emboldened action on another. Blacks, frustrated by high unemployment and poverty in a generally prosperous country, rioted and set fire to inner city neighborhoods in Los Angeles (1965), Newark (1967) and Detroit (1967). Many persons were killed: thirty-four in the Watts area of Los Angeles, thirty-three in Newark and forty-three in Detroit.[53]

Milwaukee came next. On the night of July 3l, 1967, rioting and arson broke out in Milwaukee's inner city on the North Side. Within two hours Mayor Henry Maier asked Governor Warren Knowles to call out the National Guard, 2,305 of whom arrived within twenty-four hours.[54] Simultaneously, Maier imposed a city-wide twenty-four-hour curfew – the most rigid imposed in any American city – which he modified gradually.[55] On the tenth day the curfew was lifted altogether. Maier's prompt actions held down Milwaukee's casualties to four people killed and one hundred injured, including twelve police officers.

I remember my personal shock in learning of the shootings, fires, and curfew on the car radio. My family and I were returning from a pleasant weekend in Door County, 175 miles to the north. We were forbidden to enter the city for a day, and even then I could not take my customary route to work along North 3rd Street. Nor would I have dared, if permitted. Many whites feared being attacked if they traveled through the inner city. A few, such as my frequent tennis partner Peter McBride, reacted positively. He, a consummately polite, cheerful, extraordinarily successful broker at Robert W. Baird, with thirteen children to raise, told me: "We can't let the city explode. If someone will only figure out how to lessen the causes of the riots, I'd be willing to contribute twenty-five thousand dollars a year."

The riots were contagious. Less than a month later, on August 29 and 30, Father James Groppi, a fearless, flamboyant, confrontational Catholic priest and civil rights leader led a march of 200, mostly young blacks, into Milwaukee's South Side. They protested Milwaukee's racially segregated housing and the city's persistent refusal to outlaw it. The South Side had effectively prevented blacks from settling there. Hostile crowds of up to 5,000 jeered the marchers. Twenty-two people, including 122 police officers, were injured, largely from tear gas. It was a long, tense summer.

A year later, on September 24, 1968 fourteen young activists opposed to the Vietnamese war ransacked the draft board's offices on West Wells Street and publicly burned draft card records. Promptly arrested, they were convicted of looting and destroying government property and given prison sentences.

The race riots, Father Groppi's deliberately provocative marches, and the draft card burning were part of a broader Civil Rights Movement conducted primarily by young, single-minded, and passionate advocates. The Civil Rights Movement was supported by a broader youthful rebellion bearing a motto "make love, not war," the causes of which have not been fully fathomed thirty years later.[56]

In some ways, the idealistic young were a protest awaiting a cause, almost any cause, which attacked the existing establishment's decisions or their way of doing things. One example affecting me personally foreshadowed the disruptive tactics to be used by the rising opposition to building more freeways. It took place in the area bordering the University of Wisconsin-Milwaukee (UWM), which, like UWM itself, was traditionally receptive to liberal causes. In 1972, when youthful activism was at its peak, the ward elected a new alderman typical of the times. He was Edwin J. Griffin, a former Catholic priest and social worker. Griffin campaigned as being willing to listen to the rising concerns of the neighborhood. These included lack of adequate housing and other causes voiced by the young activists and their older sympathizers. In late July 1972, Griffin appointed a citizens' task force to plan the ward, saying in revealingly judgmental terms that:

> [T]he stability of East Side neighborhoods is threatened by the combined pressures from UWM, expanding hospitals [Columbia and Saint Mary's], careless apartment and commercial development, traffic, and the loss of family housing.[57]

Griffin's grassroots task force held frequent forums to obtain input from local residents. Griffin reasoned that residents, not traditional city planners and other professional staff, such as traffic experts, were best able to advise him and the city on what should be done in their ward.

One of the activists' prime targets was Columbia Hospital, a client of mine. Columbia, a venerable institution, had been built at the corner of Maryland and Edgewood Avenues in 1909 when the location lay on the city's largely undeveloped outskirts. By 1972 it was surrounded by residences. A rising tide of patients required Columbia to expand once in the 1960s. In the early '70s Columbia asked me to obtain the city's approval for another expansion. To do so would require the city to vacate, or technically abandon, Murray Avenue in the 3300 block. Thereafter, Columbia could clear space for hospital expansion by removing residences that Columbia had purchased earlier on the west side of Murray Avenue.

Griffin's task force favored protecting the neighborhood by freezing all development. It objected to Columbia's expansion, saying that scarce housing would be destroyed and not replaced. When I asked Griffin to support the closing of the Murray block as a preceding alderman had done for an earlier expansion, he replied: "I'll do whatever the task force agrees to; you have to convince them."

Never before had an alderman publicly abdicated his decision-making power to a grassroots group. Once he tipped his hand, the opposing political activists escalated their demands. For example, they insisted that Columbia move all houses slated for destruction to another part of the area served by the local high school. That would be very expensive. The buildings were massive two-story brick structures. Only after the battle was over did the activists startle me by volunteering one previously secret extra motive in saving the housing. It was to retain white students at nearby Riverside High. Destroying homes would reduce white enrollment.

They also wanted Columbia to give up any possible future expansion. They asked Columbia to sell all additional homes it had purchased for just such a possibility. Their final demand was a shocker. They unrealistically insisted that Columbia's directors, who included prominent presidents of two banks and many manufacturing corporations, make the governor and legislature reduce UWM student parking. No reduction in student parking, no hospital expansion. They said – with some truth – student parking monopolized scarce places. Residents near Columbia and UWM repeatedly complained that they and their visiting friends could not park in front of their homes because students parked there first.

The leader of the expansion's opponents, Ted Seaver, taught me, at forty-six, a major lesson. He was a blunt-speaking, extremely self-confident young man of thirty-three who personified the rebellion's strongest qualities: idealism, conviction, hard work, imagination, intolerance, calculated rudeness, and courage. When I questioned the reasonableness of his asking Columbia to solve a parking problem created by UWM students, he told me, smiling in triumph: "We are urban guerrillas fighting against your suburb-serving hospital's unjust treatment of our neighborhood; this is war; we will use any tactic necessary to win."

That answered my question. Alderman Griffin, whether naively or purposely, had given Seaver carte blanche. Columbia had no choice and, at great financial cost, gave in to all but the parking-solution demands. With me recruiting and supervising the necessary contractors, Columbia moved thirteen cumbersome houses to other locations, (eleven west of the Milwaukee River), rehabilitated them, and sold them. Columbia also surrendered ownership of the houses west of its new expansion site which it had laboriously acquired over many years. Confrontation tactics had paid off. Grass roots defeated the estab-lishment. Or, the younger generation beat the older generation. In any event, I learned the winners' tactics and was better prepared for later confrontations.

Chapter 11

Opposition Deadlocks Freeways, 1969-1975

Meanwhile, the formerly popular freeway construction ran into its first organized opposition. It erupted at a September 1965 public hearing on the proposed Lake Freeway through Juneau Park overlooking Lake Michigan. The public quickly renamed this stretch of the freeway "the Downtown Loop Closure" because it would enclose downtown by connecting the Park East Freeway to the Lake Freeway at the north end of the future Hoan Harbor Bridge. (See Map 4.) To do so, the freeway would run east from the stub of the Park Freeway East at North Jackson Street (just north of Ogden Avenue) to Juneau Park, and then south along a former railway right of way to the north end of the future bridge at Michigan Avenue.

By coincidence a prominent, gruff, go-for-the-jugular corporate attorney, Malcolm Whyte, had labored long to build a new Layton School of Art on Prospect Avenue, smack in the path of the freeway's future path. He opposed the Loop Closure all out, forcing an advisory city referendum in April 1967. Freeway supporters won by a 2 to 1 vote. Freeways were still popular.

Other older generation opponents of the Downtown Loop Closure, using radically different tactics, fared better. In 1971, they obtained a court injunction against its construction, which the Wisconsin Supreme Court upheld in 1973.[58] The court victory was based on key research by Charles Q. Kamps,[59] an environmental attorney and ardent sailor at the nearby Milwaukee Yacht Club. Kamps sought to protect Milwaukee's beautiful Juneau Park and lakefront from aesthetic and noise intrusion by a broad, busy concrete freeway. Kamps found that the park had been transferred to the county by the city in 1936 on condition that, if the land ever ceased to be used for parks and parkways, title would revert to the city. In 1971 the county favored completing expressways, and the city, under Mayor Maier, did not. Therefore the title condition made a crucial difference.[60] The Loop went no further.

While these older generation opponents were attempting to stop construction of the Downtown Loop Closure (1967-1971), youthful idealists led an all-out attack on building any additional freeways anywhere. In 1968, Ted Seaver came into the picture, four years before I locked horns with him over Columbia's hospital's expansion. He was only twenty-nine. Raised in Massachusetts, he graduated from the University of Wisconsin-Madison before starting out as a high school teacher. He then worked as a civil rights activist in Mississippi during the late l960s, before moving to Milwaukee in l968. Here he continued advocacy for the disenfranchised by serving on the staff of the Tenants' Union, a private organization that championed the rights of low income tenants. The Union drew its financial support from federal anti-poverty funds created under President Lyndon Johnson's idealistic Great Society program. Seaver was more than an activist passionately devoted to a cause; he had an extraordinary knack for identifying and publicizing issues affecting the underprivileged.

Seaver employed new methods, which alternately annoyed and baffled Expressway Commissioners and staff while, at the same time, winning the grudging respect of some elected leaders. One was Henry Maier who, as a consummate politician, intuitively sensed the political appeal of Seaver's tactics. Robert W. Brannan, chief engineer for the commission, years later summarized Seaver's disruptions of Express-way Commission meetings in general terms:

> Seaver brought Saul Alinsky [the radical Chicago guru of confrontational activism in the l960s] tactics to Milwaukee and did it successfully. He brought tactics to play that the genteel Milwaukee community was not familiar with and was offended by; but unable to respond [to] at the same time.[61]

Harvey Shebesta, then an engineer with the Milwaukee District Office of the state Highway Commission, was more graphic. Shebesta noted that the businessmen-commissioners were "gentlemen who did not know how to cope with these unprecedented disruptions." He gave a vivid word portrait of a Seaver-staged confrontation:

> The members of the Milwaukee County Expressway Commission were prominent citizens from industry, commerce, and the professions. When confronted at their meetings with the likes of Ted Seaver, and his entourage of women, occasionally including their babies, the commissioners were ill prepared to respond

except as the gentlemen they were. In their board meetings etc. they had never encountered such interruptions. As a result Seaver and his crowd could easily disrupt commission meetings. When he attended meetings he was dressed sloppily with his shirt tail hanging outside his trousers, i.e. he was dressed to fit the part of representing his 'poor' who were being forced from their homes, etc.[62]

By 1969, the Milwaukee County Expressway Commission was acquiring the last homes and businesses in the path of the proposed three-mile-long Park Freeway West. That freeway was designed to start at the Hillside Interchange near North 8th Street on the North-South Freeway (I-43) and then go westward – roughly parallel to North Avenue – to the proposed Stadium Freeway North at North Sherman Boulevard. (See Map 5.)

Seaver worked for the Tenants' Union on behalf of persons being evicted for the Park Freeway. He told me that witnessing evictions quickly spawned his opposition to further freeways anywhere:

> I came upon two female heads of households who were being evicted to make way for the Park Freeway. They were being treated awfully. The so-called replacement housing for these women and their children was infested by cockroaches. I told the Expressway Commission that they couldn't move these women until they have adequate replacement housing.[63]

Seaver waged a relentless campaign to dramatize the housing plight of families uprooted by the freeways. As his stock in trade, he staged demonstrations against evictions and was, he recalled, arrested twice,[64] which, as he said, "got good P.R."

Seaver was far more than noise. He carefully courted political allies, such as Mayor Maier, while attacking the faceless Expressway Commission. Once he challenged the governor, the Milwaukee county executive, and the mayor to a debate on housing problems, heavily centered on the freeways. Mayor Maier attended; the county executive sent a staff representative; the governor stayed away. Seaver proudly admitted that the mayor was pleased that the attack was directed at the county rather than the city.[65] In fact,

Henry J. Schmandt, an astute observer of the Milwaukee political scene in the late 1960s, accurately captured the foundation of the unique Seaver-Maier working relationship:

> Seaver is one of the few "protest activists"...who have been able to establish a working relationship...with the mayor...the principal reason is...the compatibility of the [tenant] union's approach with Maier's over-all strategy of dispersing responsibility for the city's social problems to other units of government.[66]

Maier praised Seaver as "...a bright, effective leader who is very intense on issues."[67]

There was, of course, underlying justice in several complaints by freeway opponents. People usually do not protest loudly without reason. For example, in early years, legislative and administrative action favored freeway construction over the interests of homeowners in several respects. The exact center line location and width of the proposed freeway were not disclosed until the public hearing. By then, it was too late for affected landowners to offer comment that conceivably might alter the route. Earlier disclosure and dialogue might have yielded constructive suggestions from those directly affected. More likely, earlier notice might have lessened their feeling that the government was arbitrary, inhumane, and needed restraint. Shebesta, a career highway engineer, also criticized this procedure as too harsh:

> Freeway plans were not made public until the public hearing. While the general corridors were known, the specific alignments were not revealed until the public hearing. At that point it was almost axiomatic that objections would be raised (I was [then] personally opposed to exposing plans to the public, but am now an avid supporter of the public involvement process as a means of generating support through listening to people and modifying plans where possible).[68]

Prices of homes in the inner city path of certain freeways became depressed. At first, according to Herbert A. Goetsch, Milwaukee commissioner of public works during the construction of the freeways, many homeowners welcomed the purchase of their homes by the county, which later auctioned them off to the highest bidder for removal and relocation elsewhere. That attitude changed when some property owners found it paid to contest what the government offered them. They challenged the offering price and received a higher amount.[69] Later some properties were awarded sums lower than their mortgage debt, possibly because home values declined further when more homeowners moved out of the neighborhood for other reasons.

Shebesta criticized the low awards for lost homes:

> By law in the early years we were required only to pay fair market value, which, in many cases, particularly on the near North Side was exceeded by outstanding mortgages. Thus some owners... not only wound up without a home but a debt to be paid on something which no longer existed. A more humane and considerate approach would have paid dividends. [70]

Herbert Goetsch, Milwaukee's commissioner of public works in the 1960s and '70s, believes that the economic hardship of losing homes was the principal cause of early opposition to freeways. He believes that Congress could have perhaps "saved the construction of the later abandoned freeways by authorizing the payment of 115 percent of the market value of the homes acquired."[71]

When the government started acquiring homes for the freeways, it was not required to confirm that new homes were available for those it was displacing. Gradually, Congress made desirable changes by requiring highway officials to certify that "decent, safe, and sanitary" replacement housing was available. Otherwise, stop. Or, implicitly, find housing.

In 1969 Congress enacted the National Environmental Policy Act (NEPA). The act was a whopper. It required any federally funded agency undertaking public construction to prepare a statement assessing the impact its project would have on the environment. That objective was admirable. However, NEPA was to have a far-reaching, probably unintended, effect. NEPA became a weapon – perhaps the prime weapon – by which opponents could delay freeways to death. They could insist to the agency or, more often, the courts that the costly environmental statement was incomplete, outdated, or faulty. Therefore, delay or abandon construction.

In 1969, the expressway commission, without expressly acknowledging Seaver's major role, succinctly reported a dramatic shift in the public attitude toward continuing freeway construction:

> In the early 1960s, the commission heard vocal and strident demands for accelerated freeway design and construction. In 1969, equally loud voices were heard, only this time directed toward other goals: design the freeway elsewhere, don't design it at all, build a mass transit system instead, call a moratorium on all construction, provide good housing before a single additional person displacement is made. These calls, however, were from a new constituency, those located in or along a proposed freeway, whereas the early 1960 vocalists represented a broad cross-section of the community.[72]

Seaver in late 1969 or early 1970 realized that he needed to do more than win public support through publicity generated by his staged demonstrations. He also needed allies. The freeways, until at least 1967, had broad support from elected officials, the press, the Greater Milwaukee Committee, and the Metropolitan Milwaukee Association of Commerce. Seaver wrote a paper listing the "large" amount of housing being lost to freeways. He identified six proposed freeways and looked for an opponent of each. He found six opponents who formed a working alliance called "Citizens Regional Environmental Coalition." All six were private citizens. Four were shortly to win elective posts by campaigning against pro-freeway incumbents: John O. Norquist (Wisconsin State Assembly), Mike Elconin (Wisconsin State Assembly), Cynthia (Cindi) Cukor (Milwaukee Common Council), and Dan Cupertino (Milwaukee County Board). The other two were Dr. Helmut Enkel, who lived in Wauwatosa and Dr. Robert Purtell who lived in Brookfield. Their rallying cry: freeways ruined neighborhoods by dividing them.[73] Some opponents also argued that freeways were primarily intended to reduce the commuting time of suburbanites and facilitate the departure of residents and industry from the central city. The Coalition, as Seaver recounted, obtained 20,000 to 30,000 signatures on petitions opposing more freeways.[74]

Seaver's allies soon decided to campaign door to door for elective office against the pro-freeway incumbents. What provoked Cindi

Cukor to seek elective office illustrated the times. She was secretary of the Wisconsin League of Women Voters and an ardent no-nonsense activist for liberal causes. Her pungent staccato speaking style left no doubt as to where she stood. She lived on South 44th Street in the path of the proposed Stadium South Freeway.

> I remember how I got started on the freeways like yesterday. I was looking out the window at a neighbor, Grandma Dredzwicki. There was a surveyor on her doorstep. I watched her. I went over to see if I could help, or find out what was going on. He told her he was surveying for the Stadium Freeway. It was all cooked and dried. I objected. He said "Call your Alderman." I did. His name was Jankowski. He supported freeways. He told me to "mind your own business; to stay home and mind the kids."[75]

Almost immediately, Cukor announced she would run for alderman to unseat Jankowski. The city was redistricting at the time and just happened to redraw the boundaries of Jankowski's district to exclude candidate Cukor. She moved her residence back into the district and beat him.

Many other freeway opponents, energized by passionate convictions, were elected to the legislature, Milwaukee County Board, and Milwaukee Common Council. They won even though the media and a quiet, less fervent, majority continued to favor completion of the freeways.[76] In 1972 the anti-freeway forces mounted candidates for thirteen of the twenty-five county board positions; eight were elected. The tide was starting to turn, slowly at first, and then faster. Between 1972 and 1976 many faces changed in the thirty-three member Milwaukee delegation to the Wisconsin Legislature. Sixteen new members of the senate and assembly were elected, preponderantly in their mid-twenties.[77] All strongly opposed the freeways when elected, or at least did before early 1977. Some became vigorous leaders of freeway opposition within the legislature, including Michael Elconin, elected in 1972 at eighteen, the youngest person ever elected to the Wisconsin Legislature; John Norquist, the son of a courageous Presbyterian pastor,[78] an articulate campaigner and an admiring ally of Seaver, elected in 1974 at twenty-five; and Mordecai Lee, a son and grandson of successful real estate developers and a brilliant idealistic holder of two graduate degrees, elected in 1976 at twenty-eight.

Freeway opponents, both before and after many of their leaders were elected to public office, employed numerous tactics to slow or stop freeway construction. In 1969 opponents killed the proposed Bay Freeway, which would have provided an east-west link paralleling West Hampton Avenue between the North-South Freeway (I-43) and the City of Oconomowoc in Waukesha County.[79] (See Map 3.) Politically active residents persuaded legislators at the state, county, and local levels of government to adopt resolutions opposing the Bay Freeway.[80] On December 23, 1969, the expressway commission dropped it from its list of proposed freeways. The legislature promptly prohibited the construction of the part lying within Milwaukee County. That legislation remains on the books today.[81]

Opponents also used the new Environmental Policy Act to hammer the Park Freeway West. They brought suit in federal court, claiming that an environmental impact statement had to be prepared under NEPA before construction could commence.[82] They started suit notwithstanding the fact that *before the legislation was enacted in 1969* 99 percent of the land had been acquired and 1,590 homes had been cleared at a cost of $22 million. On June 2, 1972, just days before a $6 million construction bid was to be let, U.S. District Judge John Reynolds restrained the letting of contracts, ruling that an environmental impact statement had to be prepared before construction could commence.[83] Then, to upstage the Expressway Commission's anticipated preparation of a favorable environmental impact statement, Seaver's Coalition prepared its own unfavorable impact statement and persuaded the U.S. Department of Transportation to approve and file it. The Coalition probably had the support of the powerful local Congressman Henry A. Reuss, who vociferously opposed Park Freeway West. A public hearing on the impact statement was not held until May 13, 1975, more than three long years after Reynolds' injunction. A respected, temperate civic leader, John C. Geilfuss, chairman of the Metropolitan Milwaukee Association of Commerce and president of the Marine National Exchange Bank, and George Watts, a passionate freeway advocate, spoke in favor of the freeway in a four-hour hearing. Most area residents at the hearing spoke against it. [84]

Meanwhile, freeway construction stopped until the three-and-one-half-mile Hoan Bridge over the Harbor was completed in 1977 as Interstate Highway 794. Both Mayor Maier and Congressman Reuss supported this freeway leg. They recognized that it would serve Milwaukee's city-owned Port Authority which increasingly depended upon trucking, rather than rail, to deliver cargo to and from the ships.[85] Then construction stopped again. Delays were caused by the time-consuming preparation and hearings on environmental impact statements, followed by litigation. Too, Mayor Maier resisted freeways in many small ways, such as stalling on the federally required improvement of local access streets. Maier approved of Seaver's tactics and employed him in his office from 1973 to 1976. The legislature became increasingly reluctant to appropriate more money for the state's 50 percent matching share of the expense for later, non-interstate freeways, such as Park West and Park East.

In 1974, the status of the state- and county-approved 112-mile[86] multi-year freeway construction program could be clearly divided into three stages.

1. Completed: sixty-one miles, or 54 percent, consisting of a grid of the potentially heaviest traffic arteries: North-South, East-West, Airport and Zoo Freeways.
2. Scheduled in the projected Milwaukee County budgets for construction next: seventeen miles, or 15 percent, consisting of freeway legs or parts of such legs which freeway engineers considered essential to make the system more efficient. They would do that by providing alternate routes to the East-West and North-South Freeways when predicted traffic increased substantially by 1990, twenty-five years after the planning of the freeway routes. Examples were the Park, Downtown Loop, and Stadium South Freeways.
3. Not yet scheduled in projected budgets: thirty-four miles, or 30 percent, lying generally on the outer perimeter of the county: the Stadium North Freeway to the Ozaukee County Line; the Lake Freeway South from Layton Avenue to the Racine County Line; and the Belt Freeway from the Lake Freeway in Oak Creek near Lake Michigan

westerly to the Waukesha County Line, and then north through Waukesha County to the Fond du Lac Expressway.

Work was stalled on the second or seventeen-mile package.

What could resolve the impasse?

Chapter 12

Freeway Construction Stops

By l974 the pro-freeway forces' earlier confidence had eroded. Projects had been stopped. Voters were placing freeway opponents in key positions on the county board and in the Wisconsin Legislature. Yet the business community and the *Milwaukee Journal* and *Milwaukee Sentinel* continued to favor completion of the freeways. Proponents sought to recapture the initiative. Early in 1974, Supervisor Rudolph Pohl of the Milwaukee County Board proposed a county-wide advisory referendum – YES or NO – on whether the remaining seventeen miles of the eighty-two miles of freeway budgeted by the county should be completed. Those seventeen miles (shown on Map 5) consisted of:

1. the Airport Spur Freeway between the North-South Freeway and General Mitchell Field;
2. the Park Freeway West between the North-South Freeway (I-43) at the Hillside Interchange west to the Stadium Freeway North [which, someone had failed to notice, had been dropped by the Express-way Commission in the Spring of l974];
3. the Stadium Freeway South from West National Avenue to the Airport Freeway;
4. the Lake Freeway (Downtown Loop) easterly from the Park Freeway east of the Milwaukee River to the north end of the Hoan Bridge;
5. the Lake Freeway southerly from the south end of the Hoan Bridge to East Layton Avenue.

Supervisor Cupertino, an original Seaver ally, objected to a single referendum. He felt opponents would fare better if the county scheduled a separate referendum on each of the separate proposed freeway routes. He proposed five referenda. After five months of wrangling, the county board authorized separate referenda on each of the five freeways. (See Map 5.) Business and labor organizations, the press, and Congressman Clement Zablocki (South Side) urged voters to vote "yes;" Mayor Maier, Congressman Henry A. Reuss (North Side), Seaver's Coalition, and two subsequently elected members of his Coalition, Milwaukee Alderman Cukor and County Supervisor Cupertino, urged voters to vote "no."

On November 5, 1974, in the regular gubernatorial election, 237,355 persons voted, or 48.1 percent of those eligible to vote, the lightest turnout in twenty-two years. All five referenda received substantial "yes" majorities. Even in the "freeway corridors" – that is, in the wards through which a part of a proposed freeway segment would pass and where the opponents were most vocal – the "yes" vote won in three out of five. Ironically, fervent opponents (Cukor, Norquist, Cupertino) resided in those three wards. The referenda results:

Freeway	Percent Voting YES in the Referenda County-Wide	Percent Voting YES in the Referenda in Wards in which a proposed freeway would be located (8% of all wards)
Airport Spur Freeway	58.2	41
Park Freeway West	54.2	48
Stadium Freeway South	59.4	53
Downtown Loop Freeway Closure	58.2	54
Lake Freeway	59.7	51

Both sides claimed victory, Cupertino (of Bay View) saying "There is no strict indication here people want freeways" and Milwaukee County transportation engineer Robert Brannan saying the vote showed voters "supported comprehensive transportation planning." Freeway opponents did not accept the referenda results. One exchange of views between a supporter and opponent revealed why. Shebesta confronted Assemblyman Mordecai Lee, a leader of the opponents:

"Now, can you support the freeway program?"
"Oh, no; it would be political suicide."
"Why?"
"Because those who are in favor of freeways are just a little in favor; but those who are opposed feel

passionately."[87]

On May 9, 1975, a few days before the hearing on the Park West environmental impact statement, Reuss became the first elected official to take a post-referendum position contrary to the pro-freeway referendum result. He strongly opposed construction of the Park Freeway West. (See Map 6.) He spoke with his customary mellifluous, even grandiose, style:

> The freeway is a monument to a bygone age which is not needed in a time of limited gas supplies, permanent lowered speed limits and emphasis on public transit... we are in a new transportation era far different from the Great Automotive Age for which freeways were designed.[88]

Reuss urged that the freeway land be used instead for housing, light industry, public transit, and outdoor recreation. John Schmidt, president of the State AFL-CIO and a vocal champion of freeways (because hundreds of union members worked on the freeways), criticized Reuss, quoting the 54 percent referendum vote favoring the Park Freeway West. Schmidt could speak sharply – Reuss was mistaken about the impact of limited gasoline supplies; cars on freeways burned less gas per mile than on crowded city streets. He added that the freeway corridor had "been cleared for years" and that the only future damage there "will be the waste of taxpayer dollars because of escalating prices as a result of delay."[89]

Three months later in September 1975, Milwaukee County Executive John Doyne, probably the most popular elected official in the county, proposed reviving the most-needed part of the Stadium Freeway North. The Expressway Commission had canceled the entire freeway in 1974,[90] presumably because rising opposition had blocked appropriation of the necessary funds. Doyne suggested building the southern part of the Stadium Freeway North, which would "close the gap" between its stub at West North Avenue and the southern end of the existing Fond du Lac Freeway at North 68th Street. (See segment 1 on Map 7.) Doyne's proposal became informally known as the "gap closure freeway" but was never adopted. Assemblyman Mordecai Lee immediately attacked the "gap closure" proposal because:

> It would destroy 1,500 homes,[91] slice up a thriving

community and...anyway why should commuters be facilitated anymore at a time of permanently reduced speed limits...scarce energy sources and decreasing traffic volumes. Our government should be discouraging rather than encouraging suburban commuting by car.[92]

The decisive, final freeway battle was fought over the Park Freeway West. A public hearing on the environmental impact statement took place on May 13, 1975. Both sides pushed for a government decision on the statement favorable to their purpose. However, the matter dragged on for twenty-one months until January 1977. Then the U.S. Department of Transportation rejected the statement. That killed the freeway – though the battle continued for many more months. The department, after dryly understating that there was considerable opposition to the freeway from Mayor Maier, some aldermen, county supervisors, and state legislators, declared that construction:

[W]ill sever established neighborhoods, divide residential areas from stores and services...[and] it is conceded by highway planners that the Park Freeway West without the gap closure would be of only limited utility[93]

(Significantly, as already noted, the Expressway Commission had dropped the gap closure from its plans in 1974.)

In 1975 mounting vocal opposition to freeways stopped further construction. SEWRPC leaders were alarmed. George Berteau, SEWRPC chairman, and Kurt Bauer, executive director, devised a fresh approach. SEWRPC would try to break the deadlock by creating a citizen committee consisting of even numbers of proponents, opponents, and neutrals. They hoped that the committee, a microcosm of the larger community, would forge a consensus, or at least a compromise which would lead to consensus in the larger community. The committee was to focus on the unfinished freeways in Milwaukee County.

Berteau and Bauer jointly asked me to assemble and chair such a committee. It would consist of six proponents, six opponents, and six neutrals – eighteen in all. They told me I was the man for the job because, they flatteringly declared, I worked hard, conducted orderly meetings, and enjoyed working with persons of diverse points of view. Bauer, with his Teutonic love for long, precise titles, saddled the committee with a revealing but tongue-twisting name: Citizens' Advisory Committee on the Freeway-Transit Element of Regional Land Use and Transportation Plan Reevaluation. Members called it the "Cutler" or "6-6-6" Committee.

Berteau and Bauer underestimated the difficulty of assembling a balanced committee from a deeply polarized community. Freeway opponents did not wish to join a SEWRPC committee. They detested SEWRPC. To them, it was an engine for freeways. Finally, I parlayed with Cindi Cukor in her aldermanic chambers at city hall. I told her committee membership would give her a chance to influence the future of freeways. She vented anger at the arrogance of pro-freeway proponents, including my boss, Berteau. Finally, she accepted my offer. Other opponents followed her lead. Four were members of the Seaver Coalition against freeways. Another was Bert Stitt, the serious, colorful, and amiable executive secretary of the Brady Street Merchants' Association. Finding credible neutrals in a thoroughly divided community required an extensive search. In the end, I lined up six,[94] but locating pro-freeway people among civic leaders from the business community was comparatively easy.[95]

Meantime, while the 6-6-6 Committee worked through twenty tense but civil sessions at city hall, freeway adversaries in the legislature continued their attack. In late 1976, eighteen legislators from Milwaukee County started an active campaign "using all measures" to stop further freeways in Milwaukee County.[96] One of their first efforts was to send a letter to Governor Patrick Lucey on January 3, 1997, requesting him to halt construction of the Stadium Freeway South, which he did.[97] The letter was drafted and circulated by the ever resourceful legislator John O. Norquist. This was the first of a series of events making 1977 the climactic year in the raging freeway controversy.

Also in January 1977, Governor Lucey appointed a "Park Freeway West Task Force" to develop a plan for the alternative development of the vacant, presumably never-to-be-paved Park West Freeway corridor. He picked a top-notch chairman, David Carley, and included outspoken State Representative Mordecai Lee as a member.

Carley and I had worked together for Governor Nelson in getting SEWRPC started. More important, Carley was at the time the highly regarded head of the newly created Medical College of Wisconsin. The college had recruited him because of the political savvy he had displayed on various state government assignments in Madison. The new task force, in short order, recommended the vacant land be used for housing.

In June 1977 the assembly sent a budget to Governor Lucey, which Mordecai Lee said, "assures that the stymied Park Freeway West would never be built."[98] Its cost by then had risen to $54.7 million in 1975 dollars[99] from the $44 million estimate reported two years earlier by Reuss.

In July 1977 the SEWRPC 6-6-6 Committee made its report. Traffic research had substantiated both the need for the uncompleted freeways and the validity of the opponents' concerns over lost housing, underpayment for condemned homes, divided neighborhoods, and the need for increased mass transit. In the end, the six opponents gained unanimous committee agreement for their recommendations: there must be more government help on replacement housing and several measures should be taken to discourage freeway traffic and favor transit service.

Nevertheless, the opponents remained adamantly opposed to more freeway construction. They took but they did not give. The effort at either consensus or compromise had failed. The majority recommended proceeding with the earlier planned freeways – 12 to 6 – with all proponents and neutrals voting in favor. Freeway opponents on the committee became intellectually isolated. However, the committee's report had no political impact. The decision-makers were not listening.

During the summer of 1977, leading legislative opponents took a new, more imaginative tack. They were Wisconsin State Senator (later Congressman) James Moody (on leave of absence from teaching at UWM), together with State Representatives Mordecai Lee and Michael Elconin. They worked with UWM planners and economists to find a compromise that SEWRPC's staff could rationally accept.[100] In effect, opponents from academia proposed a ten-year moratorium on freeway construction. The declared objective was to determine whether freeway capacity could be increased without further construction. They recommended various measures to create such a painless increase. One was to manage traffic flow by the now-familiar traffic lights at freeway entrances. At the end of the ten year moratorium, the community would be able to determine whether these measures had increased freeway capacity enough to accommodate SEWRPC's predicted traffic increases. Yet, in 1977, it was quickly apparent that the real objective of these suggestions was to kill further construction by stalling it for ten years. In fact, when the suggestions were quickly endorsed by powerful anti-freeway legislators, they impacted the thinking of key SEWRPC commissioners.

George Berteau, the diligent SEWRPC chairman, closely monitored the increasing hostility toward further freeway construction among Milwaukee area elected officials. He also knew that many conservative SEWRPC commissioners from outside Milwaukee County strongly believed that the painstakingly designed regional freeway system should be completed. He felt that they – from a distance – regarded freeway opponents in Milwaukee as little more than noisy, single-issue radicals. Not so Berteau. He realistically appraised the opponents' rapidly growing power. By December, Berteau proposed that the full commission recommend a ten-year moratorium on the construction of certain freeways, including the Park Freeway West and Stadium Freeway South.

SEWRPC commissioners were scheduled to vote on the recommendations on December 19. Berteau spoke to the *Milwaukee Journal* in advance of the meeting. He attempted to signal a shift in his position toward the city's growing anti-freeway sentiment. He also used the interview to try to persuade commissioners to follow his lead. He agreed with the proposed moratorium on most freeway legs but, in a gesture of conciliation to the city and legislators, suggested that the Park Freeway West be dropped altogether from commission plans. He explained why:

> While it was an important link on the freeway system, it lacked state funding and there was a problem letting the land lie fallow for ten years [as would be the consequence of the staff recommended moratorium]. [101]

A majority of the commissioners refused to follow Berteau's suggestion. By a 13 to 6 vote on December 19, they decided to keep the Park Freeway West and Stadium Freeway North "gap closure" alive until a $300,000 study could be completed. The study would measure how much the proposed deletions would in future years overload and thereby lessen the performance of the heavily traveled Marquette and Stadium interchanges.[102] (See Map 6.) In fact, by 1995 they would be clearly overloaded. Berteau and all three Milwaukee County commissioners, including me, dissented. I, as an until-then "freeway proponent," explained the dissenting vote to the *Milwaukee Journal*:

> Milwaukee now placed more value on keeping houses
> than building controversial freeways...and that linking
> Park Freeway West with the Fond du Lac Freeway
> would require moving or razing 1,100 houses and
> businesses...[103]

The Milwaukee Association of Commerce cheered the majority's recommendation; the activist legislators protested loudly. Norquist and Lee threatened to obtain legislation stripping SEWRPC of its power to "veto" federal grants deemed inconsistent with its federally financed plans.[104] They had two things very much in mind. The city was about to file an application for a federal grant to help finance housing in the abandoned Park Freeway West corridor (as recommended by the Carley Task Force). Federal law prohibited awarding federal grants found to be in conflict with federally financed metropolitan transportation plans, such as those of SEWRPC. Therefore SEWRPC's continued planning for a Park Freeway West would put it on a collision course with the city's federal grant application. Something had to give.

Berteau, seeking to head off a clash with both the city and legislators, called a special meeting of SEWRPC for December 28 to reconsider its December 19 vote. On December 22 the common council of the City of Milwaukee delayed action on its application for federal housing funds to allow SEWRPC to reverse its action on the 28th. Before the meeting Acting Governor Martin Schreiber put pressure on the commission to drop the disputed freeways. His spokesman announced that he would remove them from the state "maps" in January. [105]

On December 28 SEWRPC convened in Waukesha with prominent members of both pro- and anti-freeway forces present.

SEWRPC did reverse its position; a 10 to 7 vote agreed that the Park Freeway West and "gap closure" should not be built at all. Other uncompleted freeways should be subject to a ten-year moratorium as recommended earlier by key legislators such as Moody, Lee, and Elconin. After I voted with the majority, Lee, in an outburst of genuine emotion, embraced me, saying, "You have saved my district."

Like a just-killed snake, the Park Freeway West wriggled some more. The expressway commission refused to surrender. It asked SEWRPC to veto the city's application for housing funds from the federal government for the corridor. SEWRPC declined to do so, now thoroughly chastened by the power and retaliatory threats by grimly determined anti-freeway legislators.

While the conclusive firefight over freeways was taking place in public, something else was going on unbeknownst to the public and even to me, who would be affected by it. My third six-year appointment to SEWRPC was to expire January 1, 1978. At the end of two prior terms, incumbent governors had reappointed me by December or earlier of my term's last year. This time Acting Governor Schrieber hesitated. Senator John Norquist had written him recommending he not reappoint me. He must have thought if he could not kill SEWRPC, at least he could eliminate an apparently pro-freeway commissioner. Finally, on December 28, Schreiber reappointed me, responding to repeated requests by Mayor Maier. The mayor's chief of staff disclosed to me that Norquist's letter had caused the delay.

Thus, the freeway construction program virtually ceased by the end of 1977. The 1974 pro-freeway county-wide referendum proved to be politically meaningless, except that the referendum-approved 1.4-mile Airport Spur was completed in 1978. Thereafter no freeway segments were constructed in Milwaukee County until 1999, when a three-mile leg of the Lake Freeway was added, but it was redesigned as four lane, slower-speed Lake Parkway.

By 1978, Milwaukee County had completed sixty-one miles of the 112-mile freeway system[106] that SEWRPC's 1965 plan had recommended (Map 3). They represented 54 percent of the miles and 69 percent of the carrying capacity of the recommended ultimate 112-

mile system. The difference between percent of miles completed and of carrying capacity is due to some freeways having more lanes than others. Freeway construction between 1950 and 1978 cost approximately $412 million ($1.89 billion in 1995 dollars), of which Milwaukee County's share was approximately $110 million or 27 percent.[107]

Why was the remainder of the recommended system never built? Clearly, public support for further freeways declined sharply in the 1970s. Clearly, dedicated opponents were elected to key state and local posts between 1972 and 1976. Clearly, they felt they were not bound by the 1974 pro-freeway advisory referendum. Obviously, too, freeway opponents – including Henry Maier[108] – were more politically sophisticated and determined than proponents such as Milwaukee's business leaders. However, troubling questions remain today – stimulated by the currently overloaded freeways and arterial highways.

Chapter 13

The Wisdom of Abandoning Nine Recommended Freeways

Should Milwaukee have built any of the freeways recommended in 1965 but abandoned in 1977? To help answer this question in 1998 I asked both opponents and proponents whether their earlier opinions had been modified by subsequent events or reflection. The leading freeway opponents such as Seaver, Lee, and Cukor vigorously proclaimed their 1970s opposition to freeways as the right thing. Norquist's actions subsequent to 1977 and his 1998 book, *The Wealth of Cities*,[109] demonstrated that his original ideological opposition to freeways did not moderate. The 1970s reasoning lingers into the late '90s: Opponents maintain that none of the abandoned freeways should have been built; freeways are bad because they serve the few at the expense of the many; they harm the central city by siphoning people and industry to the suburbs (the Pied Piper argument), and by demolishing neighborhoods. They are unsightly. The elevated parts are an ugly concrete blob sullying the city's skyline.

In contrast, three leading freeway designer-proponents from the 1970s concede, in retrospect, that the government in the early period gave inadequate compensation and assistance to those whose housing was taken for freeways. These officials, all retired, were Kurt W. Bauer, for thirty-five years executive director of SEWRPC, Harvey Shebesta, for twenty-two years director of the Milwaukee District of the Wisconsin Department of Transportation, and Herbert A. Goetsch, a long-time highly respected and politically sensitive City of Milwaukee commissioner of public works under Mayor Maier. Nevertheless, the planners believe that some but not all of the Milwaukee County freeways abandoned in 1977 should have been built.

To be sure, the freeways that were completed worked reasonably well until 1991. Then, SEWRPC driver surveys recorded the average work-commute time to downtown Milwaukee at twenty minutes or less from elsewhere in the City of Milwaukee, from Brookfield in the west, and Mequon in the north. Eight years later in 1999, freeways had become seriously overloaded. The cause was a cumulative, com-pounded, annual one percent increase in traffic in the twenty years from

1977. By 1999, SEWRPC reported that 70 percent of the Milwaukee County freeway system was at or over design capacity part of each day, as compared with 22 percent in the region.[110]

By 1999, precise Wisconsin Department of Transportation (WISDOT) traffic counts revealed traffic congestion was becoming more severe. It was extending farther out on the freeway system and prevailing more hours of the day. For example, during the three-hour afternoon heavy-traffic period (3 to 6 P.M.) traffic was severely congested just south and east of the Zoo Interchange and only slightly less congested just north, west, and south of the Marquette Interchange. [111] Engineers define severe congestion as a continuous slowdown in traffic speeds (often bumper-to-bumper) and loss of freedom to change traffic lanes. For a limited time each day, intermittent traffic congestion in 1999 extended as far west on I-94 at State Trunk Highway (STH) 164 just north of Waukesha, and as far north on I-43 as the Ozaukee County line. Maps 8 and 9 show the increase in congestion. The accident rate climbed to three-and-a-half times that occurring on uncongested freeways.

The planners I interviewed explained that long delays occur because the freeway system, when operating at or over design capacity,

> becomes unreliable or unstable because any slight disruption caused by an accident or lane closing for maintenance, or even wet weather, can cause massive back-ups for miles.[112]

At the heart of the case for having built at least some of the nine recommended-but-abandoned freeways is their major purpose: to provide alternate routes in case of the correctly predicted traffic overloading and consequent pile-ups.

I asked the three transportation experts, Bauer, Shebesta, and Goetsch, to designate which, if any, of the abandoned freeways they felt should have been built to provide a freeway system that would efficiently serve the needs of the metropolitan region. They individually numbered the nine unbuilt freeways in the order of their comparative importance to moving traffic over the system – with the lowest number indicating the freeways most needed. Their rankings were in near perfect agreement. Map 7 shows the proposed routes of the abandoned freeways, listed in order of today's need.

Freeway Segment	Location	Comparative Need
Stadium Freeway North Gap Closure	Stadium North stub at W. North Ave. to W. Fond du Lac Ave. at N. 69th and W. Burleigh Streets	1
Park Freeway West	North-South Freeway at Hillside Interchange near N. 8th St. to N. Sherman Boulevard and the Stadium Gap Closure	2
Stadium Freeway South	East-West Freeway (I-94) to Airport Freeway (I-894)	3
Stadium Freeway North	N. 69th and W. Burleigh Streets to Ozaukee County Line	4
Belt Freeway	North-South Freeway in Oak Creek west to and through Waukesha County to meet USH-141 in Washington County North of the Village of Menomonee Falls	5
Bay Freeway	North South Freeway westward parallel to Hampton Avenue to the Zoo Freeway, thence westward to STH-16 Freeway to Oconomowoc	6
Lake Freeway	E. Layton Avenue south to Wisconsin-Illinois State Line	7
Belt Freeway Stub	Lake Freeway in Oak Creek west to North South Freeway	8
Park Freeway East & Downtown Loop	N. 4th Street east to N. Prospect Avenue, thence south along Lake Michigan to the Hoan Bridge	9

Clearly, the two most needed of the abandoned freeways, the Stadium Freeway North Gap Closure and Park Freeway West, were also the most politically unacceptable in 1977. Their construction would have provided alternate routes to the Marquette Interchange, East-West Freeway (I-94), and Zoo Freeway (STH 145) which became overloaded by the mid-1990s. In their path lay 2,690 homes, of which 1,590, or 59 percent, had already been purchased and removed at the time that work had been halted on the Park Freeway West a few hours before pavement bids were to be let in 1972. The timing of the stop could not have been worse. In my opinion, the community should have either built the two freeways, which were designed to function together, or never purchased and removed the 1,590 homes. That halt-start-then-reverse disrupted many residents' lives and wasted $22 million spent on acquisition, utility relocation, and grading. Today's increasingly longer and more severe traffic jams are proving that not building those two freeways was a major transportation mistake. On the other hand, the acquired right-of-way slowly returned to residential use.

In ranking the most-needed of the abandoned freeways, Bauer, Shebesta, and Goetsch collectively implied that some should not have been built at all. They explained why the four lowest-ranked abandoned freeways were the least desirable. The Downtown Loop Closure, which ranked last, was plainly undesirable. It had the least traffic justification but would have imposed the largest negative impact on existing land use: namely disfiguring Milwaukee's beautiful lakefront and adjoining recreational areas. Intervening events made the full length Lake Freeway (#7) less desirable than when initially recommended. In 1971, the Wisconsin Department of Transportation (WISDOT) chose to enlarge a competing or alternative route. Lured by then available federal funding, WISDOT added two lanes to I-94, the existing Chicago-Milwaukee route through Racine and Kenosha Counties.[113] The need for the Lake Freeway to serve Chicago-bound traffic was further lessened by another development. Illinois chose not to build its Lake Freeway, which originally was intended to meet the Wisconsin Lake Freeway at the state line.

The engineers ranked the Bay Freeway No. 6 for a pragmatic reason. The Bay Freeway was more than justified by traffic needs, but it flunked political acceptance. In 1969 the Bay Freeway encountered the most widespread, politically active opposition of any freeway segment.[114]

If, as the trio of professionals believe, it was unwise not to build at least some of the abandoned freeways *at the time planned for their construction,* is it right not to build some of them *today*? That question cannot be answered authoritatively without an elaborate, unavailable analysis of current traffic demand and the benefits and costs of adding possible freeway capacity. However, one can prudently speculate that subsequent substantial development in at least two abandoned freeway corridors has made the later acquisition of necessary land prohibitively expensive. Prime examples are the proposed Belt Freeway through Oak Creek and the eastern part of Waukesha County, and that part of the Bay Freeway that would pass through the eastern portion of Waukesha County.

Even if current analysis proved that the future economic benefit of one of the abandoned freeways exceeded its current cost, would its construction somehow become politically acceptable? Almost certainly not. A new freeway would require consensus by the public and several levels of government – local, county, state, and federal. Such agreement is unlikely in view of the enduring – even intensifying – deadlock on basic transportation decisions in the twenty-three years following 1977.

Chapter 14

Stalemate on Transportation Decisions, 1977-1999

Freeway opponents in the legislature wanted more than the historic 1977 moratorium against further freeways. They stayed on the attack more or less continuously for the next two decades. Norquist and Lee were the leaders. Between 1979 and 1983, the indomitable Norquist, by then an influential Wisconsin state legislator, unsuccessfully introduced bills in three successive sessions to reduce or eliminate what he considered to be a pro-freeway majority of SEWRPC commissioners.[115] Each of the seven counties had from 1960 been entitled to three commissioners or 14 percent of the total of twenty-one, yet Milwaukee County in 1979 contained 54 percent of the region's population.[116] Under Norquist's bills each county having a population of over 100,000 was entitled to one additional commissioner for each 100,000 persons or fraction thereof. According to that principle, Milwaukee County would obtain an additional nine commissioners, and other populous counties four, thereby increasing the commission to thirty-four members. Milwaukee County would have twelve or 34 percent.

In 1983, the State Senate Committee on Urban Affairs and Government Operations offered an amendment that would increase the total commissioners from twenty-one to twenty-nine, increase the county's membership from three to five, and give the City of Milwaukee six.[117] No other counties would gain. That change would raise Milwaukee area representation to eleven (six city, five county) or 39 percent of the commission. Milwaukee's new commissioners would presumably be anti-freeway and able to garner a commission majority. That was Norquist's true goal. Norquist sought this drastic change because, as his ally Mordecai Lee explained "We agreed: the freeway fight was the signal fight for urban survival."[118]

Norquist obviously concluded that SEWRPC's federally mandated freeway planning, which he detested, outweighed its many past progressive efforts, with which he sympathized,[119] such as successful recommendations to reduce flooding and pollution on the Milwaukee River and at the same time preserve floodlands, wetlands, and woodlands (discussed in Chapter 16).

Norquist's bills received sympathetic hearings from an assembly committee chaired by Lee, but they were never reported to the floor of the legislature. Apparently, legislators viewed Norquist's eloquence about Milwaukee's under-representation as a camouflage for a single-issue crusade against any agency or person recommending freeways. Norquist's bills, if passed, would have probably killed SEWRPC. Possibly Norquist intended his bills only to intimidate SEWRPC, but what he did after he became Mayor of Milwaukee in 1988 casts doubt on that interpretation.

In 1995 he sought to persuade Federal Highway Administration officials to decertify SEWRPC as a metropolitan transportation planning organization (MPO). Decertification would deprive SEWRPC of significant federal funds that accompany MPO status. He made his complaint to the federal officials on June 9 of that year in a face-to-face meeting and followed up with a stinging letter to Washington citing that the city with 628,000 residents had no vote on SEWRPC [Milwaukee County had three] while "the other six counties" with populations ranging from 73,000 to 300,000 each had three.[120] He then asked Bill Clinton's White House to suggest that the Secretary of the U.S. Department of Transportation decertify SEWRPC. Federal officials noted the mayor's complaint but dryly concluded that SEWRPC's composition met federal requirements. They recertified SEWRPC, adding that its environmental assessment and congestion management features in its regional transportation plan were, respectively, "state of the art" and models for the rest of the nation.[121]

Mordecai Lee, as an anti-freeway activist, had greater success than Norquist with the legislature. In 1983, Lee, by then a state senator, successfully authored an amendment to the 1983 state budget prohibiting use of state or state-controlled federal funds for widening the North-South Freeway (I-43) from four to six lanes between Bender Road in the City of Glendale to the Ozaukee County Line.[122] Lee's triumphant July 1983 press release explained his objective:

> All too often we encourage the abandonment of our cities
> in favor of outlying suburbs by constructing expensive,
> fast new highways that make commuting longer distances
> easier.

Before the legislature's Joint Finance Committee adopted Lee's I-43 amendment, a state representative from southern Ozaukee County,

Donald L. Stitt, warned Norquist and fellow committee member Lee:

> You are trying to choke off everyone moving out of the
> city to the suburbs by shutting down an extra lane on I-43.
> It won't work. They will find another way to leave.[123]

Lee's amendment proved to be the high-water mark of the anti-freeway legislators. Lee's legislation was repealed in the 1990s when the Silver Spring I-43 Interchange was modernized. Lee and I concluded in a 2000 conversation that I-43 ultimately will widen. However, Lee's 1983 amendment probably delayed that work by ten or fifteen years.[124]

Between 1977 and 1999 the construction of additional new freeways – as distinguished from new lanes – was regarded as a politically dead issue.[125] However, one largely unnoticed exception occurred. In 1986, a freeway supporter briefly emerged and to everyone's surprise persuaded the previously anti-freeway residents of Bay View to reverse their position. The problem started when the Hoan Bridge (the "bridge to nowhere") dumped greatly increased north-south traffic on Bay View's narrow streets. In reaction, Bay View, a closely knit City of Milwaukee enclave just south of the bridge, in the 1970s adamantly opposed the extension of the proposed Lake Freeway from the bridge southward three-and-a-half miles to Layton Avenue. The catalyst resolving the impasse was Harout Sanasarian, a Milwaukee County Supervisor and SEWRPC Commissioner. He refined Ted Seaver's political process of educating neighborhoods. Sanasarian arranged informational meetings to persuade Bay View neighbors that a freeway extension would help, not harm them.

Sanasarian, who did not live in the Bay View area, seemed an unlikely choice for such leadership but fit the pro-neighborhood times neatly. A conscientious, hard-working person, he had been elected first to the Wisconsin Assembly and then to the Milwaukee County Board, notwithstanding his sometimes difficult-to-understand Iraqi accent. He learned politics well. A one-time freeway opponent, he demonstrated an open mind. After appointment to SEWRPC by the Milwaukee County Board he learned from Bauer how transportation planning could solve community traffic problems. Sanasarian then decided to try educating Bay View residents on how the freeway extension would benefit their neighborhood. In 1986 he created and chaired a SEWRPC advisory committee and astutely held twelve informal educational neighborhood meetings in six months in 1986. SEWRPC staff displayed maps and charts to illustrate visually how the proposed freeway would decrease traffic on Bay View's narrow streets.

At the middle of each informal meeting, a formal public hearing recorded public sentiment. Gradually residents recognized that Bay View's narrow streets endangered children on their way to school or to the lakefront parks. The threat to their safety could be avoided by diverting through traffic to a freeway alongside a railway track. Neighborhood opposition to the freeway turned around, carrying Daniel Cupertino, the local Milwaukee County Supervisor and early Seaver ally, with the tide. The official reversal of the neighborhood position revived the freeway extension plan in the form of a four-lane Lake Parkway from the bridge to Layton Avenue. Norquist, confronted by the documented neighborhood support, grudgingly admitted: "Sanasarian was the only guy that ever beat me on the freeway issue."[126]

During the 1977-1998 stalemate years, one transportation problem dominated discussion by highway officials and frustrated motorists: what to do about traffic already flowing along the East-West corridor between Milwaukee and Waukesha County. Should some traffic travel on extra freeway lanes, by bus, or by light rail? By the mid-1990s federal and state highway officials jointly searched for ways to lessen congestion on I-94, the most heavily traveled highway in the region. By 1991, I-94 carried up to 158,000 vehicles daily, with a forecast of 189,000 by 2001.[127] The rate of accidents along the stretch between the Zoo and Marquette Interchanges reached two to three times the statewide average, 75 percent of them being rear-end crashes caused by stop and go congestion.[128]

Consultants for the Wisconsin Department of Transportation (WISDOT) conducted a fruitless East-West Corridor Transportation Study that produced ten confusing alternative solutions but no recommendation. The ten ranged from modernizing I-94 to be safer,[129] adding special lanes for buses and car pools, expanding bus service by 21 percent, and building a light rail system within Milwaukee County, to various combinations of those alternatives.

WISDOT held endless hearings on the alternative proposals for solutions. At one hearing in December 1996, the dynamic, long-term Mayor of Brookfield, Kathryn Bloomberg, summarized the dilemma in choosing among the alternatives. Her knowledge of transportation issues had been enhanced by her active role on the SEWRPC advisory committee on creating a multi-county Regional Transportation Authority (RTA), which I chaired in 1990. She had also served on the short-lived RTA (1991-1993) by appointment by Governor Thompson. She told the state at the hearing that it should provide more freeway or arterial highway capacity or, alternatively – if that was impossible – throttle back continuing growth in central and western Waukesha County. The state could mandate land use controls to decrease the rate of growth west of that area, she suggested.[130]

Many of the ten possible solutions presented in 1997 led to sharp splits among key government leaders. Norquist and Milwaukee County Executive F. Thomas Ament championed light rail, citing the impracticality of building more traffic lanes and the asserted increasing success of light rail in other cities. Governor Thompson and Waukesha County Executive Daniel M. Finley objected to light rail. Thompson cited its high cost. Finley agreed but pointedly added:

> Waukesha County's biggest need is workers. A fixed rail line to one destination here (as was proposed at the time) lacks the flexibility to move Milwaukee County workers to scattered locations in Waukesha and other counties. Light rail is not a viable means to move people and product throughout the region.[131]

Only the State Highway Department favored special bus and car pool lanes on I-94, figuring it to be the best way to acquire extra capacity. However, Finley favored extra lanes for cars, an alternative conspicuously not presented by the consultants. All favored more bus service. Most acknowledged that the Marquette and Zoo Interchanges had to be rebuilt for safety reasons, though some, including freeway opponents, showed reluctance to undertake such costly projects at all. As the dust settled, stalemate emerged. Light rail was dead; extra bus and car pool lanes were dead; extra automotive lanes were probably dead. My own prediction is that the community will learn to live with increasing congestion and a resulting decline in the quality of life.

Of the ten alternative solutions suggested by the East-West corridor consultants, only one is being carried out. Without fanfare, bus service expanded by 20 percent in the region. Many new routes were opened between the city and the counties of Ozaukee, Washington, and Waukesha, primarily to move employees (lacking cars) from the city to jobs in the outlying areas.

By the 1990s, the state, Milwaukee County, and the city increasingly and unfortunately disagreed about funding priorities on major transportation projects in the Milwaukee area. Possibly to encourage the parties to resolve their differences, Congress in 1991 dangled federal funds before them. It provided that $289 million (later declining to $241 million) of accumulated unspent federal funds might be spent upon the request of Governor Thompson after "consultation with the appropriate local government officials."[132] The parties did not agree until April 1999.

Looming above all other potential projects in importance and expense was the future reconstruction of the Marquette Interchange. Built in 1968, it was deteriorating, growing more congested and therefore less safe, and evidencing obsolete design.[133] Rebuilding was estimated to cost between $650 and $950 million and was planned to start in 2002 (later delayed to 2004), and would require four years to complete. Mayor Norquist was reluctant to see so much money spent on freeways, even if only to reconstruct them. His long-time aversion to freeways went further. He attacked one freeway leg adjacent to the interchange. Beginning in 1995 he began to advocate demolishing I-794 between the Marquette Interchange and the Hoan Harbor Bridge, and replacing I-794 with a landscaped boulevard. The mayor and city planning director Peter Park argued that demolition would eliminate an eyesore that bisected the Historic Third Ward and would enable commercial and residential development to take its place. In 1998 the city engineer let the mayor's cat out of the bag. He claimed a new advantage for tearing down I-794: its removal without rebuilding – together with *scaling back the reconstruction of the interchange* – would save $200 million, or up to one-half of the high cost of that project.[134]

In 1998 Mayor Norquist also pressed for the demolition of a second elevated downtown freeway, the seven-block Park Freeway East between North 4th and Jefferson Streets. Meanwhile Norquist and County Executive Ament wanted a light rail system, or at least greatly improved mass transit, serving downtown locations and the new Miller baseball park.

Norquist's suggestion that two downtown elevated freeways be dismantled launched a vigorous debate. I-794 in 1998 was carrying over

89,000 vehicles a day, double the amount handled by the six-lane Bluemound Road Boulevard in Brookfield. Present and past state highway officials warned that Norquist's boulevard, with its required lift bridges to allow boat traffic to proceed on the Milwaukee River, would create massive traffic jams. Former Mayor Frank Zeidler agreed, even though he had favored a boulevard in that location forty years earlier.[135] The Milwaukee County Transportation Committee also opposed demolition. In short order, the cities of St. Francis, Cudahy, Oak Creek and Franklin opposed demolishing I-794, the mayor of Cudahy pointing out that taxpayers were then spending over $100 million to build the Lake Parkway to facilitate trips downtown via I-794.

To prove the wisdom of building the Lake Parkway, its opening in late 1999 both quickly lowered traffic over narrow streets nearby and speeded up traffic between the airport and downtown. The number of cars driving on Superior Street in Bay View dropped 43 percent, from 14,300 daily to 8,200. Similar benefits extended farther south. The mayor of Cudahy reported:

> People have got their neighborhoods back, and believe me, they are happy. [Cudahy's] tax base is getting a giant boost from the new road.[136]

Trips via the new Parkway from the Milwaukee Airport to downtown took only seven minutes, less than required to travel via I-94 and over the High Rise Bridge north of National Avenue. Traffic on the bridge declined by 4,500 vehicles a day.[137] And cab fares from the airport downtown on the new shorter route cost less.

Norquist's 1998 proposal to remove the Park Freeway East stirred up less opposition than his campaign to tear down I-794. Traffic on the seven-block spur east of 4th Street was 35,000 vehicles a day and local in nature, while I-794's traffic was generally regional. Further, SEWRPC in a 1998 study estimated that the removal of Park Freeway East would have only a modest impact on nearby street congestion.[138] Most significantly, the stub's demolition would open up by mid-2003 twenty-three acres for development of apartments and condominiums, and improve access to the proposed Harley-Davidson Museum on the former Schlitz brewery site.

While the debate over demolishing two elevated freeways continued, the date was approaching when the $241 million in federally withheld transportation funds would be forfeited if the state and local governments did not agree on how to allocate it. On April 20, 1999,

Governor Tommy Thompson, County Executive Ament, and Mayor Norquist negotiated a written compromise. Each got some of what he wanted. The Park Freeway East would be demolished for $25 million; I-794 would be saved; $91 million would be spent to study and improve a mass transit system, possibly including light rail to serve the downtown area; $51 million would be spent on reconstructing the decaying 6th Street viaduct and building two ramps to make the outmoded Menomonee Valley industrial area more accessible for modern development; and $75 million would be applied toward the Marquette Interchange reconstruction. The county board by a 20-2 vote approved demolishing the Park Freeway East.

Norquist may not have given up on demolishing I-794. He campaigned nationally in 1999 to make his case that cities should be removing freeways, not building new ones. He told the *New York Times* on July 20, 1999:

> The urban superhighway should be relegated to the scrap heap of history...there is no greater form of subsidized social engineering than the interstate highways, which hasten flight out of the city without doing much to ease traffic congestion.[139]

Norquist's triumph in extracting begrudging acquiescence from state and county officials for the destruction of the Park Freeway East soon soured. Demolition was stalled by the very laws anti-freeway activists used to delay or kill freeways in the 1970s. Federal environmental laws required an environmental impact statement before any work (including *demolition*) could start. Preparing a statement required time and money. That was not all. Another federal action delayed funding of even the environmental impact statement as well as the big-three-agreed-upon study of mass transit. Activists here and in other states sued to stop spending federal transportation funds, claiming that plans illegally ignored poorer neighborhoods. The U.S. Secretary of Transportation held up all spending from mid-1999 to early 2000 while he investigated the litigation's merits. As of this writing, demolition of the Park East may not start until December 2002.

In short, even when three key political leaders agree to break part of the long transportation deadlock, opposition can delay, and even thwart, their plans. Achieving action is not simple.

Chapter 15

Myths and Facts About Transportation Solutions

In 2000 the controversy continued about what Milwaukee should, or should not, do about two growing transportation problems. Solving each problem appeals to different groups of supporters. One deplored the overcrowded, aging freeways. Another lamented the lack of adequate public transportation between the inner city and the outlying areas where jobs are increasingly located. Suggested solutions are numbingly numerous. Frustrated commuters suggested adding freeway lanes, especially to I-94. Daniel Finley, county executive of Waukesha County, agreed. On the opposite side, Mayor Norquist pushed to tear down the Park Freeway East, as was agreed by the governor, Milwaukee county executive and mayor in April 1999. F. Thomas Ament, the low-key knowledgeable Milwaukee county executive, apparently agreed with Norquist that a light rail system should be built, but Thompson, Finley, and the legislature did not.[140] WISDOT asked SEWRPC to complete a transportation study by July 1, 2001, which will estimate future regional traffic demands.

In 2000 and years afterward different political factions will maneuver to apply scarce federal transportation funds toward their preferred solution. The 1970-1977 pro- and anti-freeway arguments and myths will bubble up again. So will Mayor Norquist's scathing indictment of freeways, expressed in his 1998 book, *The Wealth of Cities*. Clearly, in the freeway debates of the 1970s, the better arguments on both sides had merit. Solomon was needed to weigh their comparative merits, but unfortunately no one consulted him.

Proponents claimed that freeways had many strong benefits: one direct; the other, indirect.[141] A professionally designed freeway system would move existing and future traffic much more rapidly and safely than surface streets not designed for such volumes. Freeways would at the same time reduce fuel consumption and polluting emissions.[142] More important, appropriate freeway routes and capacity would also indirectly advance the continued economic prosperity of the Milwaukee area. Unfortunately, a large segment of the public is not familiar with business's need for faster, more reliable delivery of cargo and services.

A knowledgeable mayor proudly promoting his city's economic development would ordinarily use his bully pulpit to point out this key fact. Norquist has not. Instead, he has constantly belittled freeways.

Freeway opponents made the same major arguments in the 1970s. It was true enough that freeways removed thousands of homes in the 1960s, always at great inconvenience and often at financial sacrifice to those moved in the early years. The next two arguments had, to be charitable, far less merit. Freeway benefits were said to represent "trivial" luxuries, like saving time getting to a job, and usually helped only a few people or outsiders such as suburban commuters. The notion that the freeways served few is pure bunk. In 1995, Milwaukee County freeways handled 6.5 million vehicle miles of traffic daily, over 40 percent of all traffic in the county.[143] This is hardly "a few people." However, this erroneous argument was the favorite contention by Mordecai Lee and Ted Seaver[144] in 1977, and it remains prevalent twenty-one years later. Each had insisted that freeways were designed to save five or ten minutes of commuting time and therefore did not justify the sacrifices they undoubtedly required. Mordecai Lee in 1998 enjoyed recounting how freeways were designed to favor speed and commuters. As to speed, he wrote:

> Freeway construction recommendations were driven by a decision of SEWRPC that freeway flow during rush hour should be relatively free flowing, albeit at less than maximum permitted speeds....One should not plan public facilities to deal with a situation that only occurs 6-12 hours a week....This [rush hour] figure (of 1-2 hours on weekdays) is a very generous one. Jerry Schwerm, who was the County Director of Public Works during part of this era, was quoted in the paper as joking that Milwaukee didn't have a "rush hour;" rather it had a "rush minute."....It was ridiculous to expect a free flow (albeit at reduced speeds) during rush hour. It was a more normal aspect of city life to have stop-and-go and bumper-to-bumper traffic during the rush hour....

As to commuters, Lee added:

> Surely, anyone had the right to choose to live in (say) Mequon, but the government didn't have an obligation

110

Norquist is right that the public transit system needs to be improved to a point where it invites much greater usage. Most key officials participating in the 1998-2000 transportation debate shared that conclusion. The dispute started with *how* to improve mass transit to a point that wins more ridership. Norquist and Tom Ament, Milwaukee County Executive, believed light rail service would increase ridership, as it appears to have done in San Diego and Portland, Oregon. Governor Tommy Thompson opposed light rail as too expensive. The State Department of Transportation was neutral. Waukesha County Executive Daniel Finley favored improved bus service over light rail. All four agreed that improved and faster bus service is needed and is more flexible in meeting shifting passenger demand.

Norquist and Ament gloss over the more important fact that while San Diego credibly projects an increase in light rail use between 1990 and 2015 of 120 percent and Portland, of 113 percent, the absolute growth in vehicular traffic will dwarf these high percentage gains. The bottom line: increased transit traffic will still constitute an insignificant percentage of overall traffic, Portland rising to 4.2 percent versus 3 percent and San Diego to 1.9 percent compared with 1.3 percent. In Milwaukee current SEWRPC projections show mass transit rising – even with an assumed seventeen-mile light rail system to 3.2 percent of all traffic contrasted with 2.8 percent in 1995.[164]

Norquist also urges light rail as a way of controlling urban sprawl in the long run – since it would encourage denser development.[165] Yes, but maybe the horse is out of the barn, since sprawl has already occurred. A short light rail system linking already heavy population centers in downtown Milwaukee may be justified, though gasoline-powered faux trolley buses may be a less expensive way of achieving the same end. I believe that government should support substantial improvements in mass transit as a long-term desirable supplement to the predominant highway element in the total transportation system. However, it is hard to imagine that transit would ever carry more than 10 percent of passengers – triple the present figure – absent a rise in the price of gasoline of four or five times, as happened in the years following the Arab Oil Embargo of 1973.[166] Meanwhile the regional highway system is becoming increasingly inadequate to handle the 94.1% of passenger miles which will be traveled by auto in 2010.[167] The highway system needs substantial improvements, as does the mass transit system. In other words, we need an improved and balanced transportation system.

Time will tell who correctly reads the future, the indomitable mayor, or the trio of transportation experts who recommended that metropolitan Milwaukee needs *both* more arterial street and highway capacity and a greatly improved transit system. Only two points are probable: construction is now so expensive that few new lanes, and almost certainly no new freeways, will get built; and Norquist, like Don Quixote, is chasing an impossible nostalgic dream – in this case, a return to the transportation system of fifty years ago. He did not ask for trolleys, but stay tuned.

(Above) Flooding along the Milwaukee River in Glendale in 1960 led to the Southeastern Wisconsin Regional Planning Commission's Milwaukee River Watershed Plan.

(*Copyrighted Photograph*, Milwaukee Journal Sentinel)

(Left) The plan in 1971 recommended the seventeen-mile deep tunnel under Milwaukee to reduce pollution caused by sewer overflows during heavy rains. The deep tunnel under construction in 1985.

(*Photograph courtesy of SEWRPC*)

Part Four

Flooding and Pollution Wars

Chapter 16

The Farsighted Milwaukee River Watershed Plan

In 1959 and again in 1960, heavy spring rains coincided with a sudden snow melt, causing the Milwaukee River to surge over its banks, flooding many homes, most conspicuously in Glendale, but also in Mequon and Thiensville. Scores of residents were evacuated, some by boats which skimmed along lakes where streets used to be. A great hue and cry arose to protect residents from possible future floods. No one troubled to ask whether they should have been aware of the flood hazard when purchasing homes in the low-lying areas.

As is so often the case with highly-publicized disasters, elected officials were quick to offer solutions, sometimes dramatically simple, even superficial. One such was my then congressman, the energetic Henry Reuss, whose congressional district included the heavily flooded lower reaches of the Milwaukee River. Possibly at Reuss's suggestion, the U.S. Army Corps of Engineers in early l964 disclosed a possible solution for the floods by releasing a preliminary report of a plan that had been under consideration for fifteen years. The Corps recommended the construction of a channel to divert the Milwaukee River's excess flood waters from a point below Saukville east to Lake Michigan, a mile and a half south of Port Washington. The Corps estimated the average annual flood damage on the river, without such a channel, at $181,000. The Corps suggested that a facility sufficient to protect against the hundred-year-recurrence flood would cost $5,350,000 to construct and only $12,000 annually (in 1964 dollars) to maintain. Soon after the Corps's recommendation was made public, forty-eight residents, led by Leroy W. Grossman, a retired Marine National Exchange Bank officer and resident of Mequon, petitioned the Wisconsin Public Service Commission (PSC) to start the statutory process to create a Milwaukee Flood Control Board having the power to build and operate the diversion channel.

The PSC held a public hearing on June 5, 1964, and issued a preliminary order on August 27 of that year to create the board. Governor Warren Knowles then appointed Grossman and Douglas D. Ziegler, a prominent West Bend businessman, to the Flood Control Board and awaited Milwaukee County's nomination of a third member, as the county was entitled to do by statute. Milwaukee County declined to do so. Proponents stated – and the PSC assumed – that 80 percent of the construction costs would be derived from a federal appropriation to be secured by Reuss, and the PSC so concluded in a final order creating the board on February 8, 1966.

On January 7, 1965, Reuss spoke approvingly of a Corps of Engineers' final report recommending the diversion channel project, but he did not mention that the channel would be approximately fifty feet deep, ninety feet wide at the bottom, 400 feet wide at the top, and 3.5 miles long, with the removed earth (spoil) being conveniently piled in giant earthen mounds on each side of the diversion channel. Many residents, led again by Grossman, praised Reuss's proposal as likely to prevent future floods. Other residents condemned the diversion channel, such as the outspoken George Watts, a well-known Milwaukee merchant who lived in Grafton on the bank of the river below the proposed diversion channel. Watts colorfully mocked the channel as a "monstrous big ditch" whose width and high earthen banks would "cut Ozaukee County in two."

Others offered solutions to Milwaukee River's problems. The City of Milwaukee in late 1964 and, the County of Milwaukee in February 1965, after quiet consultation with Kurt Bauer, favored a broader approach than the diversion channel. They petitioned SEWRPC to conduct a comprehensive study of the Milwaukee River watershed in order to resolve flooding *and* pollution problems. SEWRPC eventually proposed that the five counties embracing the 698-square-mile Milwaukee River watershed – including Fond du Lac and Sheboygan Counties, which lay outside the seven-county planning region – authorize and fund SEWRPC to study flooding, pollution, and other problems arising from competing uses of the river and its banks. SEWRPC sensibly recognized that adopting the single function approach of solving one problem risked unwittingly aggravating other river-related problems.

Subsequently, the study demonstrated that the proposed big ditch was not cost-effective, because its high price exceeded the economic benefits which would accrue and would, furthermore, have the important unintended consequence of diverting polluted river waters to Lake Michigan near Port Washington. Better to solve the pollution problem, too, and reduce flooding by less expensive non-structural methods.

By September 14, 1965, SEWRPC carefully assembled a technical advisory committee to conduct a comprehensive study of the Milwaukee River Watershed. This task was completed with my help and that of Ray Blank, a SEWRPC commissioner and popular and later long-serving chairman of the Ozaukee County Board who knew all the officials in his county. The committee included twenty-one members. Private citizens and public officials were selected who had demonstrated an interest or expertise in three paramount problems[168] that Bauer and his staff found to be accompanying the increasing use and misuse of the River and the land bordering it.

Committee members included: county board supervisors; officials administering sewage treatment plants whose discharges were polluting the river; farmers whose eroding fields and cows wading in the river and its tributaries did the same; officials from cities and villages who had permitted developers to build in low-lying flood-prone land next to the river, or who might be tempted to do so; realtors; conservationists; park officials; and concerned federal and state agencies. The committee truly represented the many interests concerned. Because Henry Reuss was a powerful member of Congress and his media campaign favoring the diversion channel had attracted many supporters, the committee carefully included Grossman as its well-known champion. In the interest of fairness and to give assure that the committee might not appear to be pro-Reuss, the most vocal opponent of the "big ditch," Watts, was also invited to serve.

Many committee members held top public or private positions, thus bringing quality and credibility to the committee's deliberations. These included three prominent, talented, long-term, civil servants: Ray D. Leary, general manager of the Milwaukee Metropolitan Sewerage District; Herbert A. Goetsch, Commissioner of Public Works, City of Milwaukee; and Howard W. Gregg, general manager, Milwaukee County Park Commission. SEWRPC also added two business executives[169] whose plants bordered the river and were potential major pollution sources. SEWRPC, sensing that the clash of competing interests for the use or abuse of the river might prove controversial, asked me as one of its most active commissioners to chair the Milwaukee River Watershed Committee.

Between late 1965 and August 1967 the committee and top notch SEWRPC staff laboriously detailed the nature and depth of the facts that the study needed to collect and analyze. Kurt Bauer and I persuaded Fond du Lac and Sheboygan Counties, which lie outside SEWRPC's jurisdiction, to join in directing and funding the study. Those two counties added five members to the committee. Rome was not built in a day. Thereafter the committee started its four years of fact-finding and analysis, culminating in a massively documented two volume, 1,139-page report.

SEWRPC retained an internationally known engineering firm, Harza Engineering Company of Chicago. Harza later advised Egypt on the huge Soviet-financed Aswan Dam on the Nile River, and Chicago on its deep tunnel solution to its severe pollution and flooding problems. Initially, Harza made a surprising suggestion for controlling flooding along the Milwaukee River. It proposed our committee consider recommending the construction of a major multi-purpose reservoir – for flood control *and* recreation – at Waubeka which straddles the boundary of Ozaukee and Washington Counties. A new dam would contain the downward rush of flood waters after snow melts and heavy rainfalls. It would also create a recreational lake serving residents and tourists.

By 1971, SEWRPC's early premonition that the committee would encounter controversy proved to be correct. Flood victims favored the reservoir. Environmentalists attacked it, arguing that man-made lakes would collect sediment and, in periods of prolonged dry weather, shrink and expose stinking mud flats. Perhaps the most effective opposition came from farmers and local officials. They opposed the lake's removing nineteen square miles, an area larger than Pewaukee Lake, from the tax rolls. They were not reassured by Harza's forecast that the lake would attract new recreational facilities more valuable than the lost tax base.

Lengthy public hearings in the Mequon City Hall became heated. Reservoir critics included a vociferously indignant businessman Robert Fiend, who lived near the proposed reservoir. The committee split evenly on a motion to delete the Waubeka Dam proposal from the committee's emerging array of recommendations. As chairman, I then cast the deciding vote for deletion, but the fight did not end there.

The Watershed Committee's recommendation required approval by SEWRPC itself, usually no more than a formality. Commissioners customarily assumed that a diversified, knowledgeable, technical committee had done thorough work. However, it did not happen that way. A SEWRPC commissioner vigorously championed restoring the Waubeka Dam proposal on behalf of flood-area Glendale voters. He was Richard Nowakowski, chairman of the Milwaukee County Board, and a scrappy, flamboyant South Sider whose campaign corruption later drove him from office. I never learned why he chose to fight for Glendale residents who lived miles away from his district. Perhaps he had heard the reservoir proposal would be voted down. Perhaps he owed or wanted a return favor from the supervisor representing Glendale. When a majority of commissioners seemed on the verge of voting to affirm our committee's deletion of the reservoir proposal, Nowakowski skillfully maneuvered to block the vote. He walked out of the meeting room thereby depriving the commission of a quorum necessary for a vote. He then glared at his fellow commissioners through a glass partition. Eventually, the equally forceful SEWRPC chairman, George Berteau, brought Nowakowski back into the room so the commission could approve our committee's comprehensive watershed plan.

Most Watershed Committee recommendations were carried out over succeeding decades. The public accepted them as both sensible and necessary. Municipalities moved to eliminate flood damage by zoning against filling and building in the natural flood plain, as had been unwisely permitted in the Glendale area by the preceding governing authorities, the County of Milwaukee, and Town of Milwaukee. The Watershed Committee reasoned that development's customary filling and building would deprive the river of its natural flood water storage area, leading to two disastrous consequences: heightening inevitable future floods and thereafter creating a demand for costly flood control measures to protect improperly located flood-prone development.

Importantly, the Wisconsin Legislature in 1971, the year SEWRPC'S Milwaukee River Watershed Report was published, enacted Section 87.30 of the Wisconsin Statutes requiring counties and municipalities throughout Wisconsin to zone against development in flood plains. SEWRPC's carefully prepared maps delineating flood plain boundaries acted as an authoritative benchmark, showing exactly where to ban building and filling. They also helped the state enforcement agency, the Department of Natural Resources (DNR), determine whether a particular county or municipality had failed to obey the statutory command. Apparently none did. The statute and SEWRPC's explanations were persuasive.

The plan recommended various methods for controlling water pollution. First, we suggested that particular municipalities upstream from Milwaukee improve their sewage treatment plants to meet specified effluent standards, such as phosphorous removal, a highly controversial issue at the time, but since proven sound. All complied. They saw the need to do so, as did the DNR. Second, we suggested that farmers adopt good soil and water conservation practices on 65,000 acres of land, with the help of state grants. Those practices included the construction of earthen bench terraces wherever necessary. Terraces would block fertilizers put on the fields in March from flowing into the river during snow melt or heavy spring rains. Perhaps one-half the farmers built terraces, which was a big help. Third, we recommended that the vast environmental corridors in the watershed, consisting of woodlands, wetlands, and floodlands essential to preserving the ecosystem, be protected by a combination of strict zoning and public acquisition of 41,600 acres. Seventy-five percent of the environmental corridors were so protected; sadly, 25 percent were not.

Our committee's largest challenge was devising methods for controlling pollution pouring into the lower reaches of the Milwaukee River. It was serious. During rainfall and after snow melt, water got into the metropolitan sewerage system, causing the discharge, fifty-two times a year, of partially diluted but untreated sewage into street gutters, ditches, and the Milwaukee River and its many tributaries. The explanation: Milwaukee in its oldest areas, plus one square mile of Shorewood, had up until the early 1920s built mains to collect both sanitary wastes and storm water, called combined sewers, but had not made the pipes large enough to carry much rainfall. Instead, they built by-passes to conduct the mains' excess during rainfalls to the river rather than having sewage back up into basements. Later, Milwaukee, in its newer sections, and its suburbs constructed separate sanitary sewers and disposed of storm water by means of street gutters, ditches, or storm sewers. However, this solution did not work satisfactorily either. Over time, rainfall entered the separate sanitary sewers by various means. In some cases rain infiltrated below ground into the partly broken old mains, in others, residents adopted the unfortunate practice of illegally connecting their downspouts or sump pumps to their sanitary sewers. Sometimes the local building inspector looked the other way. Sanitary sewers unable to handle rains for which they were not designed, from time to time, overflowed, bubbling up through manhole covers and backing up into basements. Again, many bypasses were built to prevent backups, but they diverted untreated sewage eventually to the Milwaukee River.

Any solution to these discharges of untreated sewage would be very expensive. Build larger sewers, whether combined or separate? Build larger treatment plants for the intermittent increased flow? Harza came up with a better, less-expensive solution it was already exploring for Chicago. Our sister city to the south had the same problem, only larger: one hundred discharges into Lake Michigan annually, compared with fifty-two in Milwaukee. Harza suggested, and our entire committee unanimously agreed (including all its top-level engineering members) that a huge deep tunnel be built under the City of Milwaukee. Chicago was at that time considering constructing a deep tunnel for the same purpose. The mammoth tunnel would become a reservoir, containing and storing the run-off until it could be pumped out over three or four days and treated. As

126

Chapter 17

Illinois' Unique Suit Against Milwaukee
for Polluting Lake Michigan

The year 1977 proved to be doubly historic. Determined opponents in that year finally stopped construction of further freeways. The same year ushered in an even more expensive project. State and federal courts ordered the City of Milwaukee Sewerage Commission (MSC) and the Milwaukee Metropolitan Sewerage Commission (MMSC) to undertake Wisconsin's largest public works project ever – the massive modernization of Milwaukee sewerage system. MSC provided sewage treatment for the City of Milwaukee from 1914 and MMSC had been created in 1921 to build trunk sewers to convey sewage from suburbs to MSC's treatment plant at Jones Island. My personal role in the battles over sewer modernization strikingly differed from what I tried to do in the freeway fight. My 6-6-6 Freeway Committee utterly failed in late 1977 to forge consensus among hopelessly polarized people. In contrast, in August 1977, I was pulled into a far-from-fruitless role in Milwaukee's defense against the State of Illinois' lawsuit claiming that Milwaukee was polluting Lake Michigan. Illinois sought to force Milwaukee to add extravagant, and unnecessary features to the sewer modernization ordered in 1977 by the State of Wisconsin. By 1977, Illinois' lawsuit was five years old, complex, and a real danger to Milwaukee.

Yet Milwaukee residents in 1977 were mostly unaware of the need to fix sewers. Sewers had not flunked the smell test. What stank was alewives decaying in the harbor and along Lake Michigan's shore. Water pollution was growing steadily but quietly, while Milwaukeeans continued to believe their sewer system remained a national model. After all, had not the Milwaukee Sewerage Commission built a treatment plant at Jones Island before 1920? And developed the first secondary treatment process in the United States to obtain greater purification of wastes? Had not Milwaukee pioneered and patented the conversion of after-treatment sewage waste to commercial fertilizer, called Milorganite, by a process which compresses and dries residual wastes? Milorganite was a win-win discovery; it not only brought in revenue but saved the cost of trucking and burying wastes at some remote spot. Milorganite ultimately fertilized one-half the numerous golf courses in Florida. The usually critical and clearly independent Metropolitan Study Commission, as late as 1958, praised the Jones Island treatment plant for its low operating costs and high purity standards.[173]

Milwaukee's sewer problems primarily originated through a sharp increase in the standards which the American public demanded for sewage collection *and* treatment. In the 1960s America became increasingly concerned about water and air pollution. Consequently, Congress in 1972 and Wisconsin in 1974 enacted closely inter-related statutes making it illegal to discharge waste water into lakes and streams, except pursuant to a state-issued discharge permit. Such permits described the cleanliness of the discharged water, which the permit-holder had to achieve by eliminating pollutants through treatment. Discharge standards had been established by the United States Environmental Protection Agency (EPA) to provide uniform minimum water pollution standards for the nation's waters.[174] They substantially raised the minimum level of treatment of municipal waste water discharges. Milwaukee immediately flunked the new EPA standards fifty-two times a year, on the average, when heavy rains or snow melt caused sewers to overflow, flushing raw sewage into Lake Michigan or into rivers leading to it.

In 1974 and 1975 Milwaukee and the State Department of Natural Resources failed – after extensive negotiations – to agree on the precise collection and treatment standards to be included in Milwaukee's discharge permits for its treatment plants at Jones Island and Oak Creek. Fearing that the state was demanding too much, Milwaukee unsuccessfully sued the state on July 6, 1976, challenging its authority to include some standards; the state countersued to require Milwaukee to abide by its discharge standards. In May 1977, the parties finally agreed to an order by the Circuit Court of Dane County that Milwaukee meet the discharge permits' effluent standards. The order also specified a timetable for Milwaukee's construction of facilities required to reduce overflows of untreated sewage that occur after storms less severe than the storm of record. Such overflows had to be reduced from fifty-two times a year to an average of 1.7 times a year. More frequent overflows would, according to computations by MMSD consultants later accepted by the DNR,[175] imperil the water quality of the receiving stream and Lake Michigan. The court required

Milwaukee to complete construction by July 1993 at a cost estimated in 1977 to be $1.9 billion.

In reality, costs ultimately rose to $2.12 billion, after inflation and without counting interest, but Milwaukee taxpayers paid only $1.1 billion because federal and state grants contributed 47.67 percent of the cost. Significantly, the sixteen-year sewer project cost more than five times as much as the freeways cost in the twenty-eight years between 1950 and 1978. The sewers' local share came to ten times as much as the local share for freeways.[176]

Back in 1972, Illinois, under the leadership of a popular Attorney General, William J. Scott,[177] had dramatically opened a second front in the battle to compel Milwaukee to end its water pollution. Scott claimed Milwaukee's discharges drifted south into Illinois waters, creating a health hazard for Chicago bathers and drinking water. However farfetched, Scott's cause was popular because Chicago justifiably took great pride in its lakefront which it had jealously protected from despoliation over decades.

For example, in 1900, Chicago took its first massive step to stop fouling Lake Michigan by diverting its own sewage wastes toward the Mississippi River. To do so, Chicago, flexing its big shoulders, radically reversed the flow of the Chicago River into which it dumped its untreated wastes.[178] For eight years, 8,500 laborers dug a twenty-mile canal, now forty-five miles long. The Chicago Sanitary and Ship Canal connected the Chicago River to the Des Plaines River, which flowed into the Illinois and eventually the Mississippi River. To push wastes southward and to dilute them[179] Chicago diverted up to 10,000 cubic feet per second of Lake Michigan water. Later, other states, including Michigan and Wisconsin, sued in the U.S. Supreme Court to reduce the diversion, claiming it dangerously lowered lake levels. The court allowed a diversion of 3,200 cubic feet per second. Realizing that the lower diversion did not dilute its wastes sufficiently to alleviate possible health hazards downstream, Chicago then built sanitary treatment plants but continued to ship its treated wastes through the canal. Chicago's elite in 1909 championed the famous Burnham plan to preserve the lakefront from unsightly railroad tracks and make way for several splendid museums, an aquarium, Soldiers' Field, and a yacht club, all of which make Chicago's urban lakefront the most beautiful on the Great Lakes today, except possibly for Toronto, Ontario.

In the 1970s Chicago realized that sending its wastes to the Mississippi River did not fully protect Lake Michigan. During heavy rains, its sewers overflowed, just as they did in Milwaukee, spewing untreated wastes into the lake one hundred times a year and closing beaches often. The cause: Chicago and fifty-one suburbs conveyed sanitary wastes to treatment plants through small diameter pipes originally designed to convey storm water. When Chicago outlawed privies, sanitary wastes were added to storm sewers. The resulting combined sanitary and storm water mains could transport only one-and-one-half-times the average dry day's flow.[180] Chicago in 1976 started to bore deep tunnels and reservoirs in the dolomite limestone up to three hundred feet below the city to store excess rain-swollen sewage until it could be treated after the rains stopped.[181] The project, officially called the Tunnel and Reservoir Plan (TARP) and informally dubbed "The Deep Tunnel," sought, over thirty-plus years, to reduce overflows into Lake Michigan to one every three to five years. Thus, by the time of Milwaukee's trial in 1977, Chicago had taken giant steps to protect its Lake Michigan beaches, and looked unkindly on its sister city to the north, which Scott claimed was fouling Chicago's prized lakefront.

In this setting, amid a flurry of press releases receiving favorable coverage from the *Chicago Tribune,* Scott started his suit in the U.S. Supreme Court in 1972 against Milwaukee, its two sewerage commissions, South Milwaukee, Racine, and Kenosha. Although the U. S. Constitution requires that suits between *states* be tried in the Supreme Court, that court ruled in April 1972 that a suit by a state against a *city* could and should commence in a lower federal court.

Within a month, Illinois filed a new suit in the U.S. District Court in Chicago against Milwaukee, both its sewerage commissions, three other Wisconsin cities, and Waukegan in northern Illinois. All defendants except Milwaukee and the commissions settled their lawsuits by agreeing to improve their sewage systems to the extent that Milwaukee agreed to, or was forced to do. Milwaukee was left to fight alone. A six-month trial followed.

Scott in 1974 hired a thirty-two year old private environmental attorney, Joseph V. Karaganis, to handle the trial. Karaganis was unique. Imbued with idealism fostered at the University of Chicago Law

School and repelled by police violence against anti-Vietnamese war protestors at the 1968 Chicago Democratic National Convention, Karaganis resolved to use his legal knowledge to fight for the disadvantaged. At twenty-six, he had founded a public interest law firm, backed by a Midas Muffler angel, to protect without a fee victims of environmental pollution. He promptly sued two Indiana-based steel plants and compelled them to stop polluting Lake Michigan. This victory and the *Chicago Tribune* made him a hero, for this was the Age of the Environment. Scott, himself a dedicated environmentalist and Republican, hired Karaganis, a Democrat, without ever having met him, saying, "I don't care about your politics." When I met Karaganis, he seemed a genial, wise-cracking, handsome, dark-haired, Greek-American who quickly proved to be an extremely bright, articulate environmental crusader – one who enjoyed making opposing witnesses fumble and cringe.

Karaganis now boldly sought to compel the Wisconsin city defendants to do far more than sharply reduce their discharge of pollutants into lake Michigan; he asked them to limit their overflows of untreated sewage to once in one hundred years and to comply with the unrealistically stiff treatment standards which Illinois applied to discharges into Lake Michigan. *Significantly Illinois did not apply its ultra-strict standard to discharges into other Illinois waters.* The statute did not mention that Illinois cities bordering the lake, unlike Wisconsin cities, had a geographic alternative place for dumping their wastes, the Chicago or Des Plaines Rivers leading to the Mississippi River. The tough legislative standards applied to Lake Michigan discharges could be achieved only by installing a highly expensive advanced waste treatment process.

Because Chicago since 1900 had diverted its collected wastes into rivers flowing to the Mississippi, by 1972 all but three or four suburbs copied Chicago's diversion. Significantly, Missouri had in 1906 sued Illinois for permitting Chicago's then untreated discharges to pollute St. Louis on the Mississippi River. [182]

I believed then and believe now that the Illinois legislature never expected out-of-state compliance with its new stringent Lake Michigan standards. The high cost of complying with the stringent new standards was intended to persuade a few existing treatment plants at Lake

133

Forest, Lake Bluff, and Waukegan, Illinois, to reroute their wastes into nearby Mississippi-bound rivers. This they did by 1977.[183] Milwaukee had no such alternative nearby-Mississippi-bound river into which to direct its treated wastes. Therefore, Karaganis' argument for Illinois that Wisconsin communities should abide by Illinois' Lake Michigan treatment standards was as persuasive as "do as I say, not as I do." Chicago avoided the statute by rerouting to the Mississippi.

Karaganis' knowledge and vigor made him a formidable foe on the facts, but his boldness caused him to be a bit too adventurous on the law, as we later proved. In the six months' trial in 1977 he ushered expert witnesses in a dozen fields into the courtroom.[184] They sought to demonstrate that discharges of partially treated sewage at Jones Island in Milwaukee, normally propelled south by occasional westerly winds, entered Illinois waters thirty-nine miles away without having become so diluted or far out in the lake as to not pose a health hazard to Illinois bathers and drinking water. Their testimony impressed U. S. District Judge John T. Grady, an extremely self-confident, heavy-penalty judge recently appointed by President Gerald Ford. Grady heard the case without a jury.

On July 29, 1977, Judge Grady decided that Milwaukee had indeed polluted Illinois waters in violation of every law which Karaganis claimed: federal common law, Illinois statutes, and Illinois common law. The judge's remedy was far worse: Milwaukee must (1) eliminate *all* overflows (vastly different from both the Wisconsin state court's requirement that Milwaukee reduce them to 1.7 times a year[185] and Chicago's 1977 deep tunnel objective of limiting them to once every three to five years); and (2) treat its sewage in accord with the Illinois almost-unattainable advanced-waste-treatment standards for Lake Michigan.

The drastic decision shocked Milwaukee. The judge asked Milwaukee to propose on September 9 a step-by-step timetable within which it proposed to comply with his decision. Presumably he would then include the timetable or some tougher version of it in his ultimate court order. We learned later that Grady's excessive penalties caused the U.S. Court of Appeals in Chicago to reverse him more often than any other District Judge.

In late August the Milwaukee Metropolitan Sewerage Commission unexpectedly asked me and my firm of seventy-seven attorneys, Quarles and Brady, the second largest in Milwaukee, to become lead counsel for the defense. That happened, as many good things do, because in addition to being part of a strong firm, I was at the right place at the right time. Not one coincidence, but three. Two were that I (that is, my team) had recently walloped the commission in court and, also, been hired by its major consultants. Here's how the three separate events came about. In the early 1970s a contractor, Eugene Fattore of Detroit, nearly went bankrupt during a commission tunneling job. He asked me to sue the commission for not warning him that solid rock lay deep underground in the path of the tunnel he was to dig. We won for his company a $2.5 million judgment in 1974 which shocked and impressed the commission. The case broke precedent. The commission had never before been sued for negligence in failing to disclose true underground conditions. Two respected attorneys had turned down the case as unwinnable before I was hired. I took the matter on a contingent fee basis for one of only two times in my career. The trial court held that no law made the commission liable.

Elwin J. Zarwell handled a successful appeal to the Court of Appeals, after which I offered to settle for one million dollars. Raymond Leary, the long-time, able, but in this case sadly overconfident general manager of the two sewerage commissions, rejected my offer. He shocked me by talking as if the appellate court had not just ruled that the commission was liable for such damages as we could later prove at a trial. He was in denial. That figure became $2.5 million.

The second event occurred in 1975 when the commission engaged CH2MHill, a giant national Oregon engineering consulting firm, to develop a new EPA-ordered system for charging commercial customers for the cost of treating their particular wastes.[186] CH2MHill in turn asked me to be its lawyer. CH2MHill's chief engineer, Charles V. ("Tom") Gibbs Jr., a perpetually smiling, politically astute, extraordinarily articulate engineer, employed me after obtaining favorable recommendations from well-known Milwaukee engineers.[187]

My user-charge assignment for CH2MHill required me to meet frequently with the Milwaukee Metropolitan Sewerage District's (District) officer in charge of operations, William Katz, a tall, intellectually precise, careful former engineer for the Chain Belt Company. Katz shortly became Milwaukee's principal expert witness before Judge Grady. Karaganis mercilessly cross-examined Katz with rapid-fire, fact-filled questions designed to upset even this solid witness. It succeeded. A thoroughly badgered Katz asked me if I could represent him personally in order to somehow protect him from Karaganis. I declined because an attorney for a witness could not formally participate in the trial but Katz later recommended me to represent the district when it decided to change lawyers.

The road to the third coincidence started July 27, 1977 when the Milwaukee Sewerage Commission elected a new chairman, Harry J. Williams,[188] who immediately spent a full day in Judge Grady's court to see for himself how the trial was progressing. He concluded that Milwaukee needed to present its defense more vigorously. Harry's unprepossessing appearance masked an acute intelligence, steel will, and scorching contempt for mediocrity. Williams worked at Cutler Hammer as a brilliant division controller, where employees regarded him as a smart, fair, but extremely tough taskmaster.[189]

The third occurrence culminated right after Judge Grady pronounced his bombshell decision against Milwaukee. Williams decided to find a strong law firm to take over the lead role in the defense. He, like Gibbs two years earlier, consulted many private and public sources including Norman Gill, executive director of the Citizens' Governmental Research Bureau, and Herbert Goetsch, Commissioner of Public Works for Milwaukee, on the choice of a strong firm. Strangely, Williams did not obtain input from the all-powerful Mayor Maier, who could and usually did control major Sewerage Commission decisions. Many sources nominated Quarles and Brady. At the same time, Gibbs and Katz also recommended that Williams employ me and my firm. After obtaining unanimous consent from fellow commissioners, Harry then asked Quarles & Brady, through me, to take over the lead role in what became the largest litigation in my career.

A few days later Mayor Maier invited me to his large paneled office. He and I had known each other through my regional planning commission work on the freeways and the Milwaukee River watershed committee,[190] and my having negotiated stevedore leases with the City of Milwaukee Harbor Commission on behalf of Hansen Seaway and Meehan Seaway. City Attorney James Brennan, brother of a famous Notre Dame player and coach, and several others sat alongside me on low upholstered chairs before the mayor who sat on an elevated platform. We discussed and condemned Judge Grady's unexpected, obviously expensive decision. (Months later engineers estimated the cost of complying with Judge Grady's order at one billion dollars.) Then the mayor excused all the others so he could talk to me alone. Looking me straight in the eye, he said:

> Dick, I am counting on you personally to get this damned decision reversed if you have to go all the way to the U.S. Supreme Court.

The mayor's remarks concerned me. I had already decided that Bud Zarwell should handle the litigation. He was a superb appellate lawyer. I was not. My strengths lay building a team and communicating with clients. Zarwell, moreover, had a degree in engineering from Marquette and was general counsel to several manufacturers whose high-quality products depended on superior engineering. Also, the Illinois suit was enormously complex in its facts, law, and political ramifications. Any hope of success in this high-stakes uphill battle required splitting the work among many attorneys chosen for their different specialized skills and demonstrated ability to function as a team. So I decided that I would supervise the team effort and explain the highly technical facts and law to our new clients, appointed and elected officials on both sewerage commissions. I had always enjoyed describing complex matters in simple terms, often illustrated by visual aids. I replied:

> Mayor, this case will take a team to win. I'll put our best appellate lawyers on it at once and work with them closely. The city will get the finest possible quality effort that way.

The mayor understood. While a forceful leader, he was consistently willing to let professionals perform their roles in the manner they thought best, so long as they did not lose. He shot right back: "I am counting on you to win it."

Immediately I put Zarwell in charge of the Illinois litigation with Samuel J. Recht as his alter ego. Although a seemingly improbable pair, their joint efforts had won many law suits. Recht had clerked for

Ryan Duffy, the former Chief Judge of the Seventh Circuit Court of Appeals (as it was then called), which would hear our appeal. Zarwell, a six-foot-two tall, Army brat and a highly disciplined lawyer, towered over Recht, who was very short and not at all military in his bearing. The two were the brightest lawyers with whom I ever worked. Each could anticipate and outflank the maneuvers an opponent might make in the fifth or sixth inning while I could not see beyond the third or, at best, the fourth. They had the utmost respect for each other and worked well as a team. They even seemed to relish working nights and weekends. Zarwell and Recht were exactly what Milwaukee needed to dig out of the deep hole into which it had fallen – or had been pushed.

bargainer but so were the engineers, Zarwell, and Recht. On November 11 we agreed on a twelve-year timetable detailing each step in construction through 1989.

On November 15, a stern-looking Judge Grady approved the jointly proposed timetable but then surprised us. He announced that he was editing his July 29 decision and would have the revised decision in our hands soon. We were aghast. The judge clearly intended to rewrite so as to weaken our grounds for appeal. We had worked twelve-hour days preparing an appeal based on his earlier written decision, on the 14,000-page transcript of testimony, and on numerous technical exhibits. Only a quick counter-attack might stop Grady. Zarwell bravely scolded the all-powerful judge. Zarwell insisted that the judge honor our reliance on his original official decision. The normally rapid-speaking, no-nonsense judge seemed taken aback but said that we could bring to his attention anything that prejudiced us in the revision.

We raced downstairs from the courtroom to file an appeal. That act moved the case officially from the district court to the appellate court. With the case no longer in his court, we figured that Grady lost any conceivable legal ability to change his decision retroactively.

Later, when Judge Grady insisted that he would nevertheless revise his decision, we made a daring move. Zarwell and I asked the West Publishing Company in Minneapolis, the official publisher of court decisions, not to print the second opinion if submitted. We told West that Grady had lost jurisdiction, or power, over the case owing to our appeal, and that a second decision would cause confusion in the written record. Perhaps the judge never sent his second opinion to be published; in any event, no subsequent opinion was ever printed.

Compliance with the judge's November decree would add one billion dollars to the $1.9 billion estimated cost of complying with the Wisconsin state court order of May 1977. Judge Grady's order was overkill because it was not remotely necessary to protect public health. Only Milwaukee on the Great Lakes was being held to Grady's ridiculously high requirements of no overflows except once in one hundred years, and advanced waste treatment (that is, tertiary rather than secondary level treatment). More realistic EPA standards applied to all other cities on the Great Lakes: Duluth, Detroit, Toledo,

Cleveland, Erie, and Buffalo. We determined to show the appellate court how the expert federal EPA felt Judge Grady had gone too far.

Soon after Judge Grady issued his decree, Milwaukee asked the EPA to reimburse part of the cost of building the extra facilities ordered by Judge Grady.[192] EPA predictably refused, saying they would not bring benefits to public health equal to their cost and therefore were not eligible for federal funds.[193] Incidentally, federal funds eventually paid 47.7 percent of Milwaukee's $2.12 billion ultimate cost (excluding interest) of complying with the *state* court order issued six months before Judge Grady's decree.

Once we appealed Judge Grady's decision in November, federal rules gave us only a short time in which to file our briefs. A large team of pollution experts and attorneys worked double shifts analyzing six months' trial testimony and numerous court decisions. Our appeal emphasized two basic points. We first challenged Grady's sweeping conclusion that both the federal common law of nuisance *and* the Illinois statutes and common law could apply to discharges in Wisconsin. We argued that the 1972 Federal Water Pollution Control Act had expressly established minimum discharge standards for interstate waters. Our legal briefs said that the 1972 statute preempted, or superseded, the old federal common law and, like it, rendered Illinois laws inapplicable in cases against discharges outside Illinois.

Second, our appeal attacked Grady's far-fetched finding that Milwaukee's discharges remained toxic after traveling eighty miles to Chicago over many days. That task was immense. Illinois' experts had bolstered that claim by complex testimony which, at times, was more theoretical than factual. In fact, the judge in his opinion said their testimony was so complicated that it was over his head, but Milwaukee had nevertheless done such a grievous wrong that very expensive remedial measures were necessary. Our appeal argued that Milwaukee had not harmed Illinois waters because Chicago had experienced no outbreaks of water-related diseases. (Illinois had used that very argument in successfully defending Chicago in 1906 in the U.S. Supreme Court against claims by Missouri that Chicago's sanitary wastes were polluting St. Louis.)[194] Further, Chicago's chlorination in 1977 protected drinking water from any conceivable water contamination from Milwaukee. Finally, if some highly diluted Milwaukee pollution did reach distant Illinois waters, Judge Grady's advanced treatment measures were far more extravagant than required to protect Illinois.

We highlighted the judge's lack of qualifications for prescribing the appropriate sanitary engineering solutions by quoting his judicial opinion's startlingly candid confession:

> The nature of the subject matter here...is such that my own experience and observations in life are of relatively little use to me. It is well known to all of us that the arcane subject matter of some of the expert testimony in this case was sometimes over the heads of all of us in one height or another. I would be certainly less than candid if I did not acknowledge that my grasp of some of the testimony was less complete than I would like it to be....

To show the appellate court in Chicago that Judge Grady's order was overkill, I asked the Environmental Protection Agency to notify the appellate court of its official determination that the order was not cost effective. The EPA declined but we attached a copy of their ruling to our briefs. As if to rub salt in Milwaukee's wounds, President Carter's Department of Justice filed briefs as a friend of the court advising that it supported Judge Grady's ruling that the federal common law applied in this case. That brief showed that the EPA and U.S. Department of Justice spoke with inconsistent voices: Grady's order was not federally fundable because it was not needed for public health, but the law upon which it was based should be upheld anyway.

The U.S. Court of Appeals in Chicago in April 1979[195] upheld Illinois' position that the federal common law applied in Illinois to Wisconsin discharges, but then, like Solomon, split the baby in half by holding that: (a) although the law justified Grady's ordering Milwaukee to curtail all overflows except during the once-in-a-hundred years storm, (b) the facts did not justify the expensive advanced waste water treatment. Judge Philip W. Tone, a noted environmental expert who, many believed, aspired to become a U.S. Supreme Court Justice, wrote a scholarly eighty-page opinion divided into published and unpublished parts. In a highly significant but little noted Footnote 53, Tone also held, as we had urged, that Illinois statutory and common law could not apply alongside the federal common law. He cited Justice Douglas's Footnote 9 in the 1972 Supreme Court decision telling Illinois to start this case in the lower court. Douglas had said:

> Federal common law and not the common law of the individual states is entitled to be recognized as a basis for dealing in a uniform way with the environmental rights of a State against impairment by sources outside its domain.[196]

While we regretted the court's opinion upholding no overflow in a hundred years, we were delighted with three victories: the appellate court's knocking out of Grady's requirement for advanced waste treatment saved $300 million dollars. Its holding that neither Illinois statutory or common law could apply to Wisconsin deprived Illinois of two of the three legal foundations on which Judge Grady based his decision. If we could persuade the U.S. Supreme Court to knock out the third, the federal common law, Judge Grady's decision would die. Judge Tone's reasoning in knocking down advanced treatment displayed another split-the-baby approach, all done in a masterful manner. After first giving Milwaukee a blow by declaring the federal common law applied rather than the 1972 federal statute, he made Illinois unhappy by holding in Footnote 53 that the Illinois statute and common law did not apply. Then, reversing field on *both* conclusions, he said the court could not fail to examine how federal and state statutes operated in practice. He made four points. Congress required only secondary, rather than advanced waste treatment, to be in place as late as July 1, 1983 and possibly later. Few cities had adopted advanced waste treatment. Illinois did not require advanced waste treatment for waters other than Lake Michigan (reflecting our position that Illinois was disingenuous in suggesting its statutory standards were a model for Milwaukee). Finally, the evidence supporting the need for advanced waste treatment in Milwaukee to protect distant Chicago was, in his own words, weak at best.

Soon this long case became even more bewilderingly complex. The Court of Appeals had ordered Judge Grady to revise his original order, that is, to drop the requirement of advanced waste treatment. His subsequent revision pleased neither side; both appealed to the Court of Appeals to compel the apparently stubborn judge to rewrite his order properly. Meanwhile both Milwaukee and Illinois separately sought review (under a writ of *certiorari*[197]) from the U.S. Supreme Court of the part of the Seventh Circuit's decision it had lost. Illinois sought to restore advanced waste treatment to the court order; we wanted the order reversed entirely because, we said, the federal common law on which it was based had been replaced by federal statutory law with which Milwaukee would comply. The justices grant only two percent of such requests. The solicitor general for the Carter administration opposed our request, egged on by an assistant attorney general who had recently been general counsel for the Sierra Club, an ardent environmental group. In March 1980 the Supreme Court allowed our appeal but was strangely silent on Illinois' request.

When the Court of Appeals was informed that both sides were appealing *to it* from Judge Grady's revised order and, simultaneously, *from it* to the Supreme Court on its own decision, it ordered *all proceedings* stayed – or suspended – until the Supreme Court decided the case. Unfortunately, Milwaukee was still obliged to spend large sums complying with Judge Grady's original order of November 15, 1977 which was technically still-standing and now nearly three years old. We asked Supreme Court Justice Stevens (of Chicago) to stay all *orders* to spare Milwaukee from spending large sums which the Supreme Court might decide were not necessary. He agreed in May 1980. Despite many frantic moves and counter moves, we and Karaganis remained civil. He and Recht bet five cents on whether Justice Stevens would grant our request. Karaganis promptly mailed a nickel to Recht.

We argued the case before the Supreme Court December 2, 1980. The night before, Zarwell, Recht, Andrew Barnes, James Baxter[198] and I staged a mock Supreme Court hearing in our rooms at the Hay Adam Hotel overlooking the brilliantly lighted White House. Zarwell practiced his argument while we interrupted and peppered him with the toughest questions we guessed the justices might ask. The next morning we climbed the white marble steps and entered between the imposing Corinthian columns. Inside, all was solemn and businesslike. Before we could enter the court chamber, attendants checked our credentials. Stern-faced female attendants, smartly attired in blue uniforms resembling those of Navy WAVES, quietly escorted us down the courtroom's center aisle to our seats at a rectangular table in the second row. There we sat before the black-robed justices who peered down at us from an elevated dais.

The court runs as efficiently as a Swiss watch. Attorneys for each side sit behind low tables. To avoid losing a moment of the justices' time, attorneys for the next case are required to sit at a second row of tables during the argument of the prior case. If the first case is suddenly settled or cut short, the second group of lawyers can instantly move forward and argue their case. We were allotted sixty seconds to move from the second row to the first.

Six of the nine justices, including Potter Stewart and Byron (Whizzer) White, both of whom had attended Yale Law School with me, asked searching questions of Zarwell and Karaganis. This time, Karaganis, no longer before a sympathetic Judge Grady, was too argumentative and stubbornly evasive to suit the justices. They asked precise, heart-of-the matter questions showing impressive familiarity with the complex case. They, or their top-notch law clerks, clearly had read all the voluminous briefs. Justice White asked Karaganis in mid-argument if he had not overlooked a key passage in the Supreme Court's prior (1972) decision in this case prophesying that the time might come when the federal water pollution statutes would supersede federal common law. (We were arguing the time had indeed come). Karaganis responded with a faulty version of the passage. Then White demolished his argument by pointedly quoting the true disputed text, word for word.

I sat silently through the argument and questioning, looking directly at Justice Potter Stewart. Long ago, Stewart, after skipping most sessions in one course at Yale Law School, had borrowed my typewritten notes. Then – in a revealing display of raw brain power – got the higher marks. I briefly wondered whether he remembered.

Six months after our return from Washington, in April 1981 – nine years after the case started – the Supreme Court, by a 6 to 3 vote, decided everything in Milwaukee's favor.[199] Or so we thought. Justice William O. Rehnquist, writing for himself and Chief Justice Burger, and Justices Stewart, White, and two others, first declared that the 1972 Amendments to the Federal Water Pollution Control Act had displaced the federal common law by "the establishment of a comprehensive regulatory program supervised by an expert administrative agency." Rehnquist termed the lower courts' invoking federal common law in the face of legislation supplanting it as "peculiarly inappropriate in areas as complex as water pollution control."

Then Rehnquist proved the case's complexity by bitingly quoting word-for-word Judge Grady's confession, cited in our brief that the expert testimony in this case was sometimes over the heads of all of us to one height or another.

(Grady surely had intended to delete this revealing quote in his abortive attempt to revise his decision.)

With cold logic Rehnquist ridiculed Illinois' claim that its statutes and common law could apply:

> [W]e note the inconsistency in Illinois' argument and the decision of the District Court that both federal and state nuisance law apply in this case. If the state law can be applied, there is no need for federal common law; if federal common law exists, it is because state law cannot be used.

News of Milwaukee's great victory – which received a page wide headline in the *Milwaukee Journal* – reached me in England. My wife and I were vacationing at an idyllic thatched roof inn next to the moors in Devon where Evelyn Waugh wrote *Brideshead Revisited.* The jovial innkeeper pounded on our door after midnight, saying with a straight face that (newly elected) President Reagan was calling Mr. Cutler. Even better, the caller turned out to be Zarwell elatedly reading every word of the court's decision.

A month later, May 1981, the Supreme Court denied Illinois' request to hear Illinois appeal from the Circuit Court's reversal of that part of Judge Grady's order requiring the expensive advanced waste treatment. This denial and the Supreme Court's opinion in our appeal represented twin triumphs for us. We naturally believed that they ended the matter. We logically reasoned that the Supreme Court had (1) killed the federal common law on which the Court of Appeals had upheld the no-overflows-in-a-hundred-years order and (2) affirmed by its footnote 7 the Court of Appeals' earlier nullification of Illinois state law as an alternative legal foundation for Judge Grady's order. We were wrong. We underestimated Karaganis's refusal to concede defeat. Karaganis then asked the Circuit Court, to which the Supreme Court had remanded (sent back) the case, to rule that the Supreme Court opinion did not prohibit Grady's order. Illinois sought to uphold Judge Grady's original order (both as to advanced waste treatment and no overflows) as being based on the Illinois common law and a statute which happened to apply only to communities that could duck it by diverting wastes to the Mississippi River Basin.

In March 1994, three years later, the Circuit Court, by a 2 to 1 vote, settled the remaining question in our favor. Justice Thomas Fairchild stated eloquently why a downstream state could not, parochially, apply its law against an upstream state already bound by federal law applying to interstate waters. His logic was clear and stood Illinois's argument on its head:

> [I]t seems implausible that Congress meant to preserve or confer any right of a state claiming injury (State II) [Illinois]...to seek enforcement of limitations on discharges in State I [Wisconsin] by applying the statutes or common law of State II....For a number of different [downstream] states to have independent... regulatory authority over a single discharge would lead to a chaotic confrontation between sovereign states. Dischargers would be forced to meet not only the statutory standards of all states potentially affected by their discharges but also the common law standards developed through case law in those states. It would be virtually impossible to predict the standard for a lawful discharge into an interstate body of water. Any permit issued under the Act would be rendered meaningless. In our opinion, Congress could not have intended such a result.[200]

Again, I was abroad when I learned of our final appellate court victory. This time, we were in our bunks far below deck on a storm-tossed ship between Israel and Greece. After midnight, I was summoned to the captain's bridge. The always-on-duty Zarwell was calling on the radio-telephone. He reported that the Circuit Court had turned down Illinois for the final time and ordered Grady to dismiss the case. Judge Thomas Fairchild's opinion was the second one wholly favorable to us out of a total of six separate decisions[201] in this long, unusual case. Illinois had won the first three decisions and shared the fourth (Tone's) with us. We celebrated the last two.

Still, Illinois did not give up. It petitioned the Supreme Court to review this case for the third time and reverse Fairchild's opinion that expressly stated that Illinois law was not applicable. We opposed. We had won. We submitted a short brief in October 1984 mocking Illinois by quoting the response made by Confederate Army General Bedford Forrest to an unreasonably repeated request by one of his soldiers. We wrote:

> We call to mind the statement of Gen. Bedford Forrest, the semi-literate cavalry genius of the Confederate States of America, who, after twice refusing a private's request for a furlough, scribbled on the back of the form "I told you twicest Godamnit know."

Maybe the court shared our humor. It denied Illinois' last request.

This quixotic case ultimately came to a close in September 1989, five years after the Court of Appeals had ordered Judge Grady to dismiss it, and seventeen years after Illinois had started it. Part of the protracted delay originated in a last-ditch squabble. Illinois knew it must reimburse Milwaukee for the substantial court costs Milwaukee had paid to Illinois in 1977 when Illinois won its lower court victory. But Illinois refused to pay interest on its long use of Milwaukee's money. Our firm found legal authority; and Judge Grady on August 16, 1989, ordered Illinois to return Milwaukee's money with twelve years' interest – over $100,000; thus Milwaukee received $498,000 in all in September, finally ending the case. In addition we had saved Milwaukee taxpayers one billion dollars by wiping out the Grady order, for which we charged $1.5 million in fees for services by up to twenty-eight different attorneys over twelve years. George Chester, a close friend and well known, witty partner at Foley and Lardner, our big brother rival, quipped after our Supreme Court victory: "Dick, with this case you are now famous; you can retire."

But I could not. One year after the U.S. Supreme Court decision, Senator Robert T. Stafford of Vermont, chairman of the Senate Committee on Environment and Public Works, sought to erase our victory. Did he care about Milwaukee? No. Did he overlook Milwaukee? Yes. He introduced a bill in 1982, S 431, to amend the Clean Water Act to allow litigants in a downstream state to apply their state's law in bringing suit against a pollutor's discharges in an upstream state. He had in mind litigants in his state, Vermont, who claimed damage from a public utility's discharges across Lake Champlain in New York.

Stafford's proposed legislation did not say it was not retroactive; arguably it could apply to our case up until Judge Grady dismissed our case, which it turned out, did not occur until 1989, seven years later. For five years I appeared – with the fancy title of expert witness – before committees of both branches of Congress to oppose, or seek to amend, Stafford's transparently parochial legislation. I eventually persuaded Rhode Island's highly respected Senator John Chaffee, chairman of Stafford's Subcommittee on Environmental Pollution, to propose amending Stafford's bill to exclude Milwaukee. Senator Allen Simpson of Wyoming opposed Stafford flatly. Simpson feared downstream states would sue persons in his state for consuming too much water from streams, thereby increasing their salinity downstream.

The battle in Congress between different interests was bitter, and it raged through three Congresses. Wisconsin Senator William Proxmire, a perpetual maverick who had also been my classmate at Yale, threatened more than once to filibuster Stafford's bill, derailing its otherwise certain passage in the Senate. Congressman Les Aspin of Racine, with assistance from a resourceful staffer, William Broydrick, later helpfully amended the companion House bill so that it did not apply to cases like ours – which had already been ruled on by the U.S. Supreme Court.

In 1986, the House and Senate finally passed different versions of the bill, the House's version protecting Milwaukee, the Senate's probably not. The House and Senate conferees, when reconciling their differences in the 1987 Amendments to the Clean Water Act, dropped Stafford's parochial pro-downstream state provision. Then, Senator Stafford gave up.

We had kept Senator Stafford at bay long enough to win. Senator Proxmire's environmental aide, Ruth Fleischer, with whom I worked closely, said of my lobbying efforts: "The principal factor in lobbying success is persistence. You have persistence."

The Illinois threat was finished.

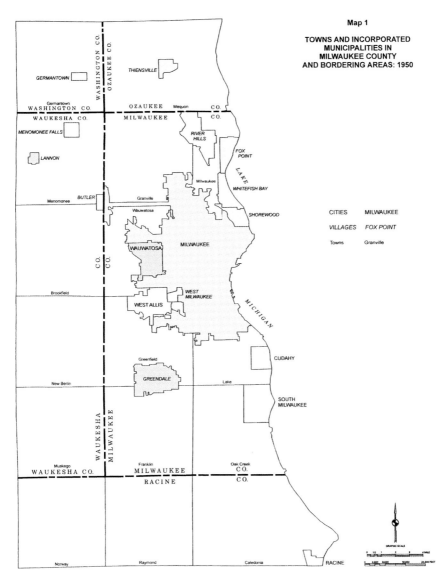

Map 1

TOWNS AND INCORPORATED
MUNICIPALITIES IN
MILWAUKEE COUNTY
AND BORDERING AREAS: 1950

CITIES   MILWAUKEE

VILLAGES   FOX POINT

Towns   Granville

Source: U.S. Bureau of the Census

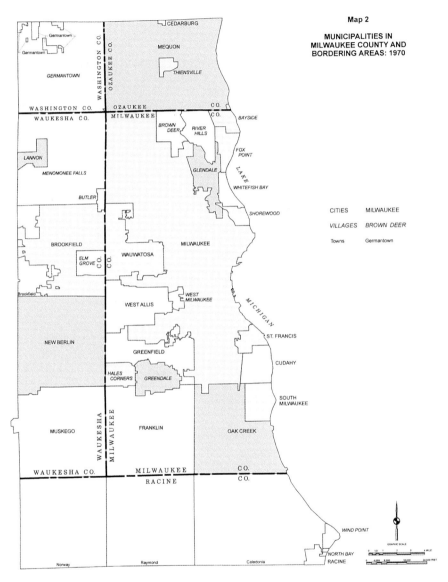

Map 2

MUNICIPALITIES IN MILWAUKEE COUNTY AND BORDERING AREAS: 1970

CEDARBURG

Germantown

Germantown

GERMANTOWN

WASHINGTON CO.

OZAUKEE CO.

MEQUON

THIENSVILLE

WASHINGTON CO.

OZAUKEE CO.

WAUKESHA CO.

MILWAUKEE CO.

BAYSIDE

BROWN DEER

RIVER HILLS

FOX POINT

LANNON

MENOMONEE FALLS

GLENDALE

LAKE

WHITEFISH BAY

BUTLER

SHOREWOOD

CITIES MILWAUKEE

VILLAGES BROWN DEER

Towns Germantown

BROOKFIELD

ELM GROVE

WAUWATOSA

MILWAUKEE

Brookfield

WEST MILWAUKEE

WEST ALLIS

MICHIGAN

NEW BERLIN

ST. FRANCIS

GREENFIELD

CUDAHY

HALES CORNERS

GREENDALE

SOUTH MILWAUKEE

MUSKEGO

FRANKLIN

OAK CREEK

WAUKESHA CO.

MILWAUKEE CO.

WAUKESHA CO.

MILWAUKEE CO.

RACINE CO.

WIND POINT

GRAPHIC SCALE

Norway

Raymond

Caledonia

NORTH BAY

RACINE

Source: U.S. Bureau of the Census

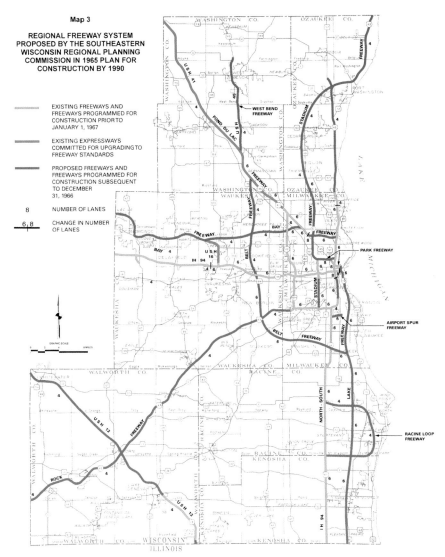

Map 3

REGIONAL FREEWAY SYSTEM
PROPOSED BY THE SOUTHEASTERN
WISCONSIN REGIONAL PLANNING
COMMISSION IN 1965 PLAN FOR
CONSTRUCTION BY 1990

EXISTING FREEWAYS AND
FREEWAYS PROGRAMMED FOR
CONSTRUCTION PRIOR TO
JANUARY 1, 1967

EXISTING EXPRESSWAYS
COMMITTED FOR UPGRADING TO
FREEWAY STANDARDS

PROPOSED FREEWAYS AND
FREEWAYS PROGRAMMED FOR
CONSTRUCTION SUBSEQUENT
TO DECEMBER
31, 1966

8   NUMBER OF LANES

6,8   CHANGE IN NUMBER
        OF LANES

Source: SEWRPC.

Map 4

**MULTI-SEGMENT DOWNTOWN LOOP FREEWAY
PROPOSED IN 1965 PLAN FOR CONSTRUCTION BY 1990**

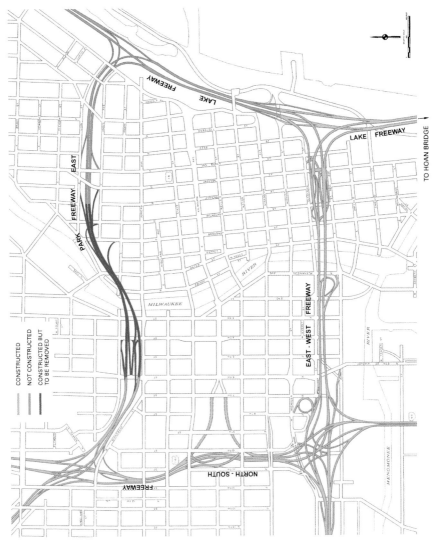

Source: SEWRPC.

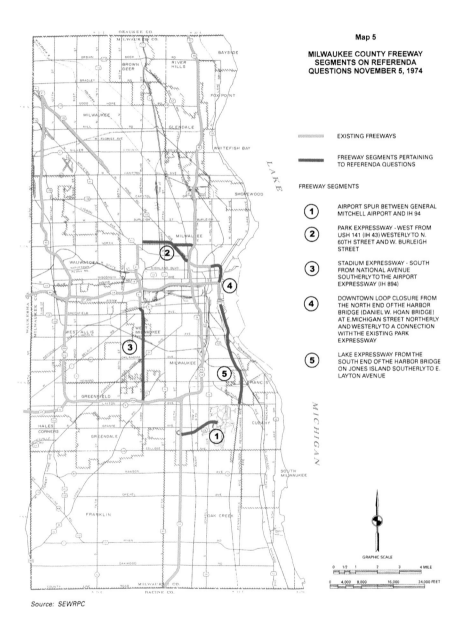

Map 5

**MILWAUKEE COUNTY FREEWAY
SEGMENTS ON REFERENDA
QUESTIONS NOVEMBER 5, 1974**

━━━━━ EXISTING FREEWAYS

━━━━━ FREEWAY SEGMENTS PERTAINING
TO REFERENDA QUESTIONS

FREEWAY SEGMENTS

① AIRPORT SPUR BETWEEN GENERAL
MITCHELL AIRPORT AND IH 94

② PARK EXPRESSWAY - WEST FROM
USH 141 (IH 43) WESTERLY TO N.
60TH STREET AND W. BURLEIGH
STREET

③ STADIUM EXPRESSWAY - SOUTH
FROM NATIONAL AVENUE
SOUTHERLY TO THE AIRPORT
EXPRESSWAY (IH 894)

④ DOWNTOWN LOOP CLOSURE FROM
THE NORTH END OF THE HARBOR
BRIDGE (DANIEL W. HOAN BRIDGE)
AT E.MICHIGAN STREET NORTHERLY
AND WESTERLY TO A CONNECTION
WITH THE EXISTING PARK
EXPRESSWAY

⑤ LAKE EXPRESSWAY FROM THE
SOUTH END OF THE HARBOR BRIDGE
ON JONES ISLAND SOUTHERLY TO E.
LAYTON AVENUE

GRAPHIC SCALE

0   1/2 1   2   3   4 MILE

0   4,000 8,000   16,000   24,000 FEET

Source: SEWRPC

Map 6

PROPOSED PARK FREEWAY WEST

Source: Milwaukee County Expressway andTransportation Commission 1977 Annual Report and SEWRPC.

Map 7

EXISTING AND PLANNED FREEWAYS FOR DESIGN YEAR 1990 AND PROPOSED ROUTES OF FREEWAYS ABANDONED IN 1977

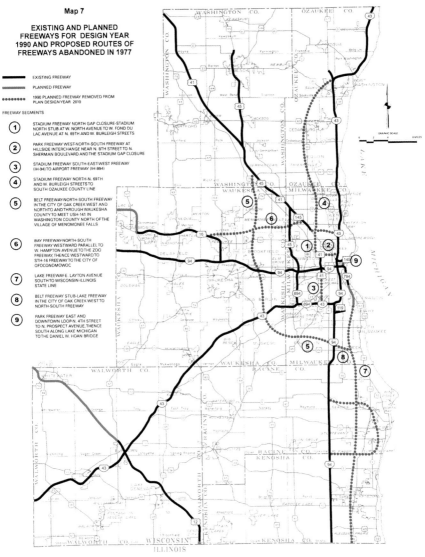

EXISTING FREEWAY

PLANNED FREEWAY

1990 PLANNED FREEWAY REMOVED FROM
PLAN DESIGN YEAR 2010

FREEWAY SEGMENTS

1. STADIUM FREEWAY NORTH GAP CLOSURE-STADIUM NORTH STUB AT W. NORTH AVENUE TO W. FOND DU LAC AVENUE AT N. 69TH AND W. BURLEIGH STREETS

2. PARK FREEWAY WEST-NORTH-SOUTH FREEWAY AT HILLSIDE INTERCHANGE NEAR N. 8TH STREET TO N. SHERMAN BOULEVARD AND THE STADIUM GAP CLOSURE

3. STADIUM FREEWAY SOUTH-EAST-WEST FREEWAY (IH-94) TO AIRPORT FREEWAY (IH-894)

4. STADIUM FREEWAY NORTH-N. 69TH AND W. BURLEIGH STREETS TO SOUTH OZAUKEE COUNTY LINE

5. BELT FREEWAY-NORTH-SOUTH FREEWAY IN THE CITY OF OAK CREEK WEST AND NORTH TO AND THROUGH WAUKESHA COUNTY TO MEET USH-141 IN WASHINGTON COUNTY NORTH OF THE VILLAGE OF MENOMONEE FALLS

6. BAY FREEWAY-NORTH-SOUTH FREEWAY WESTWARD PARALLEL TO W. HAMPTON AVENUE TO THE ZOO FREEWAY, THENCE WESTWARD TO STH-16 FREEWAY TO THE CITY OF OFOCONOMOWOC

7. LAKE FREEWAY-E. LAYTON AVENUE SOUTH TO WISCONSIN-ILLINOIS STATE LINE

8. BELT FREEWAY STUB-LAKE FREEWAY IN THE CITY OF OAK CREEK WEST TO NORTH-SOUTH FREEWAY

9. PARK FREEWAY EAST AND DOWNTOWN LOOP-N. 4TH STREET TO N. PROSPECT AVENUE, THENCE SOUTH ALONG LAKE MICHIGAN TO THE DANIEL W. HOAN BRIDGE

Source: SEWRPC.

Map 8

HISTORIC TREND IN FREEWAY TRAFFIC CONGESTION

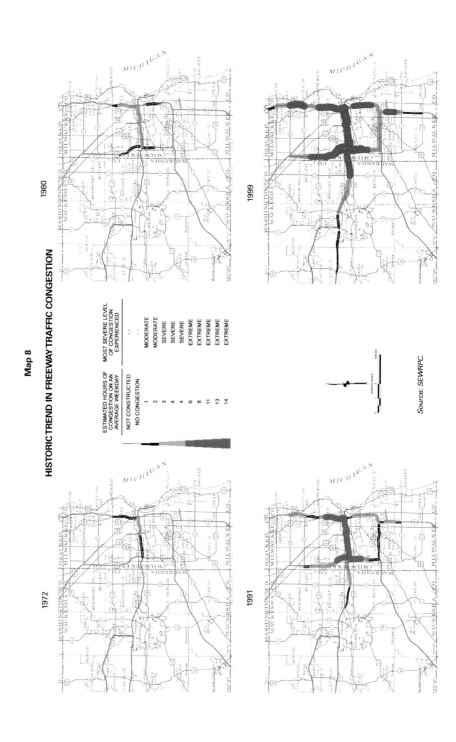

1980

1999

1972

1991

ESTIMATED HOURS OF
CONGESTION ON AN
AVERAGE WEEKDAY

MOST SEVERE LEVEL
OF CONGESTION
EXPERIENCED

NOT CONSTRUCTED

NO CONGESTION

1	MODERATE
3	MODERATE
3	SEVERE
4	SEVERE
4	SEVERE
6	EXTREME
8	EXTREME
11	EXTREME
13	EXTREME
14	EXTREME

Source: SEWRPC.

Map 9

COMPARISON OF EXISTING 1999 AND FORECAST YEAR 2020 FREEWAY SYSTEM TRAFFIC CONGESTION

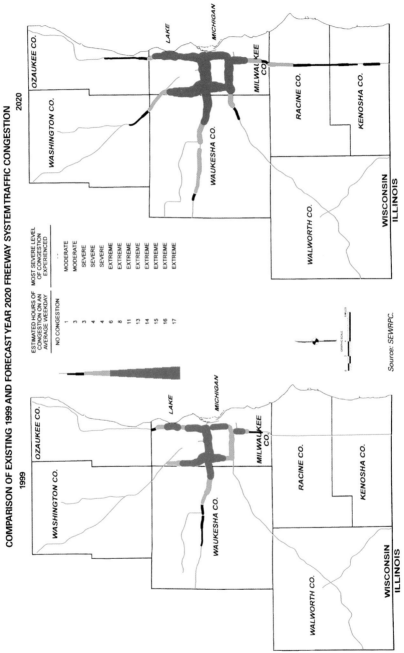

ESTIMATED HOURS OF CONGESTION ON AN AVERAGE WEEKDAY	MOST SEVERE LEVEL OF CONGESTION EXPERIENCED
NO CONGESTION	
1	MODERATE
3	MODERATE
3	SEVERE
4	SEVERE
4	SEVERE
6	EXTREME
8	EXTREME
11	EXTREME
13	EXTREME
14	EXTREME
15	EXTREME
16	EXTREME
17	EXTREME

Source: SEWRPC.

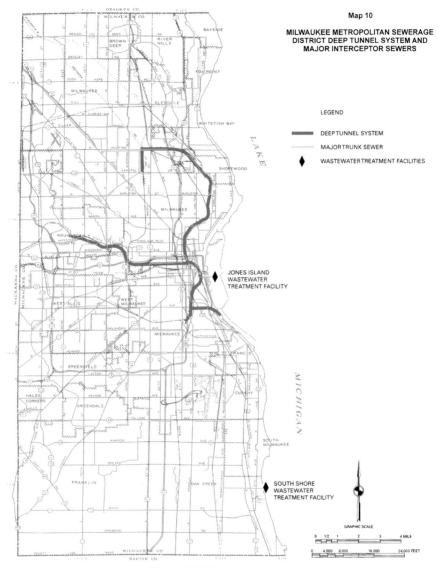

Map 10

**MILWAUKEE METROPOLITAN SEWERAGE
DISTRICT DEEP TUNNEL SYSTEM AND
MAJOR INTERCEPTOR SEWERS**

LEGEND

▬▬▬ DEEP TUNNEL SYSTEM

──── MAJOR TRUNK SEWER

◆ WASTEWATER TREATMENT FACILITIES

JONES ISLAND
WASTEWATER
TREATMENT FACILITY

SOUTH SHORE
WASTEWATER
TREATMENT FACILITY

GRAPHIC SCALE

0   1/2   1   2   3   4 MILE

0   4,000 8,000   16,000   24,000 FEET

Source: Milwaukee Metropolitan Sewerage District and SEWRPC

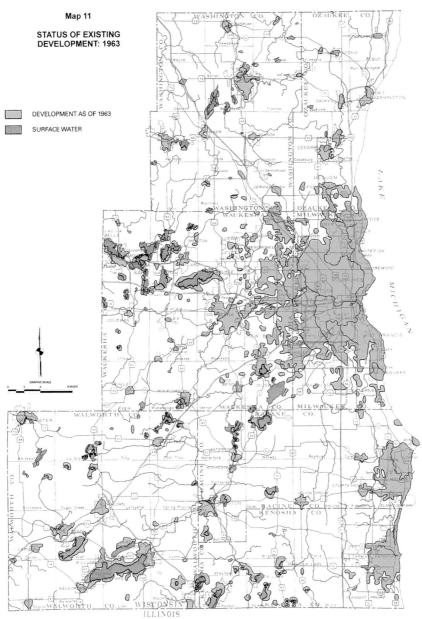

Map 11

STATUS OF EXISTING
DEVELOPMENT: 1963

DEVELOPMENT AS OF 1963

SURFACE WATER

Source: SEWRPC.

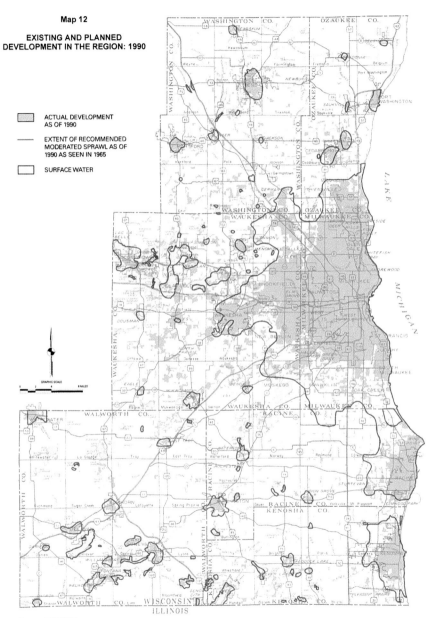

Map 12

**EXISTING AND PLANNED
DEVELOPMENT IN THE REGION: 1990**

ACTUAL DEVELOPMENT
AS OF 1990

EXTENT OF RECOMMENDED
MODERATED SPRAWL AS OF
1990 AS SEEN IN 1965

SURFACE WATER

Source: SEWRPC.

Chapter 19

Milwaukee's Massive Sewer Construction Program, 1977-1995

The tortuous path of Illinois' strange seventeen-year lawsuit against Milwaukee is relatively easy to trace. Legal battles between Illinois and Milwaukee were confined to the courts, were governed by well-established legal rules, created an extensive paper trail, and resulted in a 100 percent victory, even though all but forgotten by the public. It left no physical mark. In sharp contrast, Milwaukee's response to the agreed 1977 Wisconsin state court water pollution order left two major marks: a massive modernized sewer system and lingering angry feelings. Constructing the improved system by 1995 was the largest public works project in Wisconsin's history – even more expensive than the freeways in Milwaukee County. Yet, sewer recon-struction was completed only after countless disputes over engineering, financing, and political questions. Many fights ended in court and are not yet fully forgotten.

In November 1977, the Sewerage Commission of the City of Milwaukee and the Sewerage Commission of the County of Milwaukee (Sewerage Commissions) and their staffs were in a state of shock. Two courts, within six months, had ordered them to undertake drastic sewer clean-up programs. A few years earlier when Ray Leary was the chief engineer and general manager of both commissions (the two commis-sions for efficiency shared a common staff), Milwaukee was nationally regarded as a model. Now the states of Wisconsin and Illinois had each proved in court that the city's system had become woefully inadequate. Ray Leary had retired. Were his successors up to the task?

Mayor Henry Maier and powerful onlookers such as Bill O'Donnell, the worry-prone Milwaukee County Executive, feared sewer recon-struction could bankrupt Milwaukee. Massive federal and state contributions were needed. To be sure, Congress tantalizingly authorized reimbursement (grants) for up to 75 percent of sewer project costs. Also, the Wisconsin Legislature agreed to help fund projects where actual federal grants fell below 60 percent. However, potential grants were subject to two major qualifications. Legislators never appropriated sums anywhere near that which they authorized. Further, to obtain grants, applicants first had to persuade the federal EPA and Wisconsin DNR that their conceptual, regionally oriented plans, called Facilities Plans, would abate the water pollution they had caused. He who pays the piper calls the tune. In an ominous portent of things to come, the DNR rejected Milwaukee's first home-grown facilities plan.

In the face of numerous obstacles Milwaukee lurched forward, propelled by the threat of heavy fines for failure to comply with two highly specific court construction timetables. The commissions' first challenge was gearing up for a multi-billion dollar job.

To its credit, the Milwaukee Metropolitan Sewerage District (District) had made a major management decision even before the two court orders were handed down. In September 1976, district staff proposed a $600 million capital program to modernize collection and treatment facilities. Harry Williams, the highly respected district chairman, suggested the district might need a program manager for a task of that magnitude. County Executive Bill O'Donnell, as if on cue, appointed a task force to consider the tax implications of the capital program. It too recommended the district engage a program manager. The district agreed, advertised nationally by October 1976 for bids by engineering firms, and selected a distinguished panel[202] to interview the three best applicants.[203] CH2MHill was selected in May 1977, and a contract was signed with CH2MHill on July 5, 1977, a date between the court orders of the state in May and the federal government in November.

CH2MHill was chosen as project manager on condition that Charles (Tom) V. Gibbs, its presenter, move to Milwaukee and personally supervise the job. He had been executive director of Seattle Metro until 1974 and worked as a project manager on its construction program to bring Seattle into compliance with the new tougher environmental standards. CH2MHill brought together 850 engineers, planners, and other specialists from eight firms,[204] who, supported by back-up staff at their home offices, represented a small army temporarily hired for the project's duration. CH2MHill's team, known as the Program Management Office (PMO), was charged with planning, getting maximum grants for, and supervising the massive reconstruction effort with the help of the district's regular staff.

Nothing was easy. The Wisconsin DNR-MMSD relationship had gone downhill after the State court order. The DNR suspected the district – egged on by the ever combative Mayor Maier – was dragging its feet on compliance. The district considered the DNR overzealous and indifferent to the high costs its orders would impose on Milwaukee taxpayers.

The district's energetic, conscientious new chairman, Harry Williams, was extremely concerned about the antagonistic DNR-District relationship. He asked me – as one not tainted by the sour DNR-District relationship – to arrange a private meeting for the two of us with Anthony Earl, the secretary of the DNR (and future governor). We were to assure the DNR that the district would carry out its clean-up obligations in good faith. We did so, but I doubt this well-intended gesture accomplished much. The bureaucratic adversaries played their roles much as before.

The PMO, smoothly led by Tom Gibbs, had to integrate a new outside team with the veteran staff. As in all such forced mergers of old staff and outsiders, there were rough spots. Insiders for a long time resented the perceived arrogance of the outsiders, who they felt were running over them. They also were sullenly, if understandably, unhappy over the newcomers' higher positions and compensation. Gibbs forged excellent working relationships with both Harry Williams, the chairman, (with whom he regularly attended Milwaukee Symphony orchestra concerts), and Bill Katz, the director of technical operations and former Chain Belt executive, to whom the PMO formally reported. Eventually Katz and Harold Cahill, the most effective of the many executive directors during the tumultuous early years of the construction project, did much to soften the aloofness of the new engineers toward the old. With much hard work and considerable overtime, PMO and staff engineers in 1980 completed a facilities plan, consisting of twenty volumes.

The next hurdle was obtaining DNR approval of the plan, which seemed, to me at least, like drawing teeth. The DNR reviewed successive drafts of the district's facilities plan (whose twenty volumes took three years to complete) both for compliance with the state court order and eligibility for state grants in aid. In doing so, the DNR sometimes sought more expensive improvements than those offered by

Milwaukee. By December 1979 the DNR had appointed Jay G. Hochmuth, a thirty-two year old chemical engineer, as its Milwaukee enforcer.

Both Hochmuth and State of Illinois attorney Joe Karaganis, were thirty-two years old when they started their intensive effort to compel Milwaukee to stop polluting Lake Michigan. Probably each was more qualified in the new environmental age than older persons then available. Hochmuth was chosen in part because he had already headed DNR's enforcement effort against the paper companies in the heavily polluted Fox River Valley. Hochmuth was tough, painstakingly thorough, and did his job well. He came to Milwaukee monthly, often accompanied by Linda Borchert, a persistent, brilliant DNR attorney and Paul Guthrie, the avuncular supervisor of DNR's grant program, for meetings of the several person MMSD-DNR-EPA Grants Policy Committee. That committee hammered out the details of a grant strategy for the construction program. Hochmuth's purpose was to explain the DNR's objectives and obtain facts which might either support the district's plans or reveal needed modifications. The DNR expected the project to be done yesterday and would not tolerate foot-dragging.

For over five years (1977-1982), I participated by invitation in these important sessions. I reported regularly on the current status of the Illinois case at that time in the midst of its tortuous twelve year journey up to (1977-1981) or down from (1981-1989) the U.S. Supreme Court. And as time went on, I was able to assist Michael McCabe, the district's outstanding inside lawyer, and former Assistant City Attorney of Milwaukee, in convincing the habitually skeptical State that the district's positions were reasonable.

McCabe's innate Irish good nature and unfailing courtesy only briefly obscured the fact that he was bright, firm, and had a prodigious memory for facts, regulations, and legal principles. A consummate warrior and hard bargainer, he played his cards so close to his vest that even his allies, like me, sometimes did not know his strategy. He would almost never concede an opponent was even partly right. In contrast, I was more open and conciliatory – McCabe might have said "soft" – in negotiating with opponents. Perhaps we were an Understanding-Cop/Tough-Cop pair. Sometimes his style was more effective;

155

sometimes, mine. We made a good team, I thought. The tight-lipped McCabe, my titular boss, never said otherwise.

Often Hochmuth peppered PMO and MMSD engineers with penetrating questions about pollution facts and projections. Some staff came to resent his inquisitorial style, but he eventually responded to facts. While my knowledge of engineering was minimal, at best, I tried to help clarify issues and advance agreement by questioning engineers and attorneys on both sides; facilitating agreement eventually became my primary role.

For example, in January and February 1982 I joined McCabe and Patrick Marchese, a top-notch staff engineer in charge of planning the construction project, in the district's efforts to persuade the DNR and Department of Justice to modify the 1977 state court's stipulated timetable. The district wanted to stretch it out, or, at least, make it more dependent on the amount of federal and state grants available. Intensive discussion caused Hochmuth to articulate the DNR's previously unclear thinking, which I had duly recorded. The negotiations were shortly made obsolete by the legislature authorizing substantial supplemental additional aid for the construction program.

For years, I was also asked by the district and PMO to attend weekly PMO-MMSD staff meetings to review progress and the proposed next steps for complying with both court orders. After a while I chaired those meetings, perhaps a throwback to my chairing many technical advisory committees for SEWRPC. I remember one meeting in 1980 when a new district executive director, Harold Cahill, first appeared, seeming quite military with his crew haircut and crisp manner. Cahill was a no-nonsense administrator, well-qualified to turn an under-managed organization around. He had spent the preceding two years beefing up Detroit's deplorably weak sewerage system for the federal EPA which had taken it over. Detroit was then providing only primary treatment while Milwaukee had achieved secondary treatment as early as 1925, the first in the United States.

Norman Paulson, PMO'S strong-minded public relations advisor, suggested I offer to turn over the chair to Cahill because he was, after all, the top dog. Cahill declined, saying "Keep on doing just what you have been doing."

Between 1977 and 1980 the district's new team, finding its way, made many major planning decisions. The first decision grew out of the court's orders to reduce sharply the discharge of untreated sewage into streams and Lake Michigan during rainfalls and snow melts. The desired result could theoretically be achieved by one of two major approaches: build sewer mains and treatment facilities large enough to collect, convey, and treat nearly all of the peak flows, *or* plan to reduce the ground and storm water ("clear water") entering the system and, then, size the mains and treatment facilities accordingly. The district chose the second, seemingly less-expensive approach, but as we later saw, overestimated the quantity of clear water that would be eliminated. The consequences – flooded basements and by-passes of untreated sewage – showed up in 1997-2000.

To measure the quantity of unwanted water, the district televised sewer main interiors and injected smoke into the sanitary sewer mains. Smoke appearing above the street or ground disclosed illegal storm drain connections and defects in the main or sewer laterals on private property. In the end, the district formulated a plan by which *municipalities* within the district (which owned the normal sewer mains while the district owned the large trunk sewers) would, according to PMO estimates (approved by MMSD), reduce the invading water by an estimated 13 percent through a host of measures. *Municipalities* would disconnect storm drains, repair leaking or broken mains, and seal manhole covers to prevent storm water from entering the mains. *Municipalities* would require *homeowners* to disconnect roof and foundation drains from the sanitary sewer system.[205] However, the plan could do little to encourage or require homeowners to repair privately built broken laterals connecting with public sewers.[206] Laterals averaged sixty feet in length and added up to many more miles than the better constructed and maintained public mains.

Kurt Bauer, whose SEWRPC staff had in 1979 completed a Regional Water Quality Management Plan as a precursor to the district's facilities plan, told the PMO that it had over estimated the extent to which municipalities could (*or politically would*) reduce invasive storm and ground water. He warned that municipalities would be disinclined to do all they were asked, especially after the clean-up program had passed its peak of public awareness and support. Bauer was right, as we see when we look at the late 1990s.

The most troublesome problem was how best to reduce the court-condemned overflows. They occurred in the densely populated but relatively small geographic area served by the older combined sewers as well as in the newer nine-times-as-large area served by separate sanitary sewers. Milwaukee, like Chicago and other cities, had first built "combined" sewers, so-called because they conveyed combined sanitary wastes and storm water in one pipe. That was the state of the art between 1880 and 1920 when Milwaukee built them as an improvement over dumping untreated sewage into its rivers.[207] The combined sewer area in 1980 included twenty-four square miles of the older parts of Milwaukee and all of the Village of Shorewood where 47 percent of the district's population lived. Later, Milwaukee and the suburbs – also like other cities – built the two systems separately in the 209 square mile newer areas That change saved the cost of carrying some storm water to the treatment plant, but it did not prevent overflows from the new separate and old combined sewers. Few cared about overflows then. Pollution had not reached 1977 levels and tougher federal pollution standards were enacted in 1972. By 1977, the overflows consisted of 600 million gallons annually from the separate sanitary sewers and 7.5 billion gallons, or twelve-and-one-half times as much, from the combined sewers.

The City of Milwaukee, once the court orders compelled it to care about overflows, had trouble deciding how to reduce them. There were good reasons. The state and federal court orders set different standards for MMSD to follow in the two service areas. The state order required the elimination of overflows in the separate sanitary sewer area, but required only their abatement, or curtailment, in the combined sewer area. The federal court in Chicago flatly forbade overflows in both areas. The extra cost of complying with the federal standard in the combined sewer area was $700 million. In early 1979 the engineers initially recommended one solution for one area; a different one for the other. They recommended a deep tunnel solution for the separate sewer area and stuck with it. They proposed that MMSD separate the combined sewers into sanitary and storm sewers. However, six months' further planning changed their minds. They then chose the deep tunnel instead. The commissions, walking lock step with the engineers, also switched positions on the combined sewers' remedy between May 1979 and June 1980. There were reasons for the flip flop.

158

Doubtless the court orders' rapid timetables forced engineers and commissions to act too rapidly on a complex problem. Fortunately, all picked the right solution in the end. But 1979 saw public disclosure of different proposals for treatment. They came about in this manner. The PMO had set up two engineering groups, one to suggest solutions for the separate sewer area, the other, for the combined sewer areas. Two engineering groups proposed radically different ways to get rid of overflows in their respective geographic areas. One suggested temporarily storing the *separate* sewers' overflows in deep tunnels carved in the limestone under Milwaukee; the other suggested separating the combined sewers into sanitary and storm sewer systems. Sewer separation required tearing up 500 miles of streets in the combined sewer area and making costly modifications to external and internal plumbing systems on approximately 60,600 residential buildings and 2,750 larger buildings.[208] Further, plumbing changes on private property had traditionally been paid for by property owners. How to entice or compel owners to act?

Shortly before May 10, 1979, the District staff and PMO recommended sewer separation, saying it was more cost-effective than deep tunnels. It was cheaper based on the engineers' conceptual design. The District held a public hearing on May 10, 1979, on the *combined* sewer overflow proposal. The hearing was stormy and indicated widespread virulent opposition to several emerging practices or policies of the District.

The fiery, politically astute Mayor of the City of Franklin, Theodore Fadrow, led the charge. Fadrow argued it was unfair to charge any municipality but Milwaukee and Shorewood for solving the problems of combined sewers which lay wholly within their borders. His argument was repeated by an Oak Creek alderman and a trustee from the Village of Brown Deer who said his board, hitting the nail on the head, urged that the cost of the CSO (combined sewer overflow) solution "be borne by municipalities and homeowners." Fadrow added that – somewhat incomprehensibly – many municipalities also opposed *both* sewer separation and the deep tunnels. This remark obliquely signaled that municipalities might take the district to court. Fadrow even suggested the commissions disobey the federal court order, only to be reminded by Zarwell, then managing the district's appeal from the Chicago federal court order, that U.S. Marshals and the National Guard could back up the federal court.

Fadrow pushed the district's chairman, Dr. Raymond Kipp (who had succeeded Williams), a gentle Marquette professor, into admitting that the district was considering a PMO recommendation to charge taxpayers in the district the whole capital cost for all phases of the massive construction. The opposition promptly suspected that the city-dominated district was planning to make suburban taxpayers bear a large fraction of the several-hundred million-dollar-cost of curing a CSO problem they had not caused.

Fadrow was not done. He asked whether the district's sewer separation proposal meant that the district would install sewer laterals on private property. Dr. Kipp replied that the district had not yet decided, which only fueled Fadrow's suspicion that the district was trying to subsidize at suburban expense the cost – usually paid by the property owner – of installing new laterals in the old part of Milwaukee and all of Shorewood.

Fadrow, skillfully playing to the crowd, also lambasted the district for having lost track of the value of money and spending $1.5 million a month on consultants. His political bottom line: the sewer construction program would cost Franklin taxpayers 150 percent of what they paid for all other city services. Pensioners would not be able to pay. Two county supervisors, Harout Sanasarian and Michael Mett, also emotionally attacked the consultant's fees as being excessive, as if they were experts on the market rate for nationally-recognized engineers brought in to solve a two billion dollar problem.

Harry Williams, the conscientious accountant and chairman of the City Sewerage Commission, became flustered by the repeated accusations of reckless spending. He explained that public records showed that the district had been audited up to its ears and the consultants charges found to be valid. An exasperated Williams then asked Norman Gill, who never missed an important public meeting, how the district could convince "public officials that we are not a bunch of crooks." Fadrow's speech and a favorable crowd reaction cast a shadow of things to come.

Two weeks later the district approved sewer separation for combined sewers but wavered on one point. They asked their staff to study means by which the expensive disruptive modifications of plumbing systems on private property could be avoided.[209] (Two years later, in May 1981, the district, seemingly insensitive to growing suburban support for Fadrow's objections to subsidizing sewer laterals, adopted a Sewer Rehabilitation Program. For $160 million, this program would do at least part of the extensive plumbing work on private property throughout the entire district, such as relaying laterals, and disconnecting sump pumps and roof laterals.)

By November 1979, the engineers, in the course of refining several overflow-solution alternatives for the troublesome combined sewers, reversed course. They now suggested deep tunnels were a better answer than sewer separation. The two commissions agreed on June 5, 1980, after protracted further investigation and debate. The PMO found that deep tunnels already planned for the *separate* area could, if enlarged in diameter from twenty to thirty feet, surprisingly also handle the much larger overflows from the *combined* area without substantially lengthening the tunnel system. The reason? Overflows in the separate area were occasional and small. The increase in the tunnels' diameter would increase storage capacity by 2.25 times without significantly increasing construction costs. The full capacity of the enlarged tunnel previously planned for the separate area would be used only occasionally for the separate sewer area. It could reduce overflow from the combined sewers from fifty-two to two times year. Further, those two overflows – because they would occur only after heavy rains – would be too diluted to jeopardize the water quality of receiving streams. The engineers, as they put it, "married," or merged, the deep tunnel solution for the separate area with the solution for the combined area. The deep tunnel's location is shown on Map 10.

Yet the marriage solution fell short of the federal court-ordered elimination of *all* overflows and also needed DNR approval. To be home free, the District had to persuade the DNR and the federal court in Chicago to permit two combined sewer overflows a year. Otherwise, the tunnel would have to be further enlarged.

Fortune then smiled on the district. The Supreme Court in April 1981 virtually knocked out the legal basis for Judge Grady's draconian federal order in the Illinois lawsuit.[210] The Wisconsin DNR, on Hochmuth's recommendation, and as well as the EPA, conditionally accepted allowing two overflows a year, pending studies to verify that they would not endanger federal water quality standards. By 1987, SEWRPC's massive Estuary Study (of the consequences of pollution in the wide mouths, or estuaries, of the Milwaukee, Menomonee and Kinnickinnic Rivers,) required by the Federal Clean Water Act gave technical support for the twice-a-year overflow standard.[211]

Specifically, the PMO and staff proposed seventeen miles of deep tunnels mined through the bedrock underlying Milwaukee at depths up to three hundred feet below the surface. The tunnels acted as a reservoir; they could store excess sewage, swollen by invasive storm water, until it could be pumped to the treatment plants when post-rain flows were lower. The commission described how an augmented deep tunnel solution would solve the vexatious CSO problem:

> Two major new sewers passing through the combined sewer area would be used to store combined sewer overflows on an infrequent basis – perhaps several times a year during periods of heavy run off. These facilities would consist of large diameter sewers which would not only carry sewage but also have the capacity to store overflows during wet weather. This is referred to as in-line storage.[212]

The PMO calculated that the proposed tunnel or in-line storage solution to both separate and combined overflows in two geographic areas would cost less than the initial May 1979 plan for separating the combined sewers in one area and building a deep tunnel in another. Engineers expected the tunnel to cost $496 million[213] versus $574 million to separate the combined sewers. The $574 million was broken down to $514 million for separation plus $60 million to prevent polluted run-off, including dead animals, animal feces, oil, and salt, from entering the rivers.

By June 5, 1980, the commissions – after diligently receiving input from every conceivable source – concluded that in-line storage was the best solution for CSO and the overall system. Former chairman Harry Williams recalled in 1999 that one of many factors in their decision was the experience of another Wisconsin city.

> Contact with officials in Superior, Wisconsin, where separation had been chosen, elicited strong aversion to the road tie-up, public dissatisfaction with the mess,

and dust created, plus unexpected cost complexities not foreseen. They were overwhelming in their statements that they would have chosen other alternatives given the opportunity to decide again.[214]

The commissions' search for a CSO solution became highly controversial between 1979 and 1982. After the commissions, on a second try, chose the deep tunnel solution, opponents continued to champion sewer separation. If the commissions had reversed their position once, they could do it twice. Local contractors vigorously favored sewer separation and bad-mouthed the deep tunnel. They lacked the capital resources and large boring machine required to carve a tunnel deep down in the limestone. They lobbied local elected officials hard and won some converts.

County Executive Bill O'Donnell was one of those who favored the sewer separation alternative, believing it was cheaper (commission staff initial calculations had said it was, but were later withdrawn), or that the deep tunnels would not do the job. After all, tunnel storage was a new and relatively unproven concept. Would the tunnels leak, contaminating drinking water? The contractors wrote that the tunnels might contaminate the wells on which 40 per cent of the community depended for drinking water.[215] Suppose the pumps broke? Or power failed? How would the district lift the stored overflows to the treatment plant? Could the deep tunnel prove to be too expensive? The contractors quoted the Comptroller General of the United States as predicting (incorrectly, as it turned out) that the Chicago deep tunnel project, because of high costs, would never be finished.[216]

Disagreement over who would pay for the CSO solution was far more serious. As early as the May 10, 1979, hearing, Franklin's voluble mayor, Theodore Fadrow, had warned that municipalities would make every effort to oppose district-wide financing for the CSO solution. That was the first shoe to drop. The second fell on September 18, 1980, when Franklin and eventually fourteen other municipalities served by the district sued.[217] Eleven were from inside Milwaukee County and four from eastern Waukesha County. They sought to enjoin the district from separating the combined sewers and charging its cost on a district-wide basis. It did not matter that the district on June 5, 1980 had already discarded sewer separation. The suburbs, or their counsel, who were noted for their conviction that the city continuously plotted to undermine or get even with suburbs,[218] suspected the district might reinstitute it.

The complaint, parroting the contractors' assertion that the deep tunnel might pollute ground water and prove very expensive, predicted the tunnel would never be finished.[219] The fifteen suburbs also sought to enjoin the $160 million Sewer Rehabilitation Program's plan to construct sewer laterals on private property at public expense.[220] They felt that Milwaukee and Shorewood should pay for the entire cost of solving the combined sewer overflow problem. They had caused the overflow problem. The solution "did not benefit" the fifteen municipalities.

The suburban suit was not the only bad news. The county and the state each dropped bombshells on the district. In May 1980 an exasperated County Executive William O'Donnell threw kerosene on the fire. He made a crude effort to control costs. He vetoed funds required to keep construction on the court-ordered timetable. His underlying motive was to force a sweeping change in how the district was governed. He wanted sewer commissioners to be elected. That was his formal position; informally he parochially desired to relieve the county bond rating of the burden of future sewer bond issues. The state and the district sued the county and O'Donnell, asking for a ruling that O'Donnell and the county board must approve the financing requested by the district. O'Donnell's action and the suburban lawsuit each threatened compliance with the 1977 state and federal court clean-up orders. On March 10, 1981, the Circuit Court declared O'Donnell's action invalid, but he won his political point by starting a political discussion over governance. Hot debate preoccupied the community, the legislature, and the governor for two years. (That governance battle and its far-reaching outcome are a separate story, which I cover in the next chapter.)

On June 26, 1981, the State of Wisconsin intervened in the suburban lawsuit to prevent it from interfering with compliance with the state court clean-up order of May 1977. On September 2, it was the state's turn to drop its own bombshell. The DNR became angered that the suburban lawsuit and O'Donnell's vetoing-needed-funds jeopardized compliance with the 1977 court order. It took a drastic step. It placed a moratorium on all sewer extensions by municipalities served by the

164

district. New homes could not be built. Builders and their workers were idled; prospective home buyers were frustrated. The moratorium effectively pressured metropolitan Milwaukee leaders to resolve the varied concerns of the county (governance), suburbs (wishing not to be charged for any part of CSO elimination), and DNR (a stalled clean-up program). The DNR lifted the moratorium on September 16, 1982.

The CSO controversy became so heated it reached the desk of Governor Lee Sherman Dreyfus. His highly respected Secretary of Development, Chandler McKelvey, a former officer of Sentry Insurance Co. of Stevens Point, issued a key report on April 1, 1981 – twenty-seven days before the Supreme Court effectively knocked out the expensive Grady federal court order. McKelvey recommended that the state give additional state aid, over ten years, equal to 50 percent of the cost of solving CSO overflows, "depending on the outcome of the United States Supreme Court appeal."[221] The Wisconsin Legislature ultimately appropriated $240 million toward the cost of the CSO solution, doubtless thereby facilitating an agreed dismissal on February 12, 1982 of the lawsuit by fifteen suburbs. The suburbs, however, obtained a provision in the settlement agreement that the district would not separate the combined sewers (which it did not intend to do), nor undertake plumbing work on private property at public expense. In return, the suburbs agreed, at DNR insistence, that they would obey any orders from the district to rehabilitate their own sewer mains.

Construction of the tunnels started in 1986 but was not finished until 1994, three years behind schedule and $108 million over budget. How so? In 1987, the North Shore leg flooded while under construction. Fractures in the bedrock caused ground water to flow into the tunnel, flooding out a tunnel-boring machine and stopping work. Also, water seeping into the tunnel lowered ground water levels under downtown businesses, causing building foundations, walls, sidewalks, and sewer connections to crack. The district sued CH2MHill for $58 million in 1996, claiming their engineers were negligent in not taking flooding and seepage into account in planning the tunnel.[222] The district claimed CH2MHill knew or should have known that the bedrock was so badly fractured that lining the tunnel with concrete would be necessary. Without admitting liability, the CH2MHill consortium settled for $24 million or 40 percent of the claim. One local consortium member then went bankrupt.

Except for the North Shore tunnel fiasco, the massive construction program, as distinguished from its deep tunnel element, miraculously remained generally on schedule and on budget. Outside audits upheld all practices criticized by some. Alexander Grant & Co. said the construction program was well-managed (1980); Arthur Young, in an audit requested by the DNR, found the compensation of engineering firms "reasonable" (1982); and the U.S. General Accounting Office declared the deep tunnel storage sewer concept to be sound. By 1994 the deep tunnels were completed and the two treatment plants modernized. After many tribulations, the massive sewer program *appeared* to be a great success. All rivers flowing into the harbor became cleaner. Stocked lake trout swam up Milwaukee River, and fathers and sons fished for them near the North Avenue Dam site, as they had done before pollution came. The project had taken eighteen years and $2.1 billion without interest and $2.8 billion with interest. For a short time after 1994 Bradford Beach was no longer occasionally closed because of an excessive fecal coliform count – as had happened in the 1970s. Mayors Maier and Norquist (after his election in 1988) sponsored the building of river walks along the Milwaukee River in the late 1980s and 1990s. By 1997 apartments and condominiums sprang up along the river and many more followed by 2000. Living downtown was becoming fashionable again. A cleaner river helped.

Milwaukee got a rude surprise in the late 1990s. Sewers again backed up into basements during heavy rain. Municipalities in turn resumed dumping raw sewage into rivers. Sewage in a basement is more dangerous to public health and political careers than in a waterway. The public, the press, and elected officials became frustrated and angry. The backups and overflows questioned the previously apparent success of the modernized sewer system. Were overflows not supposed to stop when the large storage deep tunnels went into operation in 1994?

What happened? Simply put, two factors operated to overload the system: a complex, interrelated combination of possible old and recent errors by various governments or agencies and, for sure, exceptional rainfall.

Contrary to the general public's perception, the big tunnels were only a part – although a major part – of the sewer improvements intended to prevent backups and curb overflows. After 1994, the twenty-eight municipalities served by MMSD were supposed to – according to the MMSD Year 2010 Facilities Plan – take multiple steps to reduce clear water entering the sanitary sewer system. Those measures included repairing deteriorating sewers and designing sewers for new development in a manner more resistant to the entry of clear water. Also municipalities were supposed to inspect private laterals between homes and sewer mains and insist faulty ones be corrected. Laterals are a major source of clear water intrusion. Their mileage is several times greater than that of municipal sewer mains; their construction and maintenance, of lower quality.

MMSD planning in 1980 for the sewer modernization program assumed that municipalities could and would eliminate a certain percentage of clear water from the sewerage system. The DNR, in approving the MMSD Facilities Plan, agreed the assumption was realistic. However, one prominent official, Kurt Bauer, then executive director of SEWRPC and a former municipal engineer, warned that the assumption was optimistic. He felt the assumption led MMSD to build less sewer conveyance and storage capacity than actually needed. He noted sewer construction and maintenance is expensive and, especially, municipalities are reluctant to force unwilling homeowners to repair faulty laterals. Such laterals are located largely on private property where repair or replacement is highly disruptive and costly.

In any event, whether the assumptions were optimistic or not, some municipalities did a good job in minimizing clear water entering their sewers. Others, seeking to avoid politically unpopular local expense, delayed or under-performed on sewer maintenance and improvements for years. For example, the acceptable wet weather flow in municipal sewers systems is six times that of dry weather. That ratio zoomed up to twenty to forty times in some municipalities, according to MMSD monitoring[223] – way too high. The laggard municipalities changed their attitude in 1997-2000 when sewer backups generated an urgent local demand for solutions.

Those were the major possible human errors. Now, for the rainfall. Unusually heavy storms in June 1997 and August 1998 deluged *local areas* within the district. They were the once-in-250-year and once-in-500-year variety, or 9.8 and 11.8 inches of rainfall respectively, in twenty-four hours. These storms exceeded the storm of record measured over the entire district area, the benchmark used in designing the tunnel system. That benchmark assumed a once-in-forty-years rainfall of 4.25 inches in twenty-four hours. In 2000, three heavy rains occurred again. Ten inches of rain fell in May 2000, the most ever in that month. July 2000 was the fifth-wettest July.

Sewer back ups caused all governments responsible for parts of the sewer system to take prompt short-term actions to control damage. Suburbs resumed bypassing raw (but diluted) sewage into waterways to avoid backups in basements. MMSD increased its own bypassing downstream. That measure reserved more of the deep tunnel storage capacity for heavy flows from upstream sanitary sewers. In the first eight months of 2000, MMSD bypassed raw sewage four times and partially treated sewage from its treatment plants twelve times. MMSD even bypassed once when the deep tunnel was only one third full, later explaining that it was saving in-line (tunnel) storage against predicted additional rainfall, which never came.

The press tauntingly quoted Chicago as saying it never bypasses until its big tunnels are full. Chicago's case is different. MMSD is subject to a Dane County 1977 court order prohibiting overflows in its separate sewer area (while allowing limited ones from the much smaller combined sewer area). Chicago operates under no similar court order. Further, it serves only combined sewer areas.

MMSD and the suburbs explained the causes of overflows and bypasses differently. MMSD attributed them to the unprecedented rainfall and, primarily, to too much clear water getting into municipal sewers (city and suburban). Suburban leaders and their engineers denied clear water in suburban sewers was a major cause of overflows. As expected, MMSD and the suburbs also disagreed as to what long term solutions were needed. MMSD suggested municipalities should increase efforts to keep clear water out of the system. Suburbs countered that MMSD should have built or should now build larger conveyance and storage capacity. That means larger or more trunk sewers and deep tunnels. Public officials in both camps were reluctant to spend the big sums involved. That reluctance helps explain why they saw the cause of overflows so differently.

An experienced MMSD official, senior staff attorney James Petersen, and Kurt Bauer articulated for me their contrasting views on whether removal or reduction of excessive clear water could and would lead to a major reduction in overflows. Petersen pointed out that sewer basement backups originated when the rainfall-enlarged flow from one main or lateral unsuccessfully attempted to enter a connecting but already filled main. The flow then, following gravity, backed up into the nearest basement. Then, he said, suburbs built bypasses to divert the excess flow out of the sewers and spare the basements. He continued:

> Many municipalities want the district to build bigger sewers to relieve their local systems using district-wide financed funds. The district doesn't want to take on added flows because: 1) the municipalities agreed to reduce their I/I [clear water] as part of the [year] 2010 Facilities planning process [by MMSD] which, in turn, controls the size and capacity of the district's sewers, and 2) if the local...sewers (continue to) deteriorate, the district will have to build larger and larger tunnels until the whole service area becomes one huge combined sewer system in fact, if not by design.[224]

Bauer responded:

> Reducing clear water entering the local sewer systems, while desirable to some extent, will not make a substantial contribution to avoiding overflows. Such efforts, which are costly, can be expected to eliminate only about five percent of the clear water entering sewers. For two reasons. First, it's impractical to keep as much clear water out of public sewers as the district advocates. If you waterproof one part of the local system (for example, by grouting or sealing manholes, some of the clear water will run along ditches until it forces its way into the sewers (perhaps through a broken main or lateral).
>
> More importantly, most rainfall gets into municipal sewers by first entering lateral mains on private property. No one wants to tackle the job of waterproofing laterals because property owners strenuously object to the expense.[225]

In 2000, each side took steps toward long term solutions. MMSD launched a massive public information campaign to encourage municipalities and property owners to increase efforts to prevent clear water (inflow and infiltration) from getting into the sewer system. In July 2000, MMSD offered to finance $800,000 of pilot projects by eight municipalities to test the effectiveness of alternative methods for keeping clear water out of sewer systems. Municipalities accepted the offer. They and others expedited efforts to reduce clear water inflow. Mayor Norquist proposed, but after a howl of protest, one day later abandoned, a requirement that city property owners, before selling their property, repair leaky lateral pipes at an estimated cost per property ranging from $2,000 to $20,000.

It is not as simple as either MMSD or the municipalities suggest.

Jay Hochmuth, the DNR watchdog when the system was being designed and built in the 1980s, told me, in May 2000, after I summarized conflicting analyses by MMSD and suburbs "I agree with some of what each of the participants say; we encourage the parties to get together; the system was good but probably not good enough. "[226]

On March 15, 2001, Hochmuth authored a report to the board of the Wisconsin Department of Natural Resources analyzing recent sewer overflows in Wisconsin with particular attention to the MMSD service area.[227] Hochmuth, an experienced expert, made certain factual findings and sometimes deliberately opaque recommendations. His report put events in perspective. Specifically, he found that there were thirteen overflow events between 1994 and 2000. Only three were warranted by excess rainfall.[228] That is the bad news. On the other hand, overflows from the combined sewers area dropped from forty to sixty a year before 1994 to an average of 2.5 afterwards though they had risen to a less comfortable six in 1999 and five in 2000. Those frequencies contrasted with average annual overflows of seventy in Boston, thirty in Indianapolis, forty-five in Pittsburgh, 100 in Portland, Oregon, and 106 in St. Louis.[229]

Hochmuth recommended MMSD enlarge the diameter of relief sewers to increase storage capacity and that the suburbs complete sewer upgrades and projects to lessen leakage into suburban sewers. He recommended that MMSD undertake $180 million in improvements in addition to the $919 million already scheduled for the next ten years. Hochmuth tellingly advocated that the proper authority (the Dane County court, DNR, or MMSD – depending on the particular project involved) establish timetables for completing all projects by 2012.[230] MMSD challenged his recommendations as bringing minimal improvements to water quality at an unjustified public expense.

Certain elected officials attacked the DNR report as too favorable to MMSD. They suggested an independent audit. Greater Milwaukee has not heard the last of technical and political disputes about how best to manage its sewers.

Chapter 20

A Furious Battle Over Who Governs Sewers

The high cost of sewer modernization project was bound to provoke a political backlash. It occurred in 1980 as noted in the prior chapter. In 1980, county leaders rebelled against the district's rising costs and antique governance. The Milwaukee rebellion had a flash point – in this case the district's request that the county furnish $55.7 million to keep construction on the court-ordered timetable. But the real seeds for this rebellion were sown many years earlier when the legislature created a pseudo taxation-without-representation issue. It required the county to issue bonds or raise taxes to raise funds for district construction projects on which the county had no vote. In fact, during the Depression, the Wisconsin Supreme Court had twice instructed earlier rebellious county boards that they had no choice but to issue bonds when the district requested funds for construction.

In the intervening years, however, the state constitution had been amended to create the position of the county executive. Bill O'Donnell gambled that the constitutional amendment had magically changed the old financing law. He decided he would try again. On May 20, 1980, O'Donnell refused to sign the county board's resolution authorizing $55.7 in bonds, declaring that the proposed interest of 7 percent was too high.

I could not decide which was more shocking: O'Donnell's maverick action which could force the city and cash-starved district into incurring large fines for violating two court orders, or his specious reasoning about interest rates on which he was hardly an expert. His refusal, or pocket veto, effectively killed the bond issue, and – as he intended – created a crisis necessary for the community to focus on reforming the district's complicated governmental structure.

To make matters worse, O'Donnell in 1981 again refused to sign sewer construction bond resolutions. Of course, the State of Wisconsin and district could not afford to let him get away with it. They obtained a circuit court ruling on March 10, 1981, that gave the county no choice. During O'Donnell's appeal, which he ultimately won on November 10, 1982,[231] two actions allowed the district to raise overdue funds. The Legislature in 1981 provided new funding methods, effective December 31, 1982, which avoided O'Donnell's veto power.[232] O'Donnell, influenced by his loss in the lower court, agreed with the suing suburbs in April 1981 and February 1982 to let the county borrow twice without prejudice to O'Donnell's court appeal.[233] Thus, bonds were sold twice to keep construction on schedule. Ironically, the interest rates at the time were 11.58 and 12.79 percent – America then being in a historic period of rapidly rising interest rates. O'Donnell's rash action cost the taxpayers a substantial amount, but not as much as might appear. The district paid off both bonds in a year or two.

The Milwaukee County Board, caught in the middle of the O'Donnell fight with the district and the State of Wisconsin, created a Sewerage Governance Task Force. It became known as the Ryan Task Force after its chairman, County Supervisor James R. Ryan, an outstandingly thoughtful consensus builder. The Ryan Task Force was composed of nine elected officials from the county board, City of Milwaukee, suburbs, and the state legislature.[234] It included stars such as Henry Mixter and William Broydrick. Mixter was president of the Village of Whitefish Bay, probably the most respected suburban leader of the decade. Broydrick, a new state legislator, was to later brilliantly assist Congressmen Les Aspen by helping me in my lonely campaign to prevent Congress from nullifying Milwaukee's Supreme Court billion-dollar victory in the Illinois case. (See Chapter 18.)

The Ryan Task Force heard many opinions on how best to stream-line and modernize the district's archaic governance. It reviewed the district's incremental governance history up to then. It learned the following. In 1913, the legislature had provided for the mayor's appointing five commissioners to govern the Milwaukee Sewerage Commission, which at that time served only the City of Milwaukee. In 1921, when increasing untreated suburban wastes fouled Milwaukee's three rivers leading to Lake Michigan, thereby endangering the water supply of the city and areas served by it, the legislature recognized it must act to protect public health.[235] It created the Metropolitan Sewerage Commission to extend sewer service to much of suburban Milwaukee County, and to force municipalities, in the interest of public health,[236] to use it. The governor was authorized to

173

appoint three Metropolitan commissioners, one to be nominated by the City Sewerage Commission (which treated the wastes from the suburbs) and another by the predecessor of today's Wisconsin Department of Natural Resources. Neither commission was authorized to issue bonds, so the legislature mandated that Milwaukee County finance district construction costs, as we saw at the start of this chapter. Thus, three units of government had roles in managing the sewerage system.

O'Donnell and most others favored merging the two commissions. He also wanted all commissioners to be elected and the county freed of its rubber-stamp, no-discretion-allowed duty to provide financing for sewerage district construction. In other words, O'Donnell sought to replace three governmental units with one, which would be governed by elected officials. O'Donnell felt that elected commissioners would be more accountable to voters. Several elected officials agreed with him, but Henry Maier vigorously disagreed. Maier favored appointing the commissioners. He correctly believed appointees were more likely to be knowledgeable on technical matters and less apt to pander to the "keep-taxes-low-at-all-costs" sentiments of the electorate. Building sewers economically over the long term required designing sewer pipes (and taxing) early for future growth. Otherwise, sewer mains would have to be expensively enlarged or duplicated. Probably for that very reason, most sewerage commissioners elsewhere in America were appointed.

Maier, true to his philosophy, upgraded the previously staff-dominated City of Milwaukee Sewerage Commission between 1977 and 1982 by appointing independent-minded Harry Williams and persons of stature[237] recommended by Norman Gill.

At the time of the Ryan Task Force's creation, I attended all meetings of the two sewerage commissions, which met jointly. I formed two opinions on how the commissions should be reorganized. Commissioners should be appointed – for all of Henry Maier's reasons. However, most commissioners tended to be too loyal, or parochial, in responding to the wishes of those who appointed them. Thus, I felt that neither the city nor the suburbs should have the power to appoint a majority of the commissioners. I recalled that the framers of the United States constitution, fearing the tyranny of the majority, had devised a remedy: majority rule would be tempered by many checks and balances. I favored letting the governor appoint regionally oriented neutrals as swing voters. For a long time I kept my ideas to myself.

Ultimately, in May 1981, the Ryan Task Force recommended that the two separate commissions be merged into an eleven-member Milwaukee Metropolitan Sewerage District (MMSD). Seven members would be appointed by the mayor of Milwaukee (because its population then comprised 63 percent or 7/11ths of the district), three of whom had to be elected officials. Four of the eleven would be appointed by the elected leaders of Milwaukee County suburbs other than South Milwaukee (not a part of the sewerage district), two of whom had to be elected officials. Thus, five of the eleven commissioners would be accountable to their constituents. The new commission could do its own financing: charge user fees, levy taxes on real estate, and issue bonds. The district would assume responsibility for outstanding Milwaukee County bonds and debt charges related to the district.

The two Sewerage Commissions drafted legislation substantially following Ryan's recommendations. It became Senate Bill 501 and passed the senate. However, a bipartisan group of legislators in the assembly, reflecting the suburbs inside and outside Milwaukee County, blocked assembly passage of Senate Bill 501. They proposed a substitute amendment to S 501 containing extraneous provisions which the DNR said represented "a comprehensive strategy to abrogate the 1977 court order under which the MMSD agreed to upgrade its sewage system."[238] These legislators came predominantly from the fifteen suburbs, such as Franklin and Brown Deer, which had brought the 1980 suit to slow down the construction program and invalidate the district's spreading the cost of the combined sewer overflow solution over the entire district. Negotiations between the suburbs, the City of Milwaukee, and the commissions continued until deadlocked in mid-1981. The parties primarily disagreed over the Ryan Task Force's recommendation that decisions be made by the majority, which assured city control. Suburban representatives, led by an influential assembly leader, Betty Jo Nelson, wanted to require a vote of a two-thirds majority to approve capital budgets. That would amount to a vote by eight out of eleven suggested commissioners, or all seven city commissioners plus one suburban vote. The city feared that four suburban representatives – by hanging together – could block capital budgets and thereby frustrate city objectives, such as district-wide financing (opposed by most suburbs) and compliance with the state court order (issued against the city and the district but not against any suburbs). The city wanted rule by a simple majority, which the suburbs distrusted. Negotiations then stalled. Neither side could muster a majority in the legislature.

Nature abhors a vacuum. New parties moved in. The DNR, noting that the O'Donnell-caused cash shortage had put the district behind on its 1981 construction schedule, tried to force the antagonists to settle their differences. On September 2, 1981, as we have seen on pages 164-165, the DNR slapped a moratorium on the extension of new sewers within the District. By November, the Greater Milwaukee Committee's Task Force (GMC), appointed earlier in 1981, moved from study to intervention. The GMC Task Force consisted of three civic powerhouses: I. Andrew (Tiny) Rader, John Kelly, and John Schmitt. Rader was president of Allen-Bradley and much more. He, often with Francis Ferguson, the high-energy president of Northwestern Mutual Life Insurance, dissolved Milwaukee's impasses in the 1980s. Kelly was a politically savvy president of a new bank. Schmitt, the long-time congenial head of the Wisconsin AFL-CIO, was both smart and blunt. He and Kelly, the GMC hoped, had Henry Maier's ear, if anyone did. At this time, "Everyone was fighting with everyone," Rader observed.

The GMC's initial strategy was to try to persuade the principal fighter, Henry Maier, to accept a compromise proposal. Kelly and Schmitt met with the mayor in his paneled office, urging him to give the suburbs a two-thirds vote on capital issues in return for their concessions on other issues. His response: a thirty-minute tirade against the suburbs. Finally, Kelly said to Schmitt: "Let's get out of here; the guy's not even listening." They left.

The GMC soon developed a different strategy to create a reform package. They would seek to persuade the legislature even without Maier's support. That was a very tall order. Ultimately it meant, among other things, converting the district's fierce critic, Ted Fadrow, into a supporter who would lobby South Side legislators for the compromise.

Rader's team was assisted by a new executive director of the GMC, David Meissner, who was perfect for the role: indefatigable, nimble, articulate, and even-tempered. As Rader and Meissner prepared for action, I told Meissner of my feeling that providing for a few appointments by the governor might remove the suburbs' fear of majority (city) rule. Meissner refined the idea and quickly got Rader's approval to try to sell it informally.[239] On December 10, Meissner, Ryan, chairman of the Task Ryan Task Force, and Broydrick, now representing the district,[240] approached key legislators as a self-appointed "mediation team." They proposed a "wild card" idea to reduce the mistrust among city and suburbs over control of the eleven appointments to the commission. The governor would appoint three; the mayor, five; the suburbs, three.[241] Henry Maier adamantly opposed losing control of the district. The wild card fizzled. The stalemate continued.

Rader, with the backing of the GMC, the MMAC (Metropolitan Milwaukee Association of Commerce), and labor, summoned legislators representing warring factions[242] to a meeting at the Wisconsin Club on February 15, 1982. The antagonists continued to bicker, getting nowhere.

Rader then locked the door and said no one could leave until agreement was reached. Then the parties hammered out a compromise in which each party got its minimum demands and no more. They split the control issue into two parts. The suburbs got the right to a vote of two-thirds for capital projects – a good check on possible majority misrule. The city received protection against the four suburban commissioners' blocking a two-thirds vote, an essential counter-check, worthy of the U.S. Constitution's politically sophisticated framers. If no budget could gather a two-thirds vote, then a simple majority could pass a budget not to exceed $40 million, the amount calculated by CH2MHill as being required to keep the construction program on its tight court-ordered timetable. The compromise also required three of the four commissioners appointed by suburbs (instead of the Ryan Task Force's two) to be elected officials, thus satisfying O'Donnell's insistence that a majority of the eleven commissioners would be elected officials.

The negotiators also offered the contract communities membership on the commission. They declined the offer a day later when Donald Roensch, the judicious, respected city engineer of Mequon, polled them. They feared that joining the district would subject them to *ad valorem* property taxation for the rising capital costs of the sewer construction program even though that offer addressed the contract communities' complaint that they were being charged without representation when the district offered them sewer service for a take-it-or-leave-it price. Incidentally, S 501 already provided that the city-suburb allocation of seats on the commission would be revised after each census to reflect their respective percentages of population in the district. That meant the 1990 or some later census, reflecting a decline in the city's population and rise in the suburbs', would have given majority control to the suburbs in Milwaukee County and to the contract communities outside. The February compromise, which Meissner labeled "a three-humped camel with five legs," was endorsed by the county board 20-2 within three days, thus isolating Bill O'Donnell. Although Maier lectured Milwaukee area legislators at city hall on the perils of the compromise, they disagreed with him by a 14-2 vote. He was also marginalized. Maier fumed against requiring three of his appointments to be "elected representatives." He expected commissioners to follow his policies. He calculated some elected commissioners would be independent and defy his will. "How do I fire a councilman?" he asked. The city's lobbyist, George Whittow, worked to defeat S 501, and, after its passage in April 1982, Maier wrote Governor Dreyfus asking him in vain to veto it. The bill passed the legislature in April 1982. State Senator Jim Moody from Milwaukee said:

> David Meissner did a magnificent job in bringing the various sides together at a number of crucial points along the way. Without the [GMC]'s help I seriously doubt whether we would have been able to pass any bill.[243]

Maier attended Governor Lee Dreyfus's televised signing of the reform legislation. Deliberately standing with his back to the seated governor, Maier peered into the cameras, and shouted:

> This is the worst piece of legislation ever passed by the State Legislature to hurt the City of Milwaukee; it takes away the authority of the city to care for its citizens.[244]

Maier then berated the GMC, the *Milwaukee Journal*, and the suburbs for fostering the act the governor was about to sign. Ryan, who was present, mused aloud to himself and Meissner:

> If ever proof was needed that the legislation was necessary, Henry Maier has just demonstrated it exactly; the city's hold on the commission is so strong it feels it can display antipathy for the communities which are paying nearly half the bill.[245]

Tenacious Henry Maier did not give up. An assistant city lobbyist, Douglas Haselow, suggested a fallback. Haselow told Bill Broydrick, the new district lobbyist, that Maier could find a way to guarantee that the city's three elected appointees would be loyal to him. He could appoint ward committeemen, because an obscure statute surprisingly defined them as elected officials along with legislators, aldermen, and county supervisors. Bill Broydrick explained this loophole to Henry Maier, who rapidly drove a truck through it. Maier encouraged three of his existing commission appointees[246] to run for election as ward committee members. They did and won. Broydrick even filed O.J. White's nomination papers for a ward election.

Maier thought he had outfoxed the legislature which, in a furious response to his mocking evasion of the spirit of their reform, quickly amended the statute to exclude ward committeemen from the definition of elected representatives. However, a stubborn and wiley Maier got the last word on the appointments. When the three commissioners' one-year terms expired, Maier declared he was unable to find qualified successors, thereby permitting them to stay in office for six more years. He was relying on a provision in the 1982 reform statute saying his appointees would serve until their successors were duly appointed. Bond counsel agreed the hold-over appointments were legal. Further, no one wanted to be politically incorrect by challenging the legality of two minority appointments, an African-American and a female. Maier's contempt for the legislature and suburbs fueled suburban distrust which energized the notorious sewer wars to follow.

The reform of district governance was a large improvement but contained the seeds of new problems. The majority picked by the city could make non-budget decisions without regard to the concerns of the suburbs in or outside the county. The majority, even if it sought to be fair and objective in its decisions, could be perceived by the suburbs as cruelly indifferent to their concerns. Some suburbs so viewed the city's majority; others, such as Wauwatosa and most North Shore suburbs, did not. That unremovable suspicion born of absolute power (on some matters) was a factor in the fourteen-year sewer wars which followed. Better that the legislature had followed the politically astute mediation committee's "wild card" suggestion of letting the governor appoint three commissioners. Or that the contract communities had not rejected the January 1982 invitation to join the district and ultimately share majority power.

Significantly, in the 1990s, the legislators frequently cited the 1982 sewer governance scheme as a "model to be avoided."[247] The subject arose during debate on how to structure the governing body for the new regionally oriented Midwest Express Convention Center in downtown Milwaukee. They chose a very different model. Members of the governing board would be chosen by many concerned constituencies, including the governor, but no one, not even the City of Milwaukee, would have a majority. Thus the legislature indirectly admitted making a major mistake in the 1982 reform of sewerage governance. Why? The legislators had by the 1990s seen that the 1982 statute had given the majority and minority powers they could abuse, and did. This time around the legislators made sure that no interest on the board could prevail without persuading others to go along. In this way they avoided the major flaw in the 1982 Sewerage Governance Act: a lack of incentive to compromise.

Chapter 21

The Sewer Wars, 1982-1996

The public – but not Mayor Henry Maier – welcomed the legislature's ending Milwaukee's fierce battle in April 1982 over who should govern the Sewerage Commission. The respite was short-lived. Within a few months another long-simmering controversy burst into flame. The central issue: how much should each community (or user of sewer service) pay toward the local share of the two-billion-dollar ongoing sewer construction program. This fight, popularly known as the sewer wars, lasted from 1982 until 1996. Numerous battles were fought before and sometimes within many governmental authorities – the Milwaukee Metropolitan Sewerage District, the legislature, the courts, and the Wisconsin Public Service Commission. Governor Tommy Thompson intervened decisively at a crucial point. The sewer wars left a lamentable legacy of destructive mistrust between the principal protagonists, the central city and suburbs served by the district outside Milwaukee County.

Any war has deep-rooted causes. This one was no different. Municipalities outside Milwaukee County had long contracted for sewer service from the district. They stood apart. They had successfully resisted a far-sighted recommendation in 1959 by the Metropolitan Study Commission that they be brought into the district and treated the same as other municipalities.[248] The contracting municipalities paid for sewer service according to the volume of waste water they delivered to the district's trunk mains at the county border. Their sewer rate per million gallons had two components: one to cover the cost of operations; the other, to pay for the district's capital investment. After 1979 the volumetric charge for operations was refined to meet new requirements of the federal Clean Water Act and applied to all communities within Milwaukee County as well. No problem there.

However, the contract communities paid for capital costs in one manner; the municipalities within Milwaukee County, in another. There lay the seeds for future conflict. The contract municipalities paid for capital costs according to a contractual formula for setting reasonable utility rates: approximately 2 percent of the capital cost of facilities for depreciation and 8 percent for the rate of return. Within Milwaukee County, municipalities paid their share of capital costs in proportion to the equalized value of all property within their borders. By coincidence, until 1977 the annual amounts paid for capital costs by comparable suburbs inside and outside Milwaukee County were approximately the same.

Nevertheless, by 1979, the contract communities became nervous. They knew the staggering cost of the new construction program would substantially increase their capital share even under the existing formula. It might double. Moreover, it might quadruple if the district made them pay on the same basis as the Milwaukee County municipalities. The reasons were simple. The contract municipalities collectively contributed 6.6 percent of the total flow to the district while accounting for 16.71 percent of the equalized value of all property served by the district.[249] Their percentage of total property value was 2.5 times their percentage of total flow. Furthermore, this disparity was expected to increase, based on predicted suburban growth.

Between November 1979 and April 1980, the district held public hearings on the evolving Master Facilities Plan for the sewer construction program. It was called the Water Pollution Abatement Program (WPAP). The plan described the WPAP, its cost, and financing through 2005. The plan's calculations were based on the existing system of charges: flow-based for the contract municipalities; property-value-based for Milwaukee County municipalities. The contracts, incidentally, permitted either the MMSD or any individual municipality to terminate them on August 31, 1984 – although they had been automatically renewed every five years since they were signed in the 1950s and 1960s. The district adopted the Master Facilities Plan on June 5, 1980.

Two months earlier, however, the district ordered its consultants to prepare an analysis of alternate methods for charging the contract communities for capital costs. The consultants' report on August 28 recommended the district charge all communities on the property value basis.[250] It gave two logical reasons. Equity required that all communities inside and outside the district should be charged on the same basis. If the contract formula were applied equally to all communities, revenues would be inadequate to pay the debt service on the bonds. That is because the formula recaptured costs over fifty years while the bonds had to be repaid within twenty years. The statutes forbade longer terms for bonds.[251] This important politically significant report was labeled: "Privileged Information for Negotiations. Do not Reproduce."

In a closed session the district, on October 9, 1980, directed its top lawyer, Michael McCabe, to negotiate with the contract municipalities to include property-value-based charges in their contracts when they expired. When the negotiations predictably failed, the district moved to a fallback position. It directed that the rate base in the contract formula be changed to include the costs of expensive projects under construction, even though not yet in operation.

Years later the contract communities discovered the August 28, 1980, report during litigation and claimed the district was duplicitous in not making it public at the time. The district had its reasons for secrecy. Releasing the report then would have triggered a political fire fight with the contract communities over rates. That battle would have delayed governmental approval of the plan and the substantial grants contingent upon that approval. The report itself had frankly speculated that premature disclosure of higher rates might cause a few contract communities to quit being customers. They might seek to obtain lower charges by constructing their own treatment plants,[252] if they could persuade the DNR to let them do so – which seemed unlikely. At a minimum, the district's lack of disclosure, when discovered years later, sharpened the communities' existing distrust for the district and its perceived boss, Mayor Henry Maier. Such distrust probably prolonged the sewer wars.

Despite the secrecy surrounding the district's change of charging policy, the contract communities in late 1980 got an inkling that a change had taken place. The City of Muskego in the southeastern corner of Waukesha County applied for a service contract with the district. The district sent Muskego a draft contract. It proposed capital charges on a property value basis. William Mielke of Waukesha was Muskego's consulting engineer. He carried the news of the district's new charging policy to other contract municipalities. Shortly he became engineering advisor to the contract communities acting as a group against the changed charge policy.

In February 1982 as noted in chapter 20, key legislators were negotiating a reform of the district's governance structure. They offered the contract municipalities a chance to join the district. The communities promptly refused, ever wary of being charged on a property value basis. However, the legislators did include two provisions relating to the charging issue. The contract communities could be charged on any basis which recognized that the district could not levy property taxes. Also, the district could expand its boundaries to include any territory it would serve within ten years, if the communities agreed.

The district wasted no time using that new power. In late 1982, the district notified the contract communities it was proposing procedural rules by which the district could expand its boundaries to include areas which it already served. In December 1982, the seven (soon to be nine) communities formed an alliance to combat the district's proposed territorial expansion. That was their formal defense.

They also counter-attacked. They championed a proposal whereby the district should base capital charges to all twenty-five (shortly to become twenty-seven) municipalities on their flow. They named their organization FLOW for Fair Liquidation Of Wastes. FLOW's objectives set off alarm bells. Converting the district's capital charges to a flow basis inside Milwaukee County could multiply sewer bills by ten times or more to "wet industries" – those consisting of brewers, tanners, food processors, printers and electroplaters and hospitals and other non-profit organizations (who paid no real estate taxes). The wet industries formed their own group called Joint Organization for Better Sewers, or JOBS.

In January 1983 the nine municipalities started suit in the circuit court for Waukesha County to nullify the district's proposed expansion rules. Later the Metropolitan Sewerage Commission passed a resolution requesting the FLOW communities to approve becoming part of the district – after which the communities amended their complaint to challenge the resolution. Still later, the parties broadened their claims to get at the heart of their dispute. The contract municipalities asked the court to compel the district to serve them on a flow basis. The district countersued to collect full charges based on property value.

The sewer wars battle lines were drawn: FLOW versus district, with JOBS allied with the district.

I was never to participate in the battle, though twice invited, once by each side. A true conflict of interest requiring me to decline in one instance; an apparent conflict in the other. My work on the Illinois-Lake-Michigan water-pollution lawsuit still continued until 1989. That precluded accepting Mequon's July 1980 invitation to help them bargain for lower rates on their service contract with MMSD. I also had to turn down a 1983 request by John Murray, president of Universal Foods Corporation and of JOBS, who asked me to represent JOBS in the Waukesha Circuit Court in defense of MMSD's position against attack by FLOW. Since my firm, Quarles and Brady, then represented many school districts in the contract communities, we felt obliged not to anger them by accepting the JOBS offer.

While the sewer wars proceeded in court, FLOW opened up a major attack on the political front. By March 1983, FLOW asked the district to study basing its capital charges to *all* communities on flow rather than property values. The district sought to ignore FLOW, which responded with a high-powered public relations campaign. FLOW's principal spokesperson was Margaret Farrow, president of the Village of Elm Grove. She was a formidable leader. Her articulate, intelligent, and moderate manner convinced many. Her argument was simplicity itself. Capital costs were incurred in proportion to the flow generated by each community or customer. Eighty percent of the sewerage systems in America charged for capital costs on the basis of flow. So, she added, did all Wisconsin municipalities which had likewise recently undertaken massive construction plans to comply with the Clean Water Act.

The district was slow to respond, and then for a long time gave infrequent and ineffective presentations of its best argument supporting a property value basis for capital charges. It was this: the facts showed that seventy percent of the construction cost was needed to cope with invasive storm water rather than – as FLOW suggested – customers' use, like taking a shower. Further, protecting the public health from sewage overflows was a public good, logically chargeable to property, like police and fire protection, all of which enhanced property values.

185

This central political-engineering argument by the district ultimately prevailed, but in the meantime, in the summer of 1983, FLOW boldly set out to ask all suburbs within Milwaukee County to support flow-based capital charges. Farrow was ably assisted by Mielke, by then FLOW's engineer (and future President of Rueckert and Mielke). On the political level, one knowledgeable observer characterized FLOW's campaign as an effort to "shift a heavy burden from the bedroom suburbs to the central city."[253] They won resolutions of support from a majority, including Whitefish Bay and my Village, Fox Point. FLOW's appeal was clear. Fox Point, like Elm Grove, had high property values; both of them would pay *half as much* under FLOW's proposal as on a property value basis.

The district already planned to levy an annual capital charge of $3.50 per $1,000 of equalized valuation until 1995. At that rate an average home in Milwaukee assessed at $40,000[254] would pay $140 annually; an average Fox Point home assessed at $127,000 would pay $420, and an average home in Elm Grove, assessed at $98,000 would pay $343. Big dollars were involved. Mielke had painstakingly prepared figures as tempting to most suburbs as Pied Piper's music. They showed that all but four of the twenty-seven suburbs then using the District's system would pay less in sewer capital charges under a flow-based system than a property value system. The City of Milwaukee would pay 22 percent more. FLOW's figures were graphic:

Allocation Alternatives for MMSD 1983 Capital Costs [255]

Community Allocation Method

	Charges based on Equalized Value	Charges based on Total Systems Flow
Elm Grove	$ 625,556	$ 364,382
Fox Point	686,572	383,127
Milwaukee	21,174,746	25,793,493
West Allis	3,194,884	3,000,772
West Milwaukee	376,951	1,152,334

Mike McCabe asked me if I had any suggestions on how the district might convince Fox Point to drop its support for FLOW's position. Perhaps he had hoped my membership on Fox Point's Plan Commission (which was not consulted) could make a difference. I told him that the district was isolated from its suburbs. It simply did not understand what arguments would appeal to them or how to campaign. I suggested the district create an advisory public information committee including politically savvy persons, such as Bill Broydrick and the acknowledged suburban leader, Henry Mixter, president of Whitefish Bay.[256] McCabe replied that the district's executive director, Hal Cahill, disliked committees because a micro managing suburban commissioner, Vinton Bacon, always showed up and interfered.

Nothing happened. Two months later a recent chairman of the Sewerage Commission, Judge Francis Wasielewski, asked me how the district was faring in the PR battle over capital rates. I replied: "Too little, too late." He said he agreed.[257] After another two months, an astute observer, David Meissner, summarized the situation more crisply:

> FLOW is highly credible to a great number of people and is beating the Sewerage District and the city to death because of inept and inadequate defense....There [however] are some strong equity and practical arguments against imposing a user charges system on the District."[258]

FLOW's winning early passive support from a majority of Milwaukee County suburbs did not foreshadow their later being willing to battle Henry Maier over the charging rate.[259] In the long run, the seventeen Milwaukee County suburbs within MMSD generally accepted a continuation of the property value basis. They had become accustomed to it over many years.

In the short run, however, FLOW did win a costly victory of sorts. It persuaded another critical audience, the newly selected four suburban commissioners on the Sewerage Commission, to take two steps on its behalf: one mild, one drastic. FLOW asked the Commission in late 1983 for something short of enacting a flow basis for capital charges. More moderately, they requested the district to commission an independent study of flow-based versus property value-based capital charges. That was the mild step. The four suburban commissioners agreed. The seven commissioners appointed by Mayor Maier refused.

The suburban commissioners included resolute leaders such as the ever-pugnacious Ted Fadrow from Franklin and Mary Wilkinson, an energetic, resourceful Wauwatosa alderwoman. They were already frustrated by Henry Maier's representatives' ignoring their opinions on many subjects. They felt both the cost of the construction and the cost of the outside engineering consultants should be reduced. They got nowhere.

By then, Maier's commissioners were stonewalling on their request for a study. Led by Wilkinson, the suburban commissioners then took the drastic step. They hijacked the MMSD budget, exactly what Henry Maier had predicted they would do when he vainly protested against their being given this power in the law reforming the commission. They used their new power to prevent the commission from authorizing bonds needed to keep construction on the court-ordered timetable. No study, no bonds. For months, they withheld the one suburban vote required to authorize a bond issue by the vote of eight of the eleven commissioners.

Lack of funds threatened the timetable and damaged staff morale. The situation became desperate. The commission's chairman, Dean Showers, on November 23, 1983, appealed to Governor Anthony Earl to call a special session of the legislature to repeal the requirement that bonds be authorized by vote of two-thirds of the commission. He wrote that some Milwaukee legislators had expressed interest in a repeal. The Greater Milwaukee Committee became alarmed at the parochial bickering and reconstituted and enlarged its Sewer Task Force. Finally David Meissner, the GMC's adroit executive director – with substantial help from Task Force members – crafted a compromise in March 1984 by which eleven commissioners authorized the bonds at one session with the understanding that the study would be discussed at a following session.

All four suburban commissioners voted for the bond issue. However, the study was not commissioned until 1985, a year later, and then it was the legislature that acted. (It seems likely the city asked the legislature to intervene – in order to avoid its commissioners reversing their prior anti-study votes. But it is possible that the legislature acted on its own.)

The legislature authorized a three-person committee to make the study. One member was to be selected by the Sewerage Commission; one, by FLOW; the third, by "industry." FLOW picked Mielke. The commission chose William Chapman, a mechanical engineer and highly regarded retired Johnson Controls vice president. After back-room collaboration between the commission and JOBS, James T. Collins of Miller Brewing Company, one of the more vocal spokesman for "wet" industries, was selected as the representative of "industry." Chapman became chairman and wrote the committee's report. The committee met eighteen times in eleven months. A majority persistently rejected Mielke's suggestions that they invite outside experts to present their views. The same majority on October 10, 1986, not surprisingly recommended that the property value basis be retained. FLOW's representative, Mielke, issued a stinging, heavily documented ninety-page minority report. Henry Maier had won the battle inside the commission, but the sewer wars raged on and would be decided elsewhere.

In mid-1984, the district notified the contract municipalities it would terminate their service contracts on August 31. Nevertheless the district continued to serve them, billing them on a property value basis. They paid on the basis of their old rates. The unpaid difference in the first year came to $15,755,728, excluding interest.[260] This large difference between amount billed and paid decreased in subsequent years. Specifically, the MMSD tax higher charge rate within Milwaukee County went down rapidly to $3 per $1,000, while the comparatively lower amount due under the contract formula soared as the district annually added more construction work in progress to the rate base. (The contract communities unsuccessfully challenged these additions in court.)[261]

The legislature and courts took alternate kicks at the cat. Hostilities intensified. The legislature in 1983, and again in 1985, passed slightly different statutes requiring the district to charge customers outside Milwaukee County on a property value basis. The Wisconsin Supreme Court on June 29, 1988, declared them unconstitutional because those provisions were improperly included in a budget bill.[262] In response, the legislature in 1989 passed a third bill (SB 65) mandating the same result, but this time enacted the bill in the proper manner.

The bill set the stage for the timely intervention by the politically astute and powerful Governor Tommy Thompson. He noted that SB 65, favoring Milwaukee, was the legislature's approach, but that the war was also simultaneously being fought in two other arenas: the PSC and in the courts. Before deciding whether to sign or veto SB 65, the governor took a comprehensive view of what had happened in the other two arenas.

This is what he learned. On January 17, 1989, after the FLOW litigation in Waukesha had dragged on for nearly six years without a decision, frustrated new parties tried a different approach. Two of the heaviest users of the sewer system, Miller Brewing Company and Universal Foods Corporation, petitioned the Wisconsin Public Service Commission to review the reasonableness of MMSD's rates. Specifically they claimed MMSD discriminated by charging one group of customers – those in Milwaukee County – on a property value basis – while collecting at the much lower flow rate from the contract municipalities. The contract communities later intervened. The PSC delayed taking up the matter, saying it was wise to wait for the Waukesha court to reach a decision on many of the same issues. It came soon.

Between March 1989 and late 1990, FLOW won a series of victories in the Waukesha County Circuit Court. Judge Robert McGraw first decided[263] that the district's attempts to include FLOW communities were void because the 1982 authorizing statute was unconstitutional, and, even if valid, the district had not followed statutory procedure. Worse yet, after a June 1989 jury verdict for FLOW, he held, in March 1990, that the district was bound (by implied promises in its facilities plan[264] and other statements in 1979-1880) to continue to serve the contract communities on the existing flow basis. He also agreed with the jury's finding that the reasonable cost of constructing facilities needed for the contract communities was recouped under the contract formula (including construction work in progress). The judge refused to defer to the PSC's legislatively recognized expertise in rate-making – a fatal legal blunder, as it turned out.

After that stunning court defeat, the district modified its tactics. It tried two strategies simultaneously. For hard ball, it appealed the decision and turned the lead role over to Allen (Sandy) Williams (no relation to Harry Williams), a partner at Foley and Lardner, Wisconsin's largest law firm. Williams had earlier been special counsel to Governor Patrick Lucey. Then he became a specialist in PSC matters. For a soft ball tactic, the district started to negotiate with FLOW on rates for the first time. A compromise seemed achievable.

Governor Thompson now acted decisively. On December 8, 1989, he vetoed SB 65 because, as he stated:

> It imposes a relationship among the affected municipalities, which only fosters continued conflict. The proposed solution, if signed, would result in further litigation... mediation/negotiation should continue... it is time for the so-called "sewer wars" to end.[265]

Thompson urged the parties to continue to negotiate a settlement or he would refer the matter to the PSC. He pointedly said that the PSC had the authority to decide the reasonableness of rates charged by utilities and sewerage commissions. In mid-March 1990, the parties did just that under the watchful eye of James Klauser, Secretary of the Wisconsin Department of Administration and Governor Thompson's talented alter ego. FLOW, after initialing the negotiated draft, surprisingly declined to sign the agreement, and was generally blamed for the collapse of the negotiations.[266] The Wisconsin Department of Administration then petitioned the PSC to reopen the Miller Brewing-Universal Foods investigation and enlarge the issue to include the reasonableness of a property-value charge basis for the contract communities.

Ten months later, on January 28, 1991, the PSC ruled that the property charge was not unreasonable. The contract communities appealed. At this moment each side had won a victory: the communities, in the Waukesha Circuit Court in March 1990; the district, in the PSC. Both decisions were appealed.

The first answer came on November 13, 1992, when the Wisconsin Supreme Court reversed FLOW's Waukesha victory. It ruled the judge should have deferred to the PSC on rate matters.

The second and final answer ultimately came when the appellate court on June 12,1994 upheld a district court's approval of the PSC finding that charging on a property basis was not unreasonable. The appellate court reasoned, echoing MMSD arguments, why sewer capital costs could be charged on the same basis as taxes:

> The PSC concluded *the principal goal* of WPAP [Water Pollution Abatement Program] was to insure protection of public health...not to enlarge capacity to meet expanding user demand [as FLOW contended]. [267] (Emphasis added.)

At this point, the accumulated charges due by the contract communities to the district were approaching nearly one hundred million dollars without interest. FLOW's twin defeats in the state's highest court and the PSC did not make it give up. In 1993 FLOW undertook one last effort to win. Senator Don Stitt, who lived in Mequon, introduced 1983 Senate Bill 282 to authorize the PSC to establish the rates the district charged the contract communities. The bill passed the assembly and in 1994 came within one vote of winning in the senate. One anticipated FLOW supporter, George Petak of Racine, surprised FLOW by voting against the bill.

In October 1996 one additional fact pushed the contract communities into settling and paying $140 million to the district for back charges plus interest.[268] Because of the substantial addition of the entire construction project to the rate base, the annual contract charges to the contract communities had by 1996 become almost as high as the property-value-based charges to Milwaukee County municipalities. Furthermore, they were certain to go higher each year thereafter. Additionally, those contract municipalities' charges would continue for fifty years, whereas the property value charges began dropping because short-term-maturity general obligation bonds utilized by the district were being paid off, thereby lowering the property tax within the district.[269]

The sewer wars had finally ended. (A chronological summary of the major skirmishes in the fourteen-year sewer wars appears in Appendix H.) The district and city won a technical 100 percent victory; however, it was bought at a high cost to regional cooperation from which the district – and especially the city – also sought to benefit.

The Menomonee River Parkway in Wauwatosa farsightedly keeps housing back from recurrent flooding in the river's natural floodplain.

(Photograph courtesy of SEWRPC)

Part Five

Urban Sprawl

Chapter 22

Urban Sprawl: What and Why

Battles are more interesting than solid achievements. Consequently, sewer wars (1982-1996) and intermittent hot arguments over improving the transportation system (1971-2000) attracted media coverage like sugar draws flies. In retrospect, those battles were but growing pains that accompanied Milwaukee's efforts to modernize its metropolitan sewers and build a good, albeit incomplete, now obsolete, freeway system.

The two giant construction projects strengthened greater Milwaukee's ability to compete for customers and talent with other metropolitan regions. However, improved sewers and better highways quietly did something else. They facilitated the century-long outward growth from Milwaukee which became known as urban sprawl in the 1950s and fueled continuous municipal turf fights over annexations and incorporations. (See Chapter 3.)

Even today, urban sprawl has no commonly accepted definition. There are reasons. Sprawl takes many forms and springs from multiple forces. These forces are primarily market-driven but not curtailed by any significant overall regulation, such as exists in Europe. No one is in charge of sprawl. Sewers and highways are much easier to describe. They are constructed by identifiable knowledgeable agencies. They are designed by engineers following basic principles such as gravity. Their locations and alignments become somewhat predictable. They require funding to initiate and sustain.

In contrast, sprawl is a big unpredictable blob with outlying speckles. Periodicals and books often discuss urban sprawl without defining it. Perhaps those writers find definitions too complex. Definitions of sprawl, when they do appear, are generally not useful.

194

urban service areas closer in, identified in the plan. SEWRPC further suggested that recommended growth areas permit three to four home sites per acre. That required lots of one quarter to one-third of an acre lots, the medium density size at which public sewer and water services usually become affordable and fixed route bus service can be provided.

Most elected officials and residents-on-the-move did not care for the suggested smaller lots. By 1990, large lot development (one to five acres) spread beyond the area recommended by SEWRPC for any development or took place in areas recommended for medium density development. Larger lots naturally consumed more land per homesite, forcing later movers to settle still farther out.[272] As a result, a SEWRPC committee that I chaired in 1992 (and describe in Chapter 24) found that:

> ...only one half the new urban residential development [but two-thirds of the dwelling units] is occurring in areas recommended for such development in the [advisory land use] regional plan, with less than one-half the new urban development being provided with public sanitary sewer and water supply services. [273]

Map 12 shows where SEWRPC in 1965 recommended that outward development occur (thin red line) and where it actually took place by 1990. The unrecommended development scattered over the landscape resembles measles' blotches on the map. While one half of the development in the seven counties occurred where not recommended, the record was far worse in certain counties. In Washington County, 74 percent or 16.5 square miles of development took place outside the recommended areas, and in Waukesha County, 53 percent or 30.9 square miles.

Outward development (both within and beyond the recommended areas) was caused by two primary and many contributing reasons. First, people wanted to live in larger houses with substantial open space. Eighty-two percent of households in Milwaukee's urbanized region said so.[274] Second, America loved, owned, and used the automobile – even more markedly in the nineties than the fifties. In 1963, 77 percent of households in Milwaukee County owned a car; in 1991, 86 percent did. Further, the percent of daily weekday trips by car rather than by mass transit increased in the four-county region from 91.7 in 1963 to 96.6 in 1991. And in the seven-county region vehicle miles traveled by car shot up by 149 percent between 1963 and 1991 – from a total of 10,324,000 to 25,693,000 miles.

Many other reasons – some called "pull" and others "push" factors – motivated people to live outside the central city and, eventually, older inner (especially industrial) suburbs, such as West Allis. Between 1950 and 2000, pull factors included less expensive land, widely available electric power, cheap gasoline, lower real estate taxes, and the availability of septic tanks where sewers did not exist and land was even cheaper.

By the 1980s, push factors came into play. People also moved out of the central city because of poor schools,[275] rising crime,[276] racism (a white perception that a growing minority population[277] contributed to rising crime, declining schools, and a drop in property values), and less-ened job opportunities. By then, there were more jobs in outlying areas, particularly in Waukesha County, Wisconsin's fastest growing county in many recent years.

It is no surprise that the Milwaukee area's recent outward growth is no more than an accelerated continuation of the century-long outward expansion of American cities that started around 1900.[278] America was then converting from an agricultural to an industrial society. People migrated to urban centers for better jobs and a more exciting life. Later, some city residents, longing for a home in the country, moved to nearby suburbs, which they reached by streetcar lines or railways radiating out from the city's center. Early railroad suburbs were pre-existing cities or villages that offered commuters convenient travel to and from work in the central cities. New York City had its New Rochelle, where I was born, its Westport, where I grew up, and Rye, Greenwich, and Stamford. Chicago featured Evanston, Winnetka, and Lake Forest. Milwaukee's few early commuters used streetcar service north to Whitefish Bay (incorporated in 1892), and Fox Point to the north (incorporated in 1926) and commuter railway service west to Wauwatosa (incorporated in 1892), Brookfield, and Oconomowoc (originally a vacation area).

After 1950, the auto became the dominant form of transportation and, not being dependent on fixed routes as streetcars and railways were, greatly facilitated access to inexpensive home sites in the countryside. New subdivisions with coveted large homes and lots leap-frogged across the landscape. New municipalities sprang up between or beyond more traditional suburbs. They, or vast expanses within their borders, were exclusively residential. Large areas lacked nearby civic centers, shops, or jobs. No wonder they were called bedroom suburbs. They differed greatly from the early railroad suburbs with their mixture of residential, commercial, and, even industrial uses. Wauwatosa and Oconomowoc prior to World War II were examples of railroad suburbs or, if you will, early bedroom suburbs.[279]

Today's New Urbanists, including an acutely nostalgic Mayor John Norquist, bemoan such exclusively residential development as sterile and dominated by auto use. Many agree. They lack the quality of life of an old-time Wauwatosa.[280]

The quality of suburban life is being questioned in additional ways. Those who moved there initially found what they sought, but their very numbers led to new problems, such as traffic congestion. Their insistence on large lots led to others, such as substantial increases in the cost of infrastructure – roads, sewers, and schools. At the same time costly infra-structure in the central city was underutilized. Too, sprawling development meant longer distances between home, schools, shops, and services, convert-ing suburban parents (mostly mothers) into seemingly perpetual chauffeurs. Households in the region with two cars and one or two children made ten trips per day; with three or more children, made twelve to thirteen trips.[281]

Finally, market forces too often sacrificed pleasing design. Builders of moderately-priced homes saved money by repeatedly using the same house plans. Look-alike single family houses in cookie-cutter subdivisions blurred the landscape. Sometimes a traveler could not tell one community from another. Nor did buyers decline to purchase monotonous looking houses. The builders correctly read their market. Commercial development too often included big box discount stores. Other communities permitted strip malls, even possibly welcomed them. The model for a confusingly mish-mash appearance currently straddles Brookfield's Bluemound Road whose six lanes resemble eight because two parallel access roads lie only a few feet away. Nor did municipalities with some exceptions, seek to control ugly commercial buildings. Lately a few are seeking to prohibit big box discount stores in the name of aesthetics. In fairness, though, is monotonous or unappealing design truly the fault of sprawl or, simply, poor taste prevailing with all concerned: developer, consenting local government, and the buying public?

Chapter 23

Consequences: Good and Bad

If more than 80 percent of greater Milwaukee households prefer a single family home with a yard, what is so wrong with sprawl? Does it really matter that sprawl's greater consumption of land forces growth even farther outward, if land is cheap and the country is so much more affluent now than formerly? These are significant questions. There are no simple answers. Nationally, endless newspaper and magazine articles and nearly five hundred books have analyzed sprawl. Authors wrote that sprawl had forty consequences, judging two-thirds to be negative; only one third, beneficial.

Fortunately for me, a team of scholars from Rutgers University, Brookings Institution, and two planning firms in 1998 wrote a comprehensive analysis of the five hundred books in the authoritative *Costs of Sprawl Revisited.*[282] *(Costs)*. This comprehensive research was financed by the Federal Transit Administration (a sponsor with a natural pro-transit bias) on the plausible hypothesis that finding authoritative data on sprawl's costs might lead to measures reducing transportation costs.

Costs' authors phrased my questions in greater detail:

> Why such interest in sprawl? Although Americans like their single-family residences, automobiles, and suburban lifestyles, there is a nagging feeling that both the aesthetics of how communities develop and the efficiency of movement within and between them could be improved. But first it must be shown to the citizenry at large that there is a problem because life is good and If it ain't broke, don't fix it ....Is there an alternative?[283]

The authors then suggested a summary answer: sprawl is too deeply ingrained to be changeable:

> Sprawl is so well-accepted by the public that AAA-rated locations for both residential and commercial development are farther out rather than closer in, and

more rather than less segregated by type of land use. Gated communities, farmettes, research parks, law offices, medical groups, mega-stores, ...restaurants all now seek peripheral locations in pursuit of the market. [284]

In my opinion, the general thrust of sprawl is probably unchangeable, but whether sprawl is "broke" or not depends on each individual's value judgment of particular impacts of sprawl. The beneficial aspects of sprawl are self-evident but, unfortunately, they occurred outside Milwaukee. The many residents who settled in the suburbs obtained what they sought: a single family house on a "large lot," better schools, and a smaller, more responsive local government. Industry, in relocating in Milwaukee's western and northern suburbs, acquired the far larger tracts that were absolutely essential for modern single-story factories with employee parking. They also generally got quicker access to vital freeways than were available at the few sites still to be found in older cities. By the year 2000, 84 percent of the value of all cargo in the USA moved by truck.[285] Too, suburbs encouraged or even developed large campus-like industrial parks.

Shopping malls in outlying areas similarly achieved their three objectives; large tracts of land, access to good transportation, and proximity to their outward-moving customers. All but one of the major Milwaukee-area shopping malls built in the past fifty years were located at sites recommended for them in the SEWRPC 1965 advisory land use plan. The other one, Southridge, missed by only a mile. Mall developers, their financiers, and SEWRPC all used identical demographic and transportation criteria in nominating sites for shopping malls; SEWRPC accurately supplied the needed supporting data, leading Donald Slichter, a president of Northwestern Mutual Life Insurance Co., which financed one or more malls, to say in the 1970s: "SEWRPC's data bank is an invaluable resource". The desire of industry and commerce to build in outlying areas provoked intense competition among receptive suburbs. It did more. That competition disclosed a weakness in Wisconsin's (and America's) local government structure and powers.

Each local government is free to make its own decisions about whether to permit the building of a new office block or shopping mall, regardless of any cost the decision imposes on neighbors. And the

locality gets to keep any property tax revenue that
results....[286]

Sprawl hit the City of Milwaukee hard. When industry,
commerce, and residents relocated outward, jobs in the city declined.
One could more accurately say that the woeful impact on the city was
caused by fundamental factors other than sprawl, which was a
consequence: obsolescence, declining schools, white flight, and
increasing affluence enabling people to move. In any event, in 1963, 88
percent of the jobs in the four county metropolitan area were in
Milwaukee County; thirty-five years later, only 62 percent. Likewise,
the City of Milwaukee's share of regional jobs declined. In 1970 the
city had 51 percent of the four-county population and 57 percent of the
jobs. By 1998 it had only 41 percent in each category.[287] Further, when
the middle class fled, the remaining population of both the County and
City of Milwaukee represented lower incomes. The figures boggle the
mind. In 1993 Milwaukee County had 19 percent of Wisconsin's
population and 47 percent of the state's welfare caseload. In only six
years, even after Wisconsin's nationally heralded W-2 welfare reform
forced mothers whose youngest child had reached eighteen to find jobs,
thereby sharply reducing welfare loads to the least employable, the
ratios abruptly changed to 18 and 79 percent, respectively.[288] Also, even
in the booming economy, children in Milwaukee County living in poverty or near poverty grew from 91,000 to 113,000 between 1993 and
1998.[289]

Milwaukee's comparative poverty, after urban sprawl took place,
is shown by another measurement. Milwaukee today has the lowest tax
base per capita ($27,462) of the sixty-seven municipalities in the
five-county region.[290] That is one-half the median tax base and one-
fourth the average of three high income suburbs: Brookfield, Elm
Grove, and Mequon. Milwaukee's tax base in the recent past has grown
at a much slower rate than that of Milwaukee County suburbs and,
especially, of Waukesha County as a whole. The City of Milwaukee tax
base even lagged behind in inflation.

Aggregate Equalized Property Value in Billions [291]

	1988	1999	1988-1999
City of Milwaukee	$12.002	$16.701	39%
Milw. County Suburbs	11.042	19.701	79%
Milwaukee County	23.044	36.438	58%
Waukesha County	11.318	27.000	139%
State of Wisconsin	126.587	266.567	111%
		Inflation	44%

David Meissner, president of the Public Policy Forum, which reported the above figures, predicted:

> We are in sight of the time [later predicted to be 2005] [292] when the total property value of Waukesha County will exceed that of Milwaukee County.

Meissner warned:

> [T]he rise in property values outside the City of Milwaukee] in turn creates an ever more pressing need for regional cooperation, so that the wealth of the entire metropolitan area can be brought to bear on the region's needs.[293]

A surprising example of what happened in Waukesha County is the rise of property value in Brookfield which I incorporated in 1954 with 7,903 inhabitants. By 1999 it had only 37,355 residents but its assessed valuation had risen, by means of Brookfield Square, Bluemound Road development, and high-priced homes, to nearly $4 billion. That total is second only to the City of Milwaukee and exceeds those of the far older and more populous cities of Wauwatosa, West Allis, and Waukesha.

Certain early industrial suburbs such as Cudahy, West Allis, and West Milwaukee suffered losses of jobs and tax base when obsolete plants were shut down or industrial expansion moved to larger sites available farther out. That shift raised unemployment and local taxes for those left behind. For example, the tax rate of all three in 1999 exceeded Milwaukee's; West Milwaukee by 42 percent and West Allis by 10 percent.[294]

Negative aspects of sprawl to the suburbs included more than residents merely having to spend too much time in their cars. Subdivisions destroyed many square miles of farmland and woodlands. Counties, towns, and municipalities did not preserve adequate green space for future generations, either by regulation or purchase.

The process by which too much green space disappeared covered many years. In 1965 SEWRPC saw the threat coming. It recommended that large areas of environmentally sensitive woodlands, wetlands and floodplains remain undeveloped. SEWRPC called them "environmental corridors" because they often formed corridors along rivers, lakes, or ridges. Fortunately, three-quarters were protected. The legislature deserves credit. In 1968 it required municipalities and counties to preserve floodplains along rivers by zoning against development.[295] Local government did so promptly, using SEWRPC's carefully prepared floodplain maps to identify boundaries. Similar protection was provided to many bogs and marshes, known as wetlands.

Protecting woodland corridors did not fare as well. Counties and the state purchased, as recommended, some woodland sites for public parks but permitted others to be invaded or destroyed by development. SEWRPC soberly reported:

> About one-quarter of the corridor lands are vulnerable to development and destruction, particularly through residential development utilizing onsite sewage disposal systems (septic tanks). The vulnerable lands are upland in nature, consisting largely of woodlands, significant wildlife habitat areas, and....steeply sloped lands.[296]

Developers and acquiescent towns and counties all too often permitted subdivisions to extend into the steep slopes of the Kettle Moraine area. For example, Washington County largely turned over zoning to its towns in the 1970s and formally surrendered all county zoning powers in 1986 – except for the floodplain and shoreland zoning mandated by the state since 1968. As a result, largely scattered development (Map 12) invaded the recommended environmental corridors after 1965. More and more subdivisions barged into wooded areas, destroying prime vistas and habitat for flora and fauna. Twenty square miles of woodlands were lost in the region, mostly in Walworth, Waukesha, and Washington counties.[297]

The diverse negative aspects of sprawl gradually led to new strategies to lessen them, especially by sprawl's most prominent victim, the City of Milwaukee.

Chapter 24

Counter-Trends and Reform Measures

Inevitably, Milwaukee's prolonged loss of population, jobs, and hunks of tax base stimulated a reaction. Mayor John Norquist sought to reduce the primary factors driving people out, such as crime and poor schools. Milwaukee's violent crime rate dropped noticeably after 1991 but not as much as in America's ten largest cities where it went down by 34 percent.[298] Milwaukee's comparatively high crime rate compared with Boston, New York, and Los Angeles, remained a puzzle.[299] Therefore, Norquist on election night in April 2000 after his opponent taunted him for Milwaukee's high crime rate, impulsively pledged to reduce it by 50 percent in two years. Significantly, Milwaukee's downtown area went without a homicide between 1992 and 1999. In 1995, Chicago took over its schools and improved them. Later, Mayor Norquist, along with Governor Tommy Thompson, helped launch a nationally prominent school choice program in Milwaukee. Norquist also broke precedent by intervening in school board elections. His efforts eliminated incumbents opposed to choice and other reform efforts, such as merit pay for teachers. Opponents had been elected with support from the teachers' union which wanted no competition from new schools.

Milwaukee, like other cities, took many steps to make the city a more attractive place to live. Some steps hit the mark. One was to encourage the building of user-friendly apartments and condominiums downtown. Another was enthusiastic public support for private efforts to renovate old neighborhoods like the Historic Third Ward, Brady Street, and Brewers' Hill. Milwaukee added 1,579 housing units downtown between 1997 and 1999. Empty nesters and young professionals provided a strong market for new apartments and condominiums, some at unusually high prices. In one converted Third Ward building buyers paid as much as $500,000 per condominium. They liked being near the arts, good restaurants, museums, and sports arenas. Also, they did not want to mow lawns. Although people continue to move mostly to the suburbs, Milwaukee happily expects its downtown population to grow by 34 per cent by 2010.[300] Twenty-five other cities expect similar or much larger increases in downtown populations; Chicago, 32 percent; Cleveland, 220 percent.[301]

Norquist, the common council, and (mostly) the private sector worked toward making downtown more appealing by building and expanding what cities do best: museums, libraries, and sports stadiums. Between 1987 and 2000 Milwaukee and private philanthropists added a new Bradley Center (primarily for the Milwaukee Bucks basketball team), Midwest Express Center, museum of science and technology (Discovery World), children's museum, and repertory theater; they rejuvenated the Third Ward with the new Broadway Theater complex and numerous art galleries and restaurants; they renovated both the Milwaukee Public Library and Marcus Center for the Performing Arts, and drew international attention to Milwaukee's emerging icon: the spectacular, sail-like Calatrava addition to the Milwaukee Art Museum overlooking Lake Michigan.

Two extraordinary philanthropists, Jane Pettit (old electric controls fortune) and Michael Cudahy (new electronics fortune), led thousands of other givers to make the building renaissance possible. The enrichment of the arts in Milwaukee in the nineties was further enhanced by Milwaukee, as America's 19th largest city, proudly mounted the second largest annual united performing arts fund. Milwaukee civic leaders enthusiastically reported that the quality of the arts in Milwaukee helped them recruit out-of-town managerial and professional talent. Regrettably, but perhaps understandably, the Milwaukee Brewers' new baseball stadium which opened in 2001, is not being built downtown despite Norquist's strong, last minute effort to move it from the County Stadium site selected by the Brewers.[302] Norquist moved too late.

In his laudable zeal for new approaches Norquist adopted major traffic incentives intended to make downtown more livable and vital. He restored on-street parking, many two-way streets, and, as we noted, championed the not-popular-with-everyone removal of the unsightly Park Freeway East spur. Restoring on-street parking was done to provide the reality and perception of more parking downtown. Street parking would also set up a buffer between pedestrians and busses along Wisconsin Avenue where the prior parking ban had converted the curb lane into a de facto bus lane. The change of many streets from one-way-only to two-way was intended to make pedestrians more comfortable on the sidewalk and in crossing the street. These changes generally followed traffic calming principles developed nationally to slow traffic for pedestrians and neighborhoods.

However, as an urban planner observed, who sympathized with Norquist's traffic policies, any change has disadvantages as well as benefits. Some people like the traffic changes. Others, including some motorists, downtown businessmen, and retired city traffic engineers, consider the changes overdone or, in some instances, misapplied. The jury is out. Parking on West Wisconsin Avenue means trucks have to double park to load into storefronts; buses pulling out from bus stops have to wait for a break in passing traffic; bus service between Prospect Avenue and 10th Street during rush hours has slowed, we are officially told, but by one minute only.[303]

In certain instances Norquist sought to over-apply traffic calming. Changing two-way streets to one-way streets is state-of-the art only if capacity is not decreased. Thus, on wide streets with four lanes it makes sense. On narrow ones, it does not. For example on streets with three lanes like State and Wells Streets from 12th to 27th Streets where the change was proposed but not implemented, it costs lanes and capacity, slowing traffic.[304] Restoring diagonal parking, as initially done on two blocks on Milwaukee and Jefferson streets, has been considered unsafe by traffic engineers for over fifty years and was nationally removed from all American municipalities except small towns. Yet, store owners, including the George Watts china shop, on being polled by the city, said they preferred diagonal parking even though it was less safe than parallel parking. By late 2000 diagonal parking was extended to streets bordering the central library and to Kilbourn Avenue, a major artery. Perhaps the mayor's nostalgia for the past outweighed any recognition of the danger of backing a car out into traffic.

If Norquist's traffic measures in some instances and to some observers defy best professional practices and are overdone, they nevertheless symbolize his fervent devotion to reinvigorating the downtown.

In 1992 when Milwaukee's downtown renaissance was progressing, the state Department of Transportation (WISDOT) showed concern about the impact of sprawl farther from the city. WISDOT sought to dampen escalating demand for highway construction, believing its capital budgets were already stretched to meet the growth in normal traffic demand. Furthermore, excessive exurban sprawl led to demand for new or wider highways. WISDOT financed *two* studies of how land use changes throughout Wisconsin might lessen sprawl.

One WISDOT study committee was appointed by Governor Thompson; the other, by SEWRPC. Thompson's committee was to examine land use throughout all Wisconsin counties outside the SEWRPC region and suggest needed changes. SEWRPC's role was different. It was to measure the extent to which actual development in the seven-county region had followed the 1965 land use plan, which WISDOT had approved as reasonable. Interestingly, in the rest of Wisconsin there was no comparable twenty-five-year-old basic regional plan against which subsequent development could be compared.

If it was found that development had not followed SEWRPC's plan, SEWRPC was to suggest methods for achieving better compliance. SEWRPC gave the committee a planner's typical tongue-twisting name: Committee on Regional Land Use Plan Implementation in Southeastern Wisconsin: Status and Needs. When they asked me to chair it, I informally renamed it "the sprawl committee." The seven counties each appointed two members interested in land use planning or transportation, including Daniel M. Finley, the Waukesha County Executive, who, many say, has ambitions to be governor.

I was invited to select seven additional members based on their regional perspective and specialized knowledge. I chose G. Andrew Larsen of the Riveredge Nature Center (for the environment), Ronald P. Siepmann of Waukesha (a conservation-sensitive subdivider, J. Michael Mooney, a planner and builder of industrial parks (for factors influencing industrial relocation), Timothy J. McElhaton, then a Public Policy Forum staff member (for municipal finance), and Herbert A. Goetsch, retired Commissioner of Public Works for the City of Milwaukee.

By 1993 we found that sprawl, as earlier noted at pages 204 and 205, had indeed extended well beyond the plan's suggested outer boundary for urban development.[305] (Shown by a red line on Map 12) We recommended several remedies. We primarily suggested that local zoning authorities in the future carry out the 1965 zoning recommendations although we could not ask them to outlaw already poorly located development. However, zoning authorities received no new incentive to carry out our renewed recommendations. Generally, they did not.

In addition, we suggested that the state act in several ways to lessen sprawl's adverse impacts. Three were key. One was for the state to help preserve prime farmland from being gobbled up by development. Between 1970 and 1985 the region lost five times as much prime farmland to development as the plan had anticipated. Maybe the plan too optimistically bucked market trends. Only one half of the remaining prime farmland had been zoned for exclusive agricultural use, despite the existence of a State Farmland Preservation Program giving tax credits to farmers to encourage such zoning.[306] In other words, prime farmland could be sold for development. We found that farmland near cities was, quite understandably, being assessed locally according to its most lucrative potential use, such as residential development. The resulting higher real estate taxes were forcing farmers to sell. We recommended that the legislature establish:

> a system whereby operating farmland within the farm-
> land preservation program would be assessed for real
> estate tax purposes upon its value for agricultural use
> only.[307]

The legislature so acted, though primarily, or exclusively, because a farmland preservation study committee of Governor Thompson's Wisconsin Department of Revenue came up with a similar recommendation. The new law currently faces a court challenge, brought predictably by a league of cities and villages which bear the brunt of the tax relief for farmers. As of 2000, farmland sale prices near cities are escalating more rapidly than inflation.[308] Maybe this social engineering effort is slated to fail.

Our "sprawl" committee's two other recommendations for state action fell on deaf ears. I know. At that time I was retired from law practice as well as from a subsequent five-year stint as an officer of the Milwaukee Innovation Center helping start-up businesses obtain capital. Thus I had ample time to lobby six of Governor Tommy Thompson's department secretaries in person, as well as potential support and opposition groups.

Both of our recommendations sought to lessen sprawl on the outer rim. The first was the simplest but most controversial. We recommended that the state moderate its planned liberalization of regulations governing the location of on-site sewage treatment systems: septic tanks. These regulations had long forbidden placing septic tanks on thin soil above rock or a high water table or on steep slopes. Leakage, which was considered more likely in such areas, could pollute well water. The State's regulations augmented local zoning (or, more aptly, lack of zoning) to keep residential development out of steep-slope woodlands and wetlands. The Wisconsin Department of Industry, Labor and Human Relations (the Department of Commerce) was in the long process of drafting a radical relaxation of these regulations. DILHR had two bees in its bonnet. One was that continuing technological advances would greatly increase the ability of enhanced septic tanks to treat wastes. Although true, this approach passes over two facts. Even improved on-site systems may fail anyway owing to lack of proper use or needed maintenance by private owners. In theory, county inspections would detect such malfunctioning tanks and cause corrections, but in reality, too few inspectors are available to do the job.

The other bee in DILHR's bonnet was political, Governor Tommy Thompson's enthusiastic laissez-faire philosophy. Allowing septic tanks where previously forbidden would open up new areas for development (true). If such development were not in the public interest (perish the thought), then local government, DILHR proclaimed, had the power to zone it (also true). However, rural communities seldom zone in anticipation of problems. They learn, painfully, when they happen. Interestingly, too, at builders' requests, the legislature had long before prohibited counties or local municipalities from regulating septic tanks more strictly than the state.

I appealed in person to DILHR'S able secretary, Carol Skornicka, and her respected long-tenured deputy secretary, to moderate their proposed radical relaxation of septic tank rules. Joining me in my presentation was a member of my committee, the Administrator of the

Land Use and Park Department of Washington County, Paul E. Mueller. He recounted examples of how county inspection staffs were too understaffed to protect public health by monitoring more failing septic tanks. There were already 500,000 septic tanks in Wisconsin, many of which were not operating properly. We got nowhere. Eight years later, in 2000, after long debate and many skirmishes among opposing interests, the radical rules were adopted as Comm 83. The League of Wisconsin Municipalities and others in 2000 challenged Comm 83's validity in court. The League's president passionately warned:

> This rule [Comm 83] could be the catalyst for the greatest explosion of sprawl we've ever seen in Wisconsin. It could also represent the greatest threat to ground water that the state has ever seen.[309]

Any land use reform, good or bad, gets challenged in court these days. Is society more litigious? Are planners more intrusive? Or is it only that increasing population and spread-out land use engenders more conflicts between competing interests such as construction, increased tax base, and local jobs versus environmental protection, quality of life, and rational land use planning?

Our less controversial recommendation for protecting woodlands won the quiet support of the long-time secretary of the DNR, George Meyer. Our suggestion was that the state protect woodlands by substantially reducing the density of development permitted in them. We sought state legislation requiring counties and towns to limit residential development in designated environmental corridors. We suggested limiting dwelling units to one per five acres. We pointed to a precedent. A 1968 Water Resources Act had required all local governments to zone against development in the identified flood plains of rivers. Its objective was logical and simple. Further, we thought it was comparable to the woodland problem. The fragile Kettle Moraine woodland ecosystem extended through many towns, as rivers do. Rivers during floods needed the flood plains as reservoirs to contain high waters. Restricting the river's overflow in one place increased the velocity of water passing downstream, increasing erosion, and, of course, raised water levels higher upstream, thereby increasing damage through higher and wider floods. The refusal of a single municipality along the river to forbid filling or

212

building in the floodplain threatened people and property in other municipalities upstream and downstream.

Based on this regional perspective, we argued that one town's permitting heavy development to sever the necessary continuous range for wildlife could undermine a neighboring town's efforts to protect various species of wildlife and vegetation. DNR Secretary Meyer agreed with our facts and logic but told me the DNR could not sponsor the bill. The legislature would regard DNR-sponsorship as motivated by a desire to increase its power. That was because the legislation would require the DNR to specify the environmental corridors to be protected, just as it identified flood plains under the flood plain legislation.

I then appealed to Governor Thompson's powerful and politically savvy alter ego, James Klauser, the Secretary of Administration. He, I hoped, could possibly persuade the busy governor to endorse one or both of our recommendations for protecting woodlands. James Klauser had lived in Delafield in Waukesha County, near the Kettle Moraine. He had also served in local government. He understood the problem. He and his staff extended my half-hour appointment to one and a half hours, but in the end said "No." Zoning, Klauser said, is the function of local government and added:

> The beginning of a solution to a problem starts with the recognition by the people affected that they have a problem. You must first convince the towns that protecting the woodlands from development is in their interest.[310]

His softly spoken rebuff ended our search for state support. I instantly recognized that it would take years – without the active backing of a highly popular governor – to persuade towns to realize the danger of uncontrolled development. Many town supervisors were farmers some of whom hoped eventually to sell to developers. They might also have believed, often erroneously, that development would bring to their town more revenues than new infrastructure would cost. Clearly Wisconsin was not ready for our suggestions. They were ahead of their time. We hoped the public would gradually recognize their merits.

Perhaps that is now happening. At least a little. In 1999, the president of the Wisconsin Senate, Fred Risser of Madison, started drafting a bill (Senate Bill 428) refining our basic recommendation that the state protect upland environmental corridors. His bill requires the Department of Natural Resources to draft standards declaring the amount and type of development that can exist in upland environmental corridors without reducing their natural values.[311] Local communities must then zone their portion of an environmental corridor consistently with the DNR's protective minimum standards. Risser plans to introduce his bill, with several co-sponsors, in 2001.

By the mid-nineties two promising movements emerged to counter sprawl's wasteful low densities and destruction of open space. The leading organizations are the Congress of New Urbanists founded by architects[312] in 1993, and of which John Norquist is a zealous member, and Smart Growth, created by the State of Maryland in 1997. The first movement is purely design-oriented; the second is focused on how government can encourage what sponsors consider more rational growth, including the New Urbanist principles. Each promotes selective or "smart" growth which recreates features of our best-loved communities or neighborhoods. Development in rural areas, according to Smart Growth disciples, should be by "conservation subdivisions" small lots, narrow streets, alleys, sidewalks, front porches, *common areas for recreation or green space*, and, hopefully less dependence on the car. The latter could be a naive hope. In fact, by 1999, 130 New Urbanist or Traditional Neighborhood subdivisions had been built or started in sixteen states, mostly in the South.[313] Wisconsin featured one, started in 1995 by the Erdmann group in Middleton, near Madison.

New Urbanism has stimulated criticism and praise. According to the *New Yorker* magazine, New Urbanist subdivisions are intended to recreate the friendly ambiance of an old-fashioned village.[314] Another critic says the New Urbanists are seeking

> The imaginary village...as an escape into the good old days, a time when many Americans believe that life was simple and safe, and townspeople knew and trusted each other.[315]

Yet another writer says it is wrong to dismiss New Urbanists – who some say should be more accurately named New Suburbanists –

as merchants of nostalgia. One observer predicts that New Urbanists' possibly most enduring contribution is that they rediscovered how to design streets and hide parking lots in order to make neighborhoods more attractive. Specifically:

> [They] operate on the belief that streets are what make cities work, not buildings...and that the absence of streets – or, rather, the replacement of streets by six or eight-lane traffic arteries – is what makes most new suburbs so unpleasant to be in.[316]

I say it is too early to judge. In my opinion, suburban or exurban subdivisions of smaller-lot-houses-closer-together, whether conservationist or New Urbanist in nature, may become mildly fashionable. I hope so. Today I live happily on a 60 x 100 foot lot after forty-seven years enjoying beautiful but maintenance-burdensome multi-acre home sites. Smart Growth's conservation subdivisions are essentially smaller lot versions of cluster subdivisions, the first of which appeared in Mequon in the early 1960s as the Lac du Cours subdivision with its artificial lake and tennis courts. I was the developer's lawyer. The year 2000 has shown signs of a small thaw in the long standing, almost universal suburban hostility to smaller lots. Brookfield and New Berlin, both pace-setting suburbs, are relaxing that requirement in certain select areas. They wish to create or revitalize central business districts with buildings closer to the street. The cities of Cedarburg and Oconomowoc continue to encourage their historic pattern of small lot development.

In 1999 the Town of Cedarburg in Ozaukee County zoned to require cluster-type development. Developers in the town are expected to put their houses closer together and provide common ownership or green space.[317] Nearby Mequon in 2000 encouraged but did not require cluster subdivisions in the two-thirds of that large city for which sewers are not planned. In 2000, the Village of Jackson has approved a New Urbanist subdivision on the Dahlmann farm. Builders report the greater Milwaukee area has a large demand for quarter acre lots.[318]

However, while these new-style small lot suburban subdivisions, are compact and may preserve green space, they fall short of their proponents' dreams in two respects. First, they are unlikely to wean America from its love affair with the car – the most convenient means of transportation ever developed. (You start when you want and choose your own route to get there, and usually arrive when intended.) Second, the scattered location of small lot suburban green-space-preserving subdivisions fails to protect continuous environmental corridors. A proponent, 1,000 Friends of Wisconsin, admits this last point:

> Conservation subdivisions surrounded by traditional subdivisions are likely to have very limited overall environmental benefits. If a natural [environmental] corridor stops at the boundary of the subdivision, it offers little or no broader environmental benefit. Protecting the site's natural features provides an amenity for the subdivision's residents, but not much benefit to the environment as a whole.[319]

New Urbanists urge that older neighborhoods inside cities be revitalized by mixing uses: homes next to schools, shops, offices, restaurants, and parks. That mixed use urban development has extensively taken place in downtown Atlanta, causing that city to gain population for the first time in thirty years.[320] October 2000 saw the opening of Milwaukee's first New Urbanist subdivision, Cherokee Pointe, containing seventy-seven single family home sites on part of the abandoned Stadium South Freeway land near West Morgan Avenue and South 43rd Street. The subdivision features narrow streets, porches, houses closer together with small setbacks from the street, a mix of housing styles (single family and condominiums), garages in the back, rolling wooded common areas, and a stream. However, owing to neighborhood opposition, the subdivision did not include shopping and thereby address the movement's fundamental goal of reducing dependence on cars.[321]

Smart Growth was launched in strong form in Maryland in 1997. It was adopted by the Wisconsin Legislature in watered-down form in the budget bill signed by Governor Thompson on October 27, 1999. Smart Growth has no precise definition. A Maryland official coined the name Smart Growth when he tired of developers calling him "anti-growth" because he turned down irrational developments. He was in favor of growth; not just "dumb growth." Maryland rewarded counties with state money for schools and roads in certain predefined growth areas[322] such as the higher density corridor encompassing the extension of the Washington, D.C., subway into Maryland.[323] Maryland also

216

encouraged the preservation of rural areas through the acquisition of preservation easements.

The State of Wisconsin included Smart Growth as a voluntary small part of a sweeping revision of the state's requirements for local planning. The act (1999 Wisconsin Act 9 and Technical Revisions, 1999 Assembly Bill 872) came as a surprise. The legislature for thirty years had rejected suggested revisions to the planning statutes. Nor had it taken any significant action regarding land use. Thus, the new act represented a mild, encouraging break with the state's policy of leaving land use planning to local government as Jim Klauser had explained to me when rejecting my SEWRPC committee's anti-sprawl proposals in 1993. The act passed because a surprisingly broad coalition of often-warring interests backed it: highly activist 1000 Friends of Wisconsin, the Wisconsin Alliance of Cities, the Builders' Association, Wisconsin Realtors, the Sierra Club, the University of Wisconsin Extension Service, counties, and towns.

Smart Growth has a strong appeal because the term means many different things to different people. It is, like sprawl, a buzzword in its imprecision. For example, the Sierra Club holds out Smart Growth to mean:

> Livable communities, designed for people rather than automobiles; closeness to nature and permanent conservation of environmental lands; viable public transit at the city and metropolitan scale.[324]

On the other hand the National Association of Home Builders says:

> Smart Growth means meeting the underlying demand for housing created by ever-increasing populations and the prosperous economy by building a political consensus and employing market-sensitive and innovative land use planning concepts.[325]

The builders wanted lower land and infrastructure costs per dwelling unit, not necessarily an objective shared by the Sierra Club.

The new act basically requires each Wisconsin municipality by 2010 to adopt a detailed comprehensive plan for development containing many elements (or sub-parts) which must be internally consistent and accompanied by in-depth supporting data. Formerly comprehensive plans, if they existed, were often sketchy, inconsistent, or ignored – all to the understandable frustration of builders. Each municipality's new plan must ambitiously address nine elements: goals, housing, transportation, utilities and community facilities, natural resources, economic development, intergovernmental cooperation, land use, and methods for implementation.[326]

Unfortunately, the Comprehensive Planning Act does little to encourage a municipality to coordinate its planning with that of its neighbors, county, and region. To be sure, its transportation plan element must explain how its goals and programs compare with state and regional transportation plans.[327] Also, its intergovernmental cooperation element must tamely "compile," rather than actively "coordinate," any of its programs for "joint planning and decision-making with school districts, adjoining local governments for siting and building public facilities and sharing public services."[328]

Significantly, however, the 1999 act does not even refer to advisory regional land use plans. That is a logically horrendous but deliberate and politically necessary omission. If prepared well, regional plans reconcile competing land uses and municipal ambitions. Elected politicians would say reconciliation is not possible without their being involved. However, my long experience suggests that local officials are unable or unwilling to take a regional approach by moderating local aspirations. That experience partly includes the failure of a committee of elected municipal officials in the 1950s even to agree on the boundary warfare facts. Instead, they bickered. Their failure in turn disgusted the Greater Milwaukee Committee and led it to recommend that the legislature create and the governor appoint the Metropolitan Study Commission, without any public officials as members. In fairness, local officials are not elected to have a regional viewpoint. Instead, they protect local interests and the power of their turf. In fact, supporters of the act shied away from mentioning regional planning. A participant realistically observed:

> To get anything passed, we needed to emphasize strong support for local control; regional planning was a bad word with many counties and towns who were part of our alliance.[329]

Regional plans, on the other hand, can provide the basis for controlling sprawl. They suggest rational land uses and transportation routes; they identify rational urban service areas; and they recommend medium and high densities within those service areas, the lack of which – or public demand for which – is a key engine for excessive outward growth.

The Comprehensive Act seeks to advance Smart Growth, but in only limited respects. As a good start, it authorizes the University of Wisconsin Extension to draft by January 2001 model ordinances to encourage Smart Growth development in both rural and urban settings. The model ordinances' overall objective is to encourage higher densities, better protection of open spaces, a broadening of housing opportunities, and less dependence on the auto.[330] Smart Growth's model ordinances are subject to approval by a senate and assembly committee. That requirement assures that the formerly aloof legislature stays involved at least into 2001.

The model Smart Growth ordinance for the rural setting will define:

> Conservation subdivisions...characterized by compact lots and open common space and where the natural features of the land are maintained to the greatest extent possible.
> The model ordinance for urban areas will define a Traditional Neighborhood Development [as] a compact mixed-use neighborhood where residential, commercial, and civic buildings are within close proximity to each other.[331]

By January 1, 2002, every city or village (but not town) of over 12,500 population will be required to enact the traditional neighborhood model ordinance but not to "map" or apply it to its land. This will by like looking without kissing. No electricity yet. The legislature deliberately stopped short of mandating that communities apply Smart Growth principles. That was wise. How much of the public wants small lots? Though the demand is small today, it will grow substantially as seventy-seven million Baby Boomers retire, many of whom will probably seek condos and small lots in traditional urban settings, including those where transportation alternatives are available.

Instead, the act chose the carrot over the stick. It provides a to-be-quantified financial incentive for communities to adopt *and implement* either or both Smart Growth ordinances. The Secretaries of Administration and of Revenue will draft the details of a Smart Growth Dividend Aid Program by early 2001 and how the legislature should fund it two years later. No one knows whether legislative funding will be generous or skimpy. In any event, municipalities will compete for dividend grants from the state. Competing applicants will receive, according to the future Smart Growth Dividend Program, "credits" from the Wisconsin Land Council in the Department of Administration. That future program will include two far-reaching features mandated by the act. Possibly they are too ambitious. One credit will be awarded for each housing unit sold or rented in the prior year which occupies a lot no larger than one quarter of an acre, and for each new housing unit that is sold at less than 80 percent of the median sale price for new homes in the county.[332] Surely the median sale price in Milwaukee County will be too low to be politically acceptable in most municipalities in the county.

No one knows whether future legislatures will appropriate more than a token sum for Smart Growth dividends. One can guess it will not be very large because the legislature appropriated only $2.5 million to help municipalities pay for mandated comprehensive planning, which may be only one fifth of annual local planning costs, according to one ball-park estimate.[333] No one knows, either, whether the credit system for Smart Growth dividends will be realistic, too idealistic, or just plain soapbox. Nevertheless, backers were enthusiastic. Brian Burke is an articulate State Senator from Milwaukee and co-chair of the powerful Joint Finance Committee, whose championship of Smart Growth got it added to the Comprehensive Planning revision. At passage, Burke greeted the new Millennium by saying:

> Across the country the tide has turned with people in
> the suburbs and exurban areas realizing that sprawl
> hurts everyone.[334]

Idealists may regret that the act is only a limited step forward. However, taking only a small step was fortunate. Sound legislative change can come incrementally as public support materializes. The act's authors hope to strengthen it by future

220

legislation. Meanwhile, certainly the existence of comprehensive plans and model Smart Growth ordinance will provide a convenient platform for educating local governments, builders and the public.

In the end, the new home buyer's liking for compact development will more than anything else determine the extent that the new ideas of Smart Growth and New Urbanism are put into practice. Perhaps local units will resist allowing Smart Growth development. If so, possibly emerging public support could remove such a roadblock. If so, how can that happen??

Chapter 25

What Can and Should We Do About Sprawl?

Yes, the legislature in 1999 did take a first hesitant step toward improving local government's planning process and nudging or at least allowing Smart Growth development. What's next? Further incremental steps for Smart Growth implementation, such as larger state financial incentives or actual mandates? Some more radical approach toward controlling sprawl than Smart Growth? Something more moderate? Or dismiss Smart Growth as a dream of visionaries and builders?

No one knows the answers yet. This is a complex field in which people's preferences for autos and homes with large lot sizes play a larger role than government incentives or regulations. Fashion in home design and lot sizes is often as unpredictable and uncontrollable as the current length of women's skirts. Remember when split-level homes were the vogue? To answer these questions about how to control sprawl, we first need to examine whether we can moderate the third major factor contributing to sprawl.

I refer to the decentralization of land use planning and decision making. Wisconsin's 72 counties, 190 cities, 395 villages, and 1,265 towns make land use decisions with almost no state oversight. As of 1998, only 29 percent of all Wisconsin local government had a land use plan, and some of them were outdated.[335] Further, until the 1999 Comprehensive Planning Act, the state provided virtually no guidelines for local governments, excepting the 1968 floodplain zoning mandate. As we have seen, this decentralization made possible many undesirable consequences: balkanized land use policies in metropolitan areas, driven by competition for new tax revenues; destruction of valuable natural resources; low-density development that squandered land, driving people farther out from cities, and so on.

Radical solutions to sprawl have been tried in other cities. Looking at their root causes and results is instructive. The most extreme approach forbids growth beyond a prescribed outer boundary. Such a remedy apparently succeeded in Paris, France, since 1945, and

222

probably, in Portland, Oregon, since 1973. More recently and less radically, two states empowered regional governments to act. Georgia created a new one in Atlanta. Minnesota gave an existing *advisory* regional government new powers. In each case the state transferred to the regional government certain formerly local land use decision-making powers (the stick) plus a bucket of state revenues (the carrot).

Specifically, Minnesota in 1997 gave the long-established seven-county Metropolitan Council in the Twin Cities area the power to withhold $650 million in state transportation and sewage funds from communities that did not comply with its advisory plans. The council had ambitious anti-sprawl objectives. It sought greater housing density (7,500 square feet per homesite, or one-sixth of an acre) and had started a $446 million light rail system, one half of which will be paid for out of federal funds.[336]

In 1999, Georgia created a Central Georgia Regional Transportation Authority (for greater Atlanta) with all fifteen commissioners appointed by a new governor who championed the legislation. The Authority has power to veto shopping malls in areas that are over-congested or lack adequate transportation, to build rail and bus systems, and to withhold state transportation funds until a county complies with its recommendations.[337] A knowledgeable observer predicted that "the Authority will decree an expansion of mass transit, decrease residential development in some outer counties, and smile on pedestrian-friendly mixed use development in the city."[338]

Other reforms were more moderate. Several states used state funds to advance particular anti-sprawl objectives, such as buying and preserving green space. New Jersey did that. Their residents in forty-three cities and six counties voted 2 to 1 to increase taxes to buy and preserve open space.[339] Connecticut and Massachusetts authorized large bond issues to buy green space. By 1998, over one hundred counties and local governments in the United States had sought voter approval for tax increases or bonds to buy undeveloped land and curb urban sprawl.[340] Going down that path, Wisconsin, in 1999, doubled the size of its fund (the Stewardship Fund) for purchasing land costing up to a total of $460 million over ten years.

Back in 1971, Minnesota enacted a complex pooling of resources for the Twin Cities region. It legislated that 40 percent of the growth in industrial and commercial tax revenues above the 1971 total received by any one municipality within the Twin Cities region would be shared with all other municipalities in that region.

However, the act was flawed. It was not needs-based. Wealthy residential communities could share in the bounty and poorer ones contribute to it. Nevertheless the concept has been much praised by those liking the concept of pooling resources. Our SEWRPC sprawl committee in 1993 recommended that such a pooling of resources approach be explored for the Milwaukee region,[341] but nothing came of it. Despite persistent efforts by the usually persuasive J. Michael Mooney of our committee, we could not obtain funding for a study to quantify the advantages of this concept. One could not effectively champion an idea without the hard facts.

Significantly, all the more radical state measures, except for those in Paris and to a lesser extent Portland, Oregon, came about because the public experienced the politically unacceptable consequences of sprawl, particularly extreme traffic congestion and smog. Milwaukee does not yet suffer and may never suffer such extreme adverse consequences. Therefore, we lack that forceful incentive to make big changes. We have been spared because our region's population has grown by a puny 12.7 percent in the past thirty-eight years compared to the Twin Cities' seven-county growth of 67 percent in the same period[342] and the Atlanta region's 100 percent growth over thirty years.[343] As Tom Ament, the low-key and very practical Milwaukee County Executive said to me in January 2000:

> After I visit Los Angeles and New York and come back
> here, I say "What traffic congestion?"

Yet, many national planners and writers enviously cite Paris and Portland as successful examples of avoiding sprawl by fencing it in. That is largely true. Examining Paris and Portland reveals many impressive results plus two factors which suggest these models would not fit Wisconsin. First, each area provided a growth boundary *before or largely before* the post-war's rapid sprawl got started. Sprawl has already spread across the Milwaukee region's landscape. Second, the economy, culture, and political forces in France and Oregon welcomed a single decision-maker in metropolitan land use decisions. In France it was the national government; in Portland it was Metro, a specially chartered metropolitan government for the Portland area. Here is what happened and why.

The contrast between development patterns around Paris and American cities is striking. From the Eiffel Tower you can see farmland on the outskirts of Paris; from the Empire State building on a clear day you can see only a thicket of buildings spilling over state lines. From the air the differences are equally spectacular. One observer says:

> One minute and a half before the plane lands in Paris you are over the countryside. But in the U.S., even if you're landing in Columbus, Ohio, you're over suburbia for fifteen minutes.[344]

The City of Chicago uses five times the space Paris requires to house approximately the same population (2.8 million versus 2.2 million). Metropolitan Chicago, with 7.8 million people in nine Illinois counties, consumes seven times as much land as is needed to jam 9.5 million French people into Paris and its suburbs. Compacting is key. A tight government-created growth perimeter in Paris bottles up American-type sprawl. However, the average Parisian family lives in cramped quarters not acceptable to Americans. When I was squeezed into a one or two passenger elevator serving supposedly posh apartments near the Arc de Triomphe in Paris, I knew Parisian apartments are too small for Americans.

The stark contrast between metropolitan Chicago's diverse sprawl and metropolitan Paris's compactness has deep roots. They reflect decades – even centuries – of social, political, and economic policies. Europe is not immune to population growth requiring more homes. Yet Europeans contain sprawl because their values differ sharply from ours. They tolerate proximity to others more than we with our love of open space. Central governments in Europe strongly control land development, while in America, state governments decentralize that power to hundreds of local municipalities, which splinter our metropolitan regions.

Britain has a national planning policy. Development rights have been effectively abolished.[345] In America they are cherished and protected from strong government controls, federal, state, or local.[346] In France, the French government has complete control over development around Paris.[347] European governments use their power both to curtail outward development and to give citizens substantial incentives to be satisfied with living closer to each other in the city.

Europe's tax policies make homes and cars far more costly than in the United States. The registration cost of a new car in the Netherlands is nine times the average cost in the United States. Unleaded gasoline in early 2000 cost $4.00 per gallon in Europe against an average of $1.28 at home.[348] By July 2000 gasoline cost $5.50 per gallon in Great Britain and $3.70 in France. The differences stem from far higher European taxes. In France, gas taxes eat up 70 percent of the price of gasoline; in the United States, 25 percent.[349] Our national government's income tax policies subsidize home purchases by allowing mortgage interest to be deducted in computing taxable income. This tax policy has no European counterpart. It has been estimated to reduce American urban density by 15 percent.[350]

European governments allocate half of their national transportation budgets to mass transit. This enabled Paris, for example, to provide mass transit throughout its metropolitan region. John Norquist can only dream of that. In contrast, Congress spends five times as much on highways as on mass transit.[351] Taxes on income and heating fuel are much higher in Europe. Cumulatively, all these European tax policies encourage their upper middle class to live in apartments or small homes instead of the spacious home of three bedrooms and a family room for Americans of comparable income.

Further, land is expensive in Europe and cheap in America. French farmers have little economic incentive to sell their land. France zealously protects their income by generous subsidies and import quotas. France wants its landscape farmed. In America, farmers near cities often favor zoning to allow their land to be developed, hoping to sell and retire on the proceeds.

Only America's most radical, comprehensive effort to control sprawl somewhat resembles that of Paris. It is Portland's widely acclaimed program for controlling sprawl. Critics even dubbed Portland "the headquarters for a reaction against anything goes development."[352]

A unique combination of political forces gave birth to Portland's effort. In 1973, the Oregon legislature, with significant assistance from a popular Republican governor, Tom McCall, enacted a Land Use Law requiring all 257 Oregon municipalities to establish outer boundaries for their future growth. Environmentalists and agriculture (the state's dominant political force) wanted to protect farm and forest from urbanization. Six years later, Portland's leaders created a directly elected metropolitan government (Metro) to manage growth through strong land use planning.

Portland also heavily funded a mass transit system that included light rail. Metro and the mass transit agency working together took three drastic actions.

In 1979, Metro, as required by state law, established an urban growth boundary, embracing by 1999 1.3 million people (only 0.5 million in Portland itself), and 320 square miles spread over three counties and 24 cities. That's thirty percent larger than the area of Milwaukee County but much smaller than our four-county Standard Metropolitan Statistical Area (SMSA) with its comparable population of 1.45 million people. Beyond Metro's boundary, which was moved slightly outward in the intervening twenty years, green space was to be preserved by zoning against development. Inside the boundary, Portland encouraged compact development by building an expensive light rail system and planning (through zoning and other measures) for high-density growth within walking distance of rail or a bus.[353]

Portland's planning achieved much. From 1979 to 1997 as the population expanded into allowable areas, the average lot size shrank from 13,000 square feet (0.3 acre) to 7,400 (one-sixth of an acre, typically 65 x 114 feet. The planners wanted to achieve a 5,700-square-foot average (one-eighth acre or 57 x 100 feet) through increased use of row houses, townhouses, and condominiums. However, squeezing a growing population into a compact area raised housing prices as did Portland's emerging from a local recession in the eighties into prosperity in the nineties. A single family lot costing $15,000 in 1991 rose to $60,000 by 1999.[354] A median single family home costing $64,000 in 1979 rose to $156,900 in 1999, a rise of 145 percent.[355]

According to a *Washington Post* story in 1997,[356] Portland also developed a vibrant downtown with strong shopping and entertainment districts and fashionable residential districts. Today, Portland is beautiful but, some say, expensive. It is blessed by views of Mount Hood and two rivers, the Willamette, which cuts through downtown and along whose banks Portland replaced a freeway with a grassy park, and the Columbia, which separates Oregon from the State of Washington.

Land had become so scarce by 1999 that Washington County, one of three counties in the Metro area, imposed a unique condition on the expansion of an Intel factory. Instead of unconditionally welcoming a pollution-free chip-making facility with high-paying jobs, the county made Intel, its largest employer, agree to accept a potential $1,000 fine for each full-time manufacturing employee it hired over 1,000.[357]

Portland's many achievements, like light rail and higher densities, did not make the automobile go away. Far from it. The number of vehicles increased more rapidly than the population. Vehicle miles went up 6 percent a year, whereas growth within the growth area grew through 1993 by only 70 percent of the planned densities.[358] According to the transit agency, only 3.6 percent of all trips and 7 percent of all work trips by 1993 were taken by transit, compared with as against 10 and 17 percent, respectively, in nearby Vancouver, British Columbia. In an area one-third more dense than Portland, Vancouver has three times the transit ridership, and virtually no freeways.

Nor was the growth boundary leakproof, another disappointment. The fastest-growing part of metropolitan Portland is in Clark County across the Columbia River in the State of Washington, where Oregon's land use law does not apply.

An outside transportation critic suggested in 1995 that Portland's effort to lessen automobile usage through compact transit-oriented development

> unintentionally demonstrated the limits of large investments in transit to influence traffic patterns.[359]

Local critics say that putting government officials in the position of picking winners and losers in the economy is an impossible task – it presumes they know exactly where urban development should be. But supporters like 1000 Friends of Oregon accurately reply: government is already socially engineering when it locates freeway interchanges on the metropolitan fringe, thereby undermining property values in the central city, or requires large lot sizes in the suburbs, thereby keeping affordable housing out. On the whole Portland's strong controls to foster compact development have been popular locally and widely praised nationally.

I conclude that Wisconsin should not and will not authorize or mandate a growth boundary around Milwaukee's metropolitan area, as Oregon did in Portland. Two reasons. Too late geographically. The horse is already out of the barn. Also, such a proposal is too radical culturally and politically.

If Portland and Paris do not offer models for Wisconsin, what, then, can and should Wisconsin do to moderate at least some of sprawl's consequences? I suggest we pursue an array of measures, but not all at one time. That strategy would deservedly risk defeat. A particular remedy should be pursued only when political support starts to emerge, like an early crocus breaking through the snow. Our sprawl committee was woefully politically premature in 1993 as well as already geographically late.

Implementing Smart Growth should be pushed first. The new coalition championing Smart Growth (primarily 1,000 Friends of Wisconsin and realtors) can bring about more compact open-space-conserving subdivisions. Progress could unfold in this manner. Builders, where permitted, can develop homes in Smart Growth subdivisions, urban or rural. Two new ones, "Cherokee Pointe" in Milwaukee, and "Dahlmann Village" in the Village of Jackson, are examples. The public can buy. Or not buy. If communities resist permitting Smart Growth layouts, then public support, if it develops, can change their minds or obtain further legislative help. Such assistance could be through carefully tailored fiscal incentives, or mandates. Incentives work better than mandates because they acknowledge the popular primacy of local control while cajoling results favored by state policy. The legislature did, after all, successfully mandate flood plain zoning in 1968 and a new basis for assessing prime farmland (enacted in 1995, to be fully phased in by 2007).[360]

In the end, more compact subdivisions will probably be accepted in a minority of suburban municipalities. If so, regional residents will benefit by having choices of lot sizes and neighborhoods. If Smart Growth catches on substantially, many indirect benefits will accrue, such as tax savings through lower infrastructure costs.

Still other adverse consequences of sprawl may yet need remedying, such as development too far out or in the wrong place, judged by the region's best interests. Woodlands in general could be protected by adopting Senator Risser's 1999 bill refining SEWRPC's 1993 recommendation that Wisconsin require a five acre minimum density for development in what the DNR might designate as prime woodland. Risser plans to reintroduce his bill in 2001. Activists like 1000 Friends of Wisconsin support it. Septic tank regulations[361] should be modified if not eventually struck down by the current court challenge. A desirable modification could defer their application until local government has had ample time to adopt zoning and subdivision regulations for the fringe areas that would become developable under the relaxed septic tank rules.

DNR staff in 2000 is developing a far-sighted proposal to preserve a "heritage area" of over 21,000 acres of woodland, wetlands, and farmland along the northern branch of the Milwaukee River near Fredonia. Preservation would be accomplished by outright purchase or conservation easements by the DNR in cooperation with farm organizations, municipalities and land trusts.[362]

However, if Smart Growth subdivisions grow (where wanted), if woodlands are protected, and if the radical new septic tank rules disappear or are modified,[363] a major engine for sprawl would remain: highly decentralized land use and transportation decision-making. At present, there is no effective popular support for transferring or moderating local government powers. The same was true forty odd years ago. It is enlightening to recall what the Metropolitan Study Commission (Metro) did in 1958-1961 when confronted with, on the one hand, steadily increasing uncoordinated local actions, and, on the other, a lack of public support for radical change. As Chapter 5 notes Metro recommended only moderate changes, but, more importantly, predicted that a growing urbanization might require radical reforms in the distant future, say 2000. Specifically, Metro, in 1959 rejected all possible reorganization alternatives to cross-boundary problems: consolidation of the City of Milwaukee and all eighteen Milwaukee County suburbs; consolidation of Milwaukee County and City; and a federated Metropolitan government like Toronto's or Miami's.

Instead, Metro in 1959 preferred advisory regional planning as a milder method for persuading local governments to coordinate their local land use and transportation policies. SEWRPC's founders hoped or assumed – and the legislature apparently agreed – that local governments would follow SEWRPC advice on land use, transportation, and water pollution matter. They reasoned that almost certainly the bigger-picture federal and state transportation and water pollution authorities would do so. They would set a pattern. Also, the state and federal governments might use their funds and regulations to encourage local compliance. Although local government did follow SEWRPC's advice on many matters, we noted on pages 196, 197, 204 and 205, that they largely ignored key SEWRPC recommendations for moderating sprawl – particularly zoning for smaller residential lots.

To be sure, one highly effective effort to control sprawl bore fruit. It originated with coordination by three big-picture agencies. The U.S. Environmental Protection Act required and funded SEWRPC to develop a regional Water Quality Management Program on condition that Wisconsin authorize an agency (which would be the DNR) with authority to enforce such a plan. The plan, when developed, advised that low-volume local sewage treatment plants be abandoned in favor of larger and more efficient regional treatment plants (like the MMSD's). Five or six local plants were accordingly abandoned. The plan, further, advised that local sewage systems should not extend mains beyond their rational service area or outer growth boundaries. The DNR agreed, and such extensions have been denied ever since.[364]

This successful anti-sprawl precedent could be the model for a similar measure. The legislature could authorize the DNR to veto septic tank installations on land where SEWRPC (or some other regional planning commission elsewhere in the state) recommends they would be inconsistent with an extension of the region's federally funded and state approved Water Quality Plan. In this way Wisconsin could build growth boundaries around multiple rational service centers in a metropolitan region rather than around one contiguous central area as in Portland. Naturally, such a proposal would be vigorously opposed by builders and many outlying local governments. Possibly a political coalition of further-in municipalities led by the likes of Mayor Norquist and Mayor Kathryn Bloomberg of Brookfield could carry the day. It is true the two mayors scarcely speak to each other because of recent sewer wars and transportation battles. However, politics can make strange bedfellows. (Builders and environmentalists surprisingly and effectively united for Smart Growth in 1999.) And Kate Bloomberg once publicly suggested the state slow down growth west of Brookfield to relieve her city of the increasing through traffic. My suggestion of a coalition is a more practical method to achieve her goal. If not, sprawl on the outer fringe will continue.

The present difficulty of obtaining support for anti-sprawl measures recalls Metro's long forgotten concern that advisory regionally planning might not in the long run be all that was needed. Two years after Metro recommended advisory regional planning in 1959 it hedged its bets. In its farewell message in 1961 Metro predicted that the *future* (say the year 2000?) might require changes in the structure of government, such as: the transfer of single government functions to Milwaukee County or the state, the county contracting to serve areas outside its borders, or even the consolidation of Milwaukee County with a neighboring county.

Metro warned:

> In many respects...it is already true that the metropolitan community transcends the boundaries of Milwaukee County....The planning of major highways, sewage disposal facilities, major parks, and other area-wide functions cannot stop at the county line.
> Moreover, as time goes on, and as the effects of urbanization spread still further, and as more and more territory becomes increasingly interdependent, the County will no longer be the logical service area for a number of functions.[365]

As if to twist the tiger's tail, Metro poignantly continued: "Waukesha County, in fact, was a part of Milwaukee County until separated by statute in 1846."

Next, Metro advised that Milwaukee County contract with neighboring counties or municipalities to mitigate the effects of governmental problems spilling over its boundaries, but recommended that:

> If these [contract] devices prove to be insufficient or *ineffectual,* serious consideration [should] be given to legislation changing the boundaries of counties in this part of the state in an attempt to achieve greater correspondence between the county boundaries and logical service areas....(emphasis added) [366]

Metro's prediction of future "ineffectual" efforts to solve cross-boundary problems accurately characterized what happened in the mid-1990s. As we saw, Milwaukee County, Waukesha County, and the City of Milwaukee deadlocked over how to relieve growing traffic congestion on the East-West corridor. (See Chapter 14.) Yet, Metro's 1961 suggestion of changes in governmental powers or boundaries, even if intellectually tenable today, totally lacks current political support. Of course, local government in 2000 will resist conceivable new suggestions for structural change as fiercely as it opposed the ones considered in 1959-1961. Dan Finley, the forceful Waukesha County Executive, spoke bluntly in 1997: "Regional government is an idea whose time will never come."[367]

I conclude that only a future crisis would foster public support for some form of regional government, possibly similar to those of Atlanta and the Twin Cities. Is some lesser reorganization desirable and feasible? Possibly, but not likely. One concept might be for the City and County of Milwaukee to consolidate. Such a merger has happened elsewhere between a city and its surrounding county: Indianapolis (in the 1950s) and more recently Charlotte, North Carolina. The pooling of county and city financial resources greatly strengthened the Charlotte school system, helping the city become attractive and grow.[368]

If anything is conceivably possible, the ambitious politicos Norquist and Finley need to make a deal. They could each back the consolidation of Milwaukee and Waukesha counties. They could claim it as their own idea, even though Metro first suggested it in 1961. Then one could become governor; the other, county executive of the expanded county. I am joking, of course. I thought of this scenario before Norquist's leadership potential declined after a former city employee filed a sexual harassment complaint filed against him and the City of Milwaukee in December 2000.

Have we learned anything? Probably three things. First, sprawl, as noted in Chapter 23, is more irresistible and beneficial than critics concede. Second, certain measures to lessen particular adverse consequences of sprawl are desirable and possible. Third, they are most likely to be adopted if pursued incrementally and after first building public support.

On the whole, the greater Milwaukee area is a wonderful place in which to work and live. We have survived the last fifty years of growing pains. Probably Milwaukee will never have to endure the far greater ones now facing more rapidly growing areas in America, such as Atlanta and the Twin Cities.

Timeline

1950-1957	Seven Milwaukee County towns all absorbed by nearby municipalities and eight new ones which are formed.
1952	City of Milwaukee starts 20-mile expressway system within the City.
1953	Milwaukee County takes over design and construction of Expressways.
1953	Boston Braves baseball team becomes Milwaukee Braves.
1954	City of Brookfield incorporates.
1956	Town of Granville votes to consolidate with City of Milwaukee, superseding invalid prior annexation of two-thirds of the Town to the Village of Brown Deer.
1957-1861	Metropolitan Study Commission recommends creation of Southeastern Wisconsin Regional Planning Commission (SEWRPC) among twenty-five suggestions for improving the efficiency of local government.
1957	City of Mequon incorporates.
10/10/57	Milwaukee Braves defeat New York Yankees for World Championship.
1960	Governor Nelson creates Southeastern Wisconsin Regional Planning Commission.
1960	City of Milwaukee population peaks at 741,324; thereafter declines, contributing to urban sprawl.
1965	SEWRPC completes regional advisory land use transportation plan including a 112-mile Milwaukee County freeway system.
1965	Braves leave Milwaukee for Atlanta.
1966	U.S., Wisconsin, and Milwaukee County governments approve SEWRPC plan.

1967	City's race riots kill four, injure 100; Father James Groppi leads marches for open housing.
1967	City advisory referendum favors by 2 to 1 building proposed freeway through Juneau park to connect with Hoan Harbor Bridge (Downtown Loop Closure).
1968	Marquette Interchange completed, linking I-94 and I-43.
1968	Activist Ted Seaver forms coalition opposing further freeway construction.
1970	Seattle Pilots baseball team becomes Milwaukee Brewers.
1971	SEWRPC Milwaukee River Watershed advisory committee recommends flood plain zoning to lessen future flood damage, and the construction of deep tunnels by the Milwaukee Metropolitan Sewerage Commission to reduce water pollution.
1972	U.S. District Court enjoins construction of Park Freeway West paralleling North Avenue west from I-43 to proposed Stadium North Freeway.
1972	Many freeway opponents are elected to state legislature and Milwaukee County Board of Supervisors.
1972	State of Illinois sues Milwaukee and MMSD for pollution of Lake Michigan by intermittent discharge of raw and partially treated sewage.
1974	Anti-freeway activist John Norquist, 25, is elected to Wisconsin Assembly.
1974	Milwaukee County advisory referendum approves construction of five planned freeways (17 miles).
1977	Of the five, only the short Airport Spur is ever built. Wisconsin, Milwaukee County and SEWRPC abandon further freeways.
5/25/1977	Dane County Circuit Court enters agreed order, in litigation between the State of Wisconsin and the MMSD, requiring the modernization of the sewer system at an ultimate cost of over $2 billion.

11/15/77	In Illinois suit, U.S. District Court in Chicago orders MMSD to build additional improvements above those ordered by the State of Wisconsin, later estimated to cost an additional billion dollars.
1981	U.S. Supreme Court nullifies legal basis for U.S. District Court's 1977 order that MMSD provide advanced waste treatment and prevent overflows more often than once in 100 years.
1982	Legislature, after mediation by Greater Milwaukee Committee of a deadlocked fight over the governance of MMSD, slightly modifies Milwaukee's control of the governing board.
Dec. 1982	Start of the sewer wars. Seven out-of-County municipalities sue MMSD to block efforts to expand its jurisdiction to include them.
8/31/84	Seven municipalities outside Milwaukee County decline to pay their share of the capital cost of the court-ordered MMSD improvements based on equalized property value and instead pay on the less-expensive volumetric (Fair Liquidation of Waste) (FLOW) basis.
1/28/91	Wisconsin Public Service Commission upholds reasonableness of MMSD's capital (construction) charges based on equalized property value.
1993	17 miles of deep tunnels (up to 300 feet below Milwaukee) completed by MMSD providing 400 million gallons storage capacity for excess sewer flows.
1993	SEWRPC advisory committee finds scattered development (sprawl) has occurred out of sync with the 1965 land use plan and suggests measures to lessen sprawl. State and local governments give cool reception to the recommendations.
6/22/94	Wisconsin Court of Appeals affirms PSC's 1991 ruling upholding MMSD charges based on property values.

1996	Wisconsin Department of Transportation consultants recommend 10 alternatives for improving transportation on East-West Corridor (I-94 from downtown Milwaukee to mid-Waukesha County). These include improving bus service, adding multi-vehicle lanes to I-94, and building a 17-mile light rail system within Milwaukee County.
1996-1997	State, Waukesha County, Milwaukee County, and the City of Milwaukee disagree on a preferred solution. Stalemate results.
Oct. 1996	Suing municipalities and MMSD settle sewer wars lawsuit. Municipalities pay $140 million for underpayments between 1985 and 1996.
April 1999	Governor Thompson, Milwaukee County Executive Ament, and Mayor Norquist agree on demolishing the Park Freeway East stub in a larger agreement allocating $241 million of U.S. funds originally appropriated for stalemated East-West corridor solutions.
Oct. 1999	Legislature passes Comprehensive Planning Act to improve planning by local governments and moderating sprawl through encouraging Smart Growth policies (more compact growth; better preservation of green space).
1997-2000	Heavy rainstorms caused sewer back-ups into basements; some suburbs bypass untreated sewage; MMSD also bypasses; questions arise about responsibility for these actions; no clear public consensus on solutions.
2000	City of Milwaukee population drops to 596,974.

Index to Maps

Maps are located after page 151.

Index to Appendices

Appendix A
(See pages 7, 196)

PRODUCTS & NUMBER OF EMPLOYEES OF
LARGER MILWAUKEE MANUFACTURERS

(Compilation by author from the *Classified Directory
of Wisconsin Manufacturers, 1951-52*)

Name of Company (Milwaukee County only)	Employees	Products, with Examples of Customers in Italics
	Brewers	
Jos. Schlitz Brewing Co.	4,000	Beer
Pabst Brewing Co.	1,900	Beer
Miller Brewing Co.	1,850	Beer
The Blatz Brewery	1,408	Beer
Red Star Yeast	655	Yeast
	Electrical Controls	
Cutler-Hammer	4,100	Electric motor controls, safety switches, appliance switches
Allen-Bradley	3,688	Electric control apparatus, radio parts
Square D	1,485	Electric motor controls, starters and contractors; special control panels; push buttons, limit switches
Line Material	770	Fuses and cutouts, street lighting arresters, capacitors, pole line hardware, transformers

Engines

Briggs and Stratton	2,600	Small, air-cooled engines; auto locks; ignition switches
Harley-Davidson	2,275	Motorcycles
Louis Allis Co.	1,585	Electric motors and generators
Evinrude Motors	565	Outboard motors

Food

Plankinton Packing	1,400	Meat and meat products
The Borden Co., Gridley Division	755	Fluid milk, ice cream, buttermilk, butter

Foundries & Welding

A. O. Smith	9,300	Large diameter pipe, automotive frames, pressure vessels, water heaters, home heating boilers (*Struts for B-17 "Flying Fortress" Bombers in WW II*)

Ladish	3,675	Forged flanges, seamless pipe fittings, forged steel fittings, custom forgings, high density alloy forgings, aircraft forgings
Globe Steel Tubes	942	Seamless steel tubing, seamless and welded stainless steel tubing, welted fittings
Inland Steel Products	894	Metal roofing, downspout gutter and accessory roofing products, metal lathe products
Grede Foundries	850	Castings; gray iron, alloy iron, carbon and alloy steel; home appliance automotive, hardware
Ampco	666	Sand castings, bronze centrifugal castings, extruded products: rod, tube, shapes

Fuel

Milwaukee Solvay Coke	577	Coke (foundry, domestic and industrial), gas, tar, ammoniacal liquor
Allis-Chalmers	16,674	Electrical; equipment tractors; turbines (*Hoover Dam*); farm machinery; condensers; pumps; milling and mining machinery

International Harvester	6,000	Diesel and gas engine parts, agricultural implements
Harnischfeger	4,025	Overhead traveling cranes; power excavators; hoists; welding equipment
Bucyrus-Erie	2,500	Power shovels; bulldozers, scrapers, oil and water well drills, dredges, railway cranes, hydraulic truck cranes (*provided 90% of the equipment for digging the Panama Canal*)
Nordberg	2,460	Diesel engines, rock and ore crushers, railway equipment,
The Heil Co.	2,400	Hydraulic dump bodies, oil and gasoline transport tanks, dairy and beverage bottle washers, beer pasteurizers
Chain Belt	2,267	Chain, concrete mixers, food processing equipment, paving machinery, sewage disposal equipment (*made Long Tom guns in WW II*)

Falk Corporation	2,100	Speed reducers, motor reducers, flexible couplings, special and heavy gear drives, marine turbine and diesel engine gear drives and clutches, propellors (*SS United States)*
Kearney and Trecker	1,662	Milling machines, pressure boring machines, cutter grinder, drill presses, table saws, band saws
Perfex Corporation	1,135	Automatic temperature controls for heating systems, refrigeration and air conditioning systems, and automatic controls for domestic appliances
Koehring Co.	1,000	Power shovels, power cranes, pavers, mixers, dumpsters, grey iron foundry
Pressed Steel Tank	1,000	Liquified petroleum gas cylinders, compressed gas cylinders, removable head barrels and drums, containers
A-P Controls Corp	935	Oil heating controls; refrigeration valves; air conditioning valves

Geuder, Paescke & Frey Co.	900	Deep drawn stampings, metal ironing tables, steel shipping containers, galvanized
Johnson Service Co.	650	Automatic temperature and humidity control systems
Lindeman & Holverson	600	Electric ranges and water heaters, oil stoves and ranges, oil
Cleaver Brooks Co.	575	Tank car heaters, commercial and industrial oil burners, steam generators, distillation units, boosters
Rockwell Manufacturing Co.	570	Power tools, wood and metal working, saws, drill presses, joiners, planers, grinders,
Mueller Furnace	500	Gas, oil and coal furnaces, boilers, fans, fittings
Badger Meter Mfg. Co.	470	Water meters, meter testers, meter testing yokes

Leather

Weyenberg Shoe Co.	1,990	Men's dress and work shoes; juvenile shoes
Nunn-Bush Shoe Co.	1,424	Men's dress shoes
A. F. Gallun	935	Calf & pigskin leathers
Albert Trostel and Sons	850	Leather for shoes, handbags, gloves; leather oil seals
Fred Osterman Co.	650	Leather and cloth heavy outer wear, leather gloves & mittens

Paper

Hummel and Downing Co. (Div. Of Cornell Paper Products)	1,397	Specialty paperboards, corrugated and solid fibre containers, folding cartons, cleated fibre cases, laundry and garment boxes
A. Geo. Schulz	537	Set-up paper boxes, transparent boxes, printed folding cartons, corrugated

Textiles

Phoenix Hosiery	2,000	Men's, women's, children's hosiery, full-fashioned hosiery,
Junior House	530	Junior and misses' dresses, skirts, blouses, sunsuits, bathing suits, playsuits

1951 EMPLOYMENT BY CATEGORIES OF MAJOR MILWAUKEE MANUFACTURERS

Category of Industry	Employees	Percent of Total
Metal Bending		
Electrical Controls	10,043	
Engines	7,820	
Foundries & Welding	16,327	
Heavy Machinery	48,473	
Total Metal Bending	82,613	78.8
Food and Beverage		
Brewing (and yeast)	9,813	9.4
Food	2,195	
Total Food and Beverage	12,008	
Miscellaneous		
Leather	5,849	
Textiles	2,500	
Paper	1,934	
Total Miscellaneous	10,283	
Grand Total	104,903	100.0

Appendix B
(See p. 24)

Milwaukee County

Shifts in Population and Area
By Municipality, 1950-1960

(Based on statistics provided by SEWRPC)

Cities Existing in 1950	Population 1950	Population 1960	Area in Square Miles 1950	Area in Square Miles 1960	% of County Area 1950	% of County Area 1960
Milwaukee	637,392	741,324	51.8	91.7	21.5	38.1
West Allis	42,959	68,157	4.5	11.4	1.9	4.7
Wauwa-tosa	33,324	56,923	4.1	13.1	1.7	5.4
South Milwaukee	12,855	20,307	4.3	4.8	1.8	2.0
Cudahy	12,182	17,975	1.9	4.8	0.8	2.0
Villages Existing in 1950						
Shorewood	16,199	15,990	1.6	1.6	0.7	0.7
Whitefish Bay	14,665	18,390	2.1	2.1	0.9	0.9
West Milwaukee	5,429	5,043	0.7	1.1	0.3	0.5
Greendale	2,752	6,843	5.6	5.6	2.3	2.3
Fox Point	2,585	7,315	2.1	2.8	0.9	1.2
River Hills	567	1,257	4.2	5.1	1.8	2.1
TOTALS	708,909	959,524	82.9	144.1	34.5	59.9

These towns disappeared between 1950 & 1960	Population 1950	Population 1960	Area in Square Miles 1950	Area in Square Miles 1960	% of County Area 1950	% of County Area 1960
Wauwatosa	23,941		14.1		5.9	
Greenfield	20,907		25.5		10.6	
Lake	18,956		14.8		6.2	
Granville	11,784		28.7		11.9	
Milwaukee	5,857		9.8		4.1	
Oak Creek	4,807		29.3		12.1	
Franklin	3,886		35.5		14.7	
TOTALS	90,138		157.7		65.5	

Cities created after 1950	Year Inc.	Population 1960	Area in Square Miles 1950	Area in Square Miles 1960	% of County Area 1950	% of County Area 1960
Greenfield	(1957)	17,636	NA	11.1	NA	4.6
St. Francis	(1951)	10,065	NA	2.6	NA	1.1
Franklin	(1956)	10,006	NA	34.4	NA	14.2
Glendale	(1960)	9,537	NA	5.7	NA	2.4
Oak Creek	(1955)	9,372	NA	28.4	NA	11.8
TOTALS		**56,616**		**82.2**		**34.1**
Villages created after 1950	**Year Inc.**					
Brown Deer [370]	(1955)	11,280	NA	8.8	NA	3.7
Hales Corners	(1952)	5,549	NA	3.2	NA	1.3
Bayside	(1953)	3,078	NA	2.3	NA	1.0
TOTALS		**19,907**		**14.3**		**6.0**
TOTALS for New Cities & Villages		**76,523**		**96.5**		**40.1**

Appendix C

(See page 24)

Shifts in Population and Area by Classifications of Municipalities

Milwaukee County

(Based on statistics provided by SEWRPC)

Community	Population 1950	Population 1960	Area in Square Miles 1950	Area in Square Miles 1960	% of County Area 1950	% of County Area 1960
Milwaukee	637,392	741,324	51.8	91.7	21.5	37.7
10 other cities & villages	143,517	218,200	31.1	52.4	12.9	21.8
Total	**780,909**	**959,524**	**82.9**	**144.1**	**34.4**	**59.5**
7 towns	90,138	NA	157.7	NA	66.4	NA
8 new villages & cities [371]	NA	76,523	NA	96.5	NA	40.2
TOTAL	**871,047**	**1,036,047**	**240.6**	**240.6**		

Appendix D
(See page 37)

Original Fifteen Members of the
Metropolitan Study Commission, 1957

John C. Lobb, chairman, executive vice president, Marine National Exchange Bank

George A. Parkinson, vice chairman, director, Milwaukee Vocational and Adult School

Irvin Knoebel, treasurer, comptroller, City of West Allis

Mrs. Sam (Mary Lou) Cook, secretary, civic activist

Harold E. Beck, business representative, Office Employees Union, AFL-CIO

Earl R. Butter, president, Butter Hardware Company

Richard W. Cutler, attorney, Wood, Warner, Tyrrell, and Bruce

Robert T. Foote, executive vice president, Red Star Yeast & Products Company

Robert E. Jensen, executive vice president, American Appraisal Company

A. S. Kliebhan, secretary-treasurer, St. Francis Savings & Loan Association

John H. Kopmeier, president, Wisconsin Ice and Coal Company

Ebner F. Luetzow, president, South Side Laundry Company

Clifford A. Randall, attorney, Zimmers, Randall and Zimmers

Willis G. Scholl, executive vice president, Allis-Chalmers Manufacturing Company

Appendix E
(See page 47)

Metropolitan Study Commission Recommendations, 1958-1961, Arranged by General Objective Implementation

A. To raise more state revenues and distribute part of them more equitably to Milwaukee County and units within the county.

Implemented Recommendations

1. 3% Sales Tax should be instituted. (Wisconsin had no sales tax previously.)

2. Withholding tax on payroll should be instituted.

3. An increase of 1% in each income tax bracket should replace the existing 20% surcharge.

4. Personal property tax on manufacturers' inventory should be abolished.

5. A significant portion of utility taxes should be "Pooled in any distribution formula" *(i.e., no longer distributed to the municipality where the utility is located).*

(The legislature adopted those five recommendations primarily because strong political forces about the same time initiated identical or similar recommendations.)

Recommendations Not Implemented

6. Motor vehicle registration fee should be increased by $2 for each $100 of wholesale book value.

7. Milwaukee County should assess the value of property and local assessment departments should be abolished. *(Defeated by the Wisconsin Assembly, 70-18 , June 6, 1961.)*

8. State should assume county public assistance burden.

9. 2/3 of a state sales tax should be distributed among counties on the basis of collections to municipalities within the county, and on the basis of school age population.

10. An alternative distribution of revenues should be considered.

B. To increase cost efficiency and promote public health by encouraging or mandating area-wide service by one central government unit.

Recommendations Implemented In Whole or Part or Indirectly

1. The Metropolitan Sewerage District's jurisdiction should be expanded to

    (a) the rest of Milwaukee County except South Milwaukee and

    (b) to Mequon, Thiensville, Germantown, Menomonee Falls, Brookfield, New Berlin, and Muskego *(legislature approved only voluntary expansion.)*

2. The Metropolitan and City of Milwaukee Sewerage Commissions should be combined.

3. The City of Milwaukee water utility should be required to sell water wholesale to any requesting municipality in the county *(indirectly implemented by the Wisconsin Public Service Commission's ordering Milwaukee to sell water to Wauwatosa, and Milwaukee subsequently agreeing to serve all requesting suburbs not having own facilities)*

Recommendations Not Implemented

4. Areas outside Milwaukee County served by the Metropolitan Sewerage District should be taxed the same as the old areas.

5. Milwaukee County should take over and operate a central county-wide refuse collection and disposal system.

6. In general – as a 1961 farewell message – any future transfers of functions to a larger area unit of government should be made to Milwaukee County and, if coordination with Waukesha County is not practicable, perhaps Milwaukee and Waukesha should be reunited as one county as they were before 1846.

C. To encourage coordination of land use planning throughout the County and the region.

Implemented Recommendation

1. Regional planning authorization statute should be amended to require a smaller governing body (18) than in the original 1955 statute (151 for seven counties).

2. A seven-county regional planning commission should be created in Southeastern Wisconsin.

Recommendations Not Implemented

3. Municipalities should be required to give advance notice to a neighboring municipality of any pending action affecting land use on their common boundary.

4. Milwaukee County should create a planning department to coordinate actions which affect land use.

D.   To facilitate cooperation between governmental units.

Implemented Recommendations

1. The statute authorizing inter-municipal cooperative agreements should be strengthened by a revision to be devised by the Wisconsin Legislative Council.

2. All seven library systems should create a single library card entitling holders to withdraw books from any library.

3. Milwaukee firefighters should offer basic training to suburban fire-fighters for a fee.

E.   To facilitate straightening jagged municipal boundaries.

Recommendation Implemented

1. After two years boundary litigation, municipalities should be author-ized to establish their common boundary by a majority vote of their governing boards *(instead of 3/4ths vote plus referenda)*.

Recommendations Not Implemented

2. Onerous legal procedures for detaching territory from one munici-pality to transfer it to another should be amplified.

Appendix F
(page 111)

SEWRPC's Methodology in Designing Freeway Capacity

SEWRPC was responsible for recommending the location and traffic capacity of each freeway segment. Freeways are a major element of the larger regional transportation system that includes surface arterials and mass transit facilities. (Freeways, which comprise far less than 10 percent of the regional arterial system, move over 40 percent of regional traffic.) SEWRPC developed a complex mathematical simulation modeling process for computing traffic demand over every freeway segment. The process, which became nationally recognized for its accuracy, utilized data reflecting land use and the origin and destination of person and vehicular trips. The models permitted the performance of each freeway segment to be accurately simulated under both existing and planned future land use and transportation system conditions. Based on this performance, SEWRPC recommended the capacity needed to move the existing and predicted future traffic volumes at the desired levels of service.

"Levels of service" are terms by which transportation engineers measure comparative performance. Levels of service range from A, which is the highest and best level, to F, the worst. Level F represents stop-and-go and bumper-to-bumper traffic conditions. Service Level A represents free-flowing freeway traffic conditions with the ability to travel safely at design speed up to 70 miles per hour and the freedom to change lanes, and pass other vehicles safely. SEWRPC consulted advisory panels of public officials and transportation experts to determine the level of service the public wanted and elected officials would probably finance. John Doyne and Herbert Goetsch were two of the public officials consulted. Doyne was the first Milwaukee County Executive; Goetsch long served Henry Maier as Commissioner of Public Works for the city. Both were highly respected.

In general, Service Level C was nominated as the desirable level of service under *average* weekday peak period conditions. Level C represents traffic conditions under which there is some restriction on the freedom to change lanes and under which the operating speed may be limited to 50 miles per hour. As a practical matter, however, Service Level C could not be attained on many segments when they were being designed. So, Level D or E was accepted. Level D represents traffic conditions marked by congestion and an increasing restriction on freedom to change lanes, with speeds limited to between 35 and 40 miles per hour. Level E represents traffic conditions marked by severe congestion, with operating speeds limited to 30 to 35 miles per hour but with the maximum capacity of the traffic lanes being achieved. Level F represents "stop and go" movement and operating speeds of 10 to 30 miles per hour.

Achieving Service Level C required, on many freeway segments, more traffic lanes and, therefore, a wider right-of-way than elected officials would accept in the 1960s and '70s. Consequently, on many key segments such as the freeways going west and north from the Marquette Interchange (I-94 and I-43,) the SEWRPC plan accepted Levels D and E. A prime example of this compromise is the North-South Freeway (I-43) segment between the Marquette Interchange and North Avenue. SEWRPC predicted the segment would be undersized for Service Level C, but the expense of widening the freeway by tearing down part of the massive Milwaukee County Court House or taking part of Marquette University's land and buildings was considered too financially and politically expensive. Consequently, the community faced a level of service varying between D and E, with lower speeds, congestion, lower safety, and start-and-stop bumper-to-bumper traffic. Today the community has to endure a Service Level F on that segment, with stop-and-go traffic and high accident rates during peak hours – partly because the planned freeway system was never completed. Some traffic could have gone elsewhere.

Of course, in early freeway years on some freeway legs at some hours of the day, speeds higher than 30 to 35 miles per hour were possible and Service Levels A through C were achieved. But that was long before traffic volumes reached and exceeded the level for which the freeways were designed.

The facts and transportation-engineering explanations in this appendix on SEWRPC methodology were provided by Kurt W. Bauer, who was executive director of SEWRPC during the period in question. The writing is the author's.

Appendix G
(see page 139)

Summary of Six Opinions as to What Law Applied in Illinois Case

In 1972, Justice Douglas declared for the U.S. Supreme Court that the ruling law in *Illinois v. Milwaukee* was the federal common law. However, he predicted that some day future federal legislation on water pollution would become so comprehensive that it would supersede federal common law. In 1973 Milwaukee asked U.S. District Judge Bauer to rule that the 1972 Federal Water Pollution Act amendments, enacted after Justice Douglas's opinion had, as Douglas predicted, superseded the federal common law. He denied the request. Judge Grady, in 1977, ruled that the federal common law continued to be apply but declared that Illinois statutes and common law did so as well. Judge Tone for the 7th Circuit Court of Appeals in l977 held that the federal common law applied but in footnote 53 held that its presence made Illinois statutes and common law inapplicable, citing Justice Douglas's footnote 9 in his 1972 Supreme Court decision. Thus Illinois lost two of the three legal foundations for its case through footnotes.

In l981, the U.S. Supreme Court accepted Milwaukee's argument that the federal statutory law (l972 version) had superseded the federal common law, and it declared in a third overwhelmingly important footnote that Illinois laws did not apply. Illinois continued to claim that Illinois law could still justify Judge Grady's order, forcing the Court of Appeals for the 7th Circuit to settle that question in 1984. Then it gave the final answer: federal statutes and *Wisconsin* statutes and common law applied but Illinois laws did not.

Incidentally, of the seventeen judges ruling on the basic legal questions in the interminably long Illinois case, judges residing in Illinois invariably sided with Illinois' position; those residing in Wisconsin always held for Milwaukee; and judges from other states favored the answer Milwaukee sought most of the time.

The federal judges at the district court and appellate court levels were predominantly from Illinois. There was only one Illinois resident on the U.S. Supreme Court (Justice Stevens, who voted for

Illinois' side) and none from Wisconsin. All politics is local as former U.S. House Speaker Tip O'Neil famously said.

Appendix H
(see page 192)

Chronology of Principal Sewer War Disputes Before Courts, Public Service Commission, Legislature, and Governor

Date	Item	Nature of Action, Legal Claim or Its Disposition
12/82	1.	District adopts rules for future annexation of areas to be served within ten years and notifies contract communities of the rules. In 1983 District proposes extending its boundaries to include all territory it serves within contract communities.
1/83	2.	Seven contract (FLOW) municipalities sue MMSD in Waukesha circuit court to nullify MMSD's rules re: potential unilateral expansion of its boundaries to include the part of their territory which it serves or would serve within ten years. Complaint amended in 1983 to challenge validity of proposed boundary extensions.
1983	3.	Legislature enacts 1983 Act 27, the 1983 budget bill, requiring contract communities to pay capital charges on a property value basis.
2/4/84	4.	MMSD notifies contract municipalities it will terminate service contracts as of 8/31/84.
8/31/84	5.	MMSD continues to provide service to contract communities without contract. MMSD bills them on the higher property value, claiming that it had statutory authority to charge for capital costs on that basis. They pay on their old contract formula basis, which is considerably less. Each year, thereafter, the communities pay a higher percentage of what they are billed – as the result of more newly-constructed facilities being added to the rate basis in the contract formula.

6. Contract communities amend their complaint (item 2) to claim MMSD must, by promissory estopped, renew their service contracts on the prior flow volumetric basis. MMSD files cross-claims to recover its share of the capital cost on a *quantum meruit* basis, which it defines as the equal of the property value formula.

1985   7. Legislature enacts 1985 Act 29, the 1985 budget bill, requiring contract communities – even if they have no service contracts – to pay on a property value basis.

6/29/88   8. Wisconsin Supreme Court holds the 1983 (item 3) and 1985 (item 7) statutes unconstitutional. *Brookfield v. MMSD*, 144 Wis. 2d 896 (Brookfield I).

1/17/89   9. Miller Brewing and Universal Foods petition the PSC to determine that the MMSD's rates favor or discriminate in favor of the contract communities, because MMSD does not collect the sums it bills to the communities while collecting property-based charges from them. Contract communities later intervene. PSC goes slow because of action by contract communities (item 2) pending in Waukesha Circuit Court.

3/89   10. Circuit Court for Waukesha County (on pretrial motions) rules that:

(A) MMSD's resolutions including contract communities within its boundaries are void because (i) 1982 authorizing statute is unconstitutional as it applies to boundaries and, anyway (ii) MMSD did not follow statute's procedure in expanding its boundaries to include contract communities; and

6/2/89   (B) the court will not defer to the PSC on determining reasonableness of rates (item 9) and (after a jury trial);

262

3/13/90		(C) MMSD is estopped from charging on any basis other than a flow-based charging basis – because MMSD had represented it would do so during the November 1979-June 1980 public hearings on the Master Facilities Plan for planning and financing the Water Pollution Abatement Program (WPAP); and

(D) MMSD is not entitled to collect more than payments received which were based on the contract formula (item 5). Reason: the reasonable value of the capital cost of the facilities provided by MMSD for services for 1985-1988 does not exceed such payments.

6/5/90   11. After long post-verdict wrangling, both sides appeal,

7/5/90   The winner is FLOW because the court did not apply its favorable holding to years after l988.

12. Governor Tommy Thompson assigns Howard Bellman to mediate an agreement. A tentative agreement was reached but soon falls apart.

10/89   13. Legislature approves SB-65 authorizing MMSD for the third time, 1983 and 1985 being the earlier ones (see items 3 & 7) – to charge communities outside the District on the basis of property value.

12/8/89   14. Thompson, believing the parties can still talk, concludes that SB-65 interfered in the negotiations. He vetoed SB-65, stating the parties should negotiate a settlement or he will refer the matter to the Public Service Commission.

2/5/90   15. The Wisconsin Department of Administration and the parties ask PSC to delay its investigation pending the completion of the parties' negotiations. In mid-March 1990 the parties negotiate a settlement under the watchful eye and presence of James Klauser, secretary of the Wisconsin Department of Administration and Governor Thompson's alter ego. When this, too, falls apart, Thompson apparently feels publicly embarrassed and concludes the collapse originated with FLOW's professional advisors, Charles Mulcahy and William Mielke.

| 3/90 | 16. | The Wisconsin Department of Administration petitions the PSC to reopen the dormant Miller Brewing – Universal Foods case (item 9) and broaden the issues to consider the reasonableness of MMSD rates. This became 9308-SR-101. |

1/28/91   17.   PSC issues a sweeping ruling directed to the reasonableness of charges after 1988 – which had not been considered by the circuit court (item 10). It holds that the MMSD's charging outside its boundaries for capital costs on the basis of property values is within its authority and is not unreasonable or unjustly discriminatory. In doing so the PSC relies on statutes not considered by the circuit court in reaching an opposite conclusion. 9308-SR-101.

18.   FLOW appeals the PSC decision.

11/13/92   19.   Wisconsin State Supreme Court reverses Waukesha Circuit Court, in *Brookfield v. MMSD*, 171 Wis 2d 400, (Brookfield II). It reconciles the contrary rulings of the Waukesha Circuit Court (item 10) and the PSC (item 17). It holds that the circuit court should have deferred to the PSC on the reasonableness of rate matters; and that:

A. the circuit court should dismiss the contract communities complaint; and

B. the MMSD can start a collection action within 60 days (see opinion's footnote 3); and

C. the proper procedure for the contract communities would be to complain to the PSC that the capital charges were unfair; and

D. reverses the court's ruling on the MMSD's resolutions enlarging its boundaries (item 10 (A) (I)), holding that the validity of that procedure should properly be decided by the PSC, not the court.

1/3/93   20.   Waukesha Circuit Court affirms the PSC ruling. (Snyder, J.).

21.   Contract municipalities appeal.

| 6/22/94 | 22. | Court of appeals (Snyder, J.) affirms circuit court's upholding the PSC ruling, noting that FLOW does not appeal the PSC finding that capital cost recovery on property values is not unreasonable. Instead it argues that MMSD was not authorized to so charge because a provision of its enabling statute said that charges, "to the extent practicable," should be "proportionate" to the cost of the sewerage system that the district may reasonably attribute to the user." The court declares: |

"The PSC concluded that the principal goal of the WPAP was to ensure the protection of the public health and compliance with state and federal water quality standards, not to enhance capacity to meet expanding user demand. Therefore, such costs are not closely linked to usage because WPAP provides a 'public good," i.e., a public good to the entire public rather than a private good which is limited to direct purchasers of service. FLOW does not contest PSC's conclusion that the capital costs associated with WPAP are unrelated to use. Since capital costs are not attributable to users, the proportionality requirement of Sec 66.91 (5) 2.... relied on by FLOW, is not mandatory."

Also other statutory sections authorize the use of property values in setting charges. *Brookfield v. PSC*, 186 Wis 2d 129, 136. (June 22, 1994)

| 1993-4 | 23. | Margaret Farrow, state senator and former head of FLOW, attempts to pass a bill requiring MMSD to charge FLOW communities on the basis of volumetric use. It fails by one vote (George Petak's) in the senate. |

| 10/96 | 24. | MMSD and FLOW negotiate to pay $140 million to carry out the PSC court-affirmed ruling that property-based charges from 1985 to date are reasonable and authorized. |

Appendix I
(See page 196)

Growth and Dispersion of Population
Milwaukee Standard Metropolitan Area (SMA)
(Milwaukee, Waukesha, Washington & Ozaukee Counties)

County	Population 1950	Percent 1950	Population 1975	Percent 1975	Population 2000	Percent 2000
Milwaukee	871,047	85.9	1,009,618	72.1	940,164	62.6
Waukesha	85,901	8.5	255,769	18.3	360,767	24.0
Washington	33,902	3.3	74,344	5.3	117,493	7.8
Ozaukee	23,361	2.3	60,721	4.3	82,317	5.6
Total	1,014,211	100	1,400,452	100	1,500,741	100
City of Milwaukee	637,392		670,665		596,974	
The City of Milwaukee's population peaked at 741,324 in 1960						

Endnotes

Chapter 1

1. See Appendix A: Products & Numbers of Employees of Larger Milwaukee Manufacturers

Chapter 2

2. Avery Wittenberger, *Milwaukee Journal*, Stadium Edition, April 8, 1953, p. 2.
3. "Perini Will Not Sell Brewers to Anyone but Fred Miller," *Milwaukee Journal*, March 8, 1953, Sports, p. 2.
4. Lloyd Larson, "Boston Braves Transfer Near Final O.K., Fred Miller to Become Part Owner," *Milwaukee Sentinel*, March 14, 1953, Sec. 1, p. 1.
5. In 1954 I moved from Porter's firm to Wood, Warner, Tyrrell and Bruce, which, after combining with Olwell & Brady and the passage of time, became Brady, Tyrrell, Cotter, and Cutler. It, in 1974, became Quarles & Brady, after merger with Quarles, Clemmons, Herriot, Teschner, & Noelke. Before changing law firms in 1954 I turned down a surprise offer from three directors of the Marine National Exchange Bank (today Bank One). I was to become a vice president in charge of their trust department and "to compete with John C. Geilfuss to succeed Eliot Fitch as president." I did not believe they were serious about the opportunity to become president but, six months later, the bank hired John Lobb, who clea
6. rly expected to succeed Fitch, but did not. Geilfuss did. (Lobb appears in a later chapter.)
6. After attendance exceeded 1 million persons the County would receive 10 percent of all gross concession revenues and a sliding percent of ticket revenues starting at 5 percent and reaching 10 percent for attendance over 2 million. Milwaukee County File 65-943, p. 1593. Also, *Milwaukee Sentinel*, April 9, 1970, part 1, pp 5, 8. In the highest year, 1983, the County received $2,037,397 in parking fees plus $630,693 from ticket sales and $591,923 from concession sales, a grand total of $3,259,813. Email from Paul A. Baniel, Vice President – Finance, Brewers, May 1, 201; confirmed in telephone call to author from F. Thomas Ament, Milwaukee County Executive, May 4, 2001. Of course, the County's gross receipts were much lower in other years, but always included substantial parking fees.
7. Verified by Bud Selig in a handwritten note, January 8, 1999.
8. Offering letter of Allan H. Selig to William R. Daley, chairman of the Pilots, September 23, 1969, and report of a "hand shake" agreement by Edmund Fitzgerald to the Brewers board, October 11, 1969.
9. "Injunction Bars Pilots' Move Here, A. L. Fights Seattle Suit," *Milwaukee Sentinel*, March 18, 1970, Part 1, pp. 1, 6.
10. R. Goff Beach, Duane Bowman, and Oscar G. Mayer of Madison; Charles Gelatt, Eugene W. Murphy and John Murphy of La Crosse; and William Buchanan and Bruce B. Purdy of the Fox River Valley.
11. Actually, four separate appraisals were prepared by four knowledgeable baseball men, two from the Brewers' staff and two from other teams (in order to lessen the chance the Internal Revenue Service would claim that the "inside" appraisals were "MAI" (made as instructed). The appraisals ranged below and above the average figure of $10,200,000.

267

12. Such large deductions were made possible by the fact that the appraised value of the players= contracts was slightly more than twice the amount of the equity, and tax law allowed deductions in excess of actual investment, to the extent of the partnership indebtedness, which exceeded $5 million. Thus, a 4 percent, or $200,000 limited partner in the then 70 percent federal income tax bracket could, over several years, reduce his taxes by approximately $280,000 (4% x $10,200,000 x 70%).

13. The Internal Revenue Service disallowed part of the deductions but was overturned by U.S. District Court Judge John Reynolds in 1981. His decision was sustained on appeal in 1983. "Selig's Secrets," *Milwaukee Magazine*, April 1994, p. 19.

14. The twenty-one investors were listed by name in the 1970 opening day baseball program. They were: Albert B. Adelman, Ben Barkin, R. Goff Beach, Duane Bowman, William Buchanan, William R. Daley, Ralph Evinrude, Edmund B. Fitzgerald, Edwin E. Foote, Charles Gelatt, Herbert Kohl, Charles A. Krause III, Oscar G. Mayer, Jr., Eugene W. Murphy, John Murphy, Bruce B. Purdy, Allen H. Selig, Everett G. Smith, Roswell N. Stearns, Robert Uihlein, and Jack Winter. Adelman was shortly replaced by Evan Helfaer, the true owner of his interest, and Kohl by Charles D. James.

15. Milwaukee County File, 65-943, p. 415.

Chapter 3

16. *Municipal Boundary Problems - Report of Land Use and Zoning Committee of the Metropolitan Study Commission*, p. 6, 7, February 23, 1959. (As chairman of the committee I wrote the report).

17. Cutler, Richard W., "Characteristics of Land Required for Incorporation or Expansion of a Municipality," *1958 Wisconsin Law Review*, 7.

18. Ibid., 10.

19. An astute reporter, Ed Bayley, later dean of the University of California at Berkeley School of Journalism, wrote almost daily stories and the *Journal* published front-page editorials, both supporting town residents= preference for annexation to Fox Point, River Hills, and Bayside rather than to Glendale.

20. Maier, Henry A., *The Mayor Who Made Milwaukee Famous* (Madison Books, Boston Way, Md., 1993), 18.

21. Cutler, 35.

Chapter 4

22. "Study Appointments Receive Warm Praise," *Milwaukee Journal*, October 13, 1957, part 1, p. 16.

Chapter 5

23. Metro's budget was a skimpy $30,000 for the first two years – far below the figure recommended by the Greater Milwaukee Committee – which enabled it to hire only a twenty-four-year-old planner for research. Eventually the commission received $125,000 over four years from the state, city, and suburbs, and private donations. Henry J. Schmandt and William H. Standing, *The Milwaukee Metropolitan Study Commission,* (Indiana University Press, 1965), 112, 114. Schmandt served UWM from 1959-1976, ultimately becoming professor of Urban Affairs.

268

24. Entitled by Marquette: "Revenue Needs and Trends in Milwaukee County; the Distribution of Shared Taxes and Aids Among Governmental Units within Milwaukee County."

25. Schmandt, endnote 23.

26. *Major Recommendations of the Metropolitan Study Commission,* October 1957-June 1961, p. 17.

27. *Annual Report of the Metropolitan Study Commission to the Governor,* pp. 22-23, October 13, l958,

28. Ibid., 39.

29. 1973 O.A.G., p. 136. The attorney general relied on opinions of the Wisconsin and U.S. Supreme Court upholding the validity of vocational school boards and county school boards whose members were appointed rather than elected.

30. I could not find any records of the executive committee or its creation.

31. Then called *The London Economist.*

32. *Report,* p. 2. (endnote 27).

33. Schmandt, 21 (endnote 23).

34. Ibid., 131.

35. Ibid., 136.

Chapter 6

36 Cutler, 32, endnote 17.

37. *In re City of Beloit,* 37 Wis. 2d 637, 155 N.W. 2d 633 (1968).

Chapter 7

38. *The Report of the Task Force [Tarr Task Force] on Local Government Finance and Organization in Wisconsin,* January 1969, ch. VIII p. 1.

39. Ibid., 2.

40. Pleasant Prairie v. Local Affairs & Development, 113 Wis 2d 327, 339, 334 N.W. 2d 893, (1983)

41. Tarr Task Force, ch VIII, p 1.

42. Ibid, 5.

Chapter 8

43. Schmandt, endnote 23.

44. A land information system is a system of spatially referenced information and computer programs that is used to acquire, store, manipulate, analyze, and display spatial data such as land use, soils, flood hazard, assessed valuation and other data.

Chapter 9

45. Vehicle registrations grew in the city from 131,963 in 1945 to 212,316 in 1953 and in the county from 177,969 to 296,977. By 1998, they had risen to 366,197 and 603,375, respectively. Thus, from 1945 to 1998 registrations grew by 2.77 times in the city and 3.34 times in the county. Source: Milwaukee City and County Vehicle Registrations, Wisconsin Motor Vehicle Department.

46. *Preliminary Plan for a Comprehensive Expressway System for the City of Milwaukee*, Amman & Whitney, September 1952, p. 11.

47. Ibid.

48. Roosevelt envisaged a national highway system as a massive public works program, employing veterans returning after World War II. *Roads and Bridges*, June 1996, p. 39.

49. Most planners, some engineers, and probably Ike himself favored bypassing cities. Interview with Kurt Bauer, August 1998.

50. *Roads*, 40.

51. "ISTEA's Principal Author, Senator Moynihan, Shares Views," *U.S. Mayor*, December 23, 1996, p 3.

52. In 1968 the county board resolved to appropriate no more than $8.5 million annually for freeways. county expenditures had averaged above $10 million annually in the mid-sixties. The Expressway Commission warned that the county's reduced funding "will now control progress." *1968 Annual Report*, Milwaukee County Expressway and Transportation Committee, p 2.

Chapter 10

53. Maier, 63.

54. Ibid., 64.

55. Ibid., 81.

56. In *The Fourth Turning*, (Broadway Books, N.Y. 1997) William Strauss and Neil House suggest that rebellions against authority occur every eighty to one hundred years.

57. *Milwaukee Journal*, July 30,1972, pt. 2, p 11.

Chapter 11

58. Cobb v. Milwaukee County, 60 Wis.2d 99, 208 N.W.2d 848 (1973).

59. Kamps did not handle the lawsuit because many clients of the firm where he worked, Quarles, Herriott, Clemons, Teschner & Noelke (Quarles and Brady after 1974), favored freeways. He and others hired David Walther to direct the litigation. Walther later became the unsuccessful candidate for mayor against Henry Maier in 1968.

60. Technically, the Supreme Court declared, in passing, that the expressway commission could buy or condemn the city's reversionary rights in Juneau Park. However, by 1973 construction of the Park Freeway, which was designed to connect with the Lake Freeway, had been enjoined by the U.S. District Court until an environmental impact statement could be prepared. When the statement was finished in 1977, the Park Freeway was killed by the Federal Highway Administration. See page 89.

61. Letter to author from Robert W. Brannan, June 30, 1998.

62. Letter to author from Harvey Shebesta, June 30, 1998.

63. Transcript of telephone interview with Seaver, May 16, 1998, which he confirmed in writing.

64. Seaver received two columns of welcome publicity for his cause by being charged on September 13, 1968 with criminal damage to property for breaking a seal to turn

on gas for a poor tenant family whose landlord had not paid the bill. *Milwaukee Journal*, September 14, 1968, pt. 1, p. 7. On February 2, 1973 Seaver was arrested for disorderly conduct in refusing, with many others, to vacate the city Redevelopment Authority office at closing time. *Milwaukee Journal*, February 9, 1973, Part 2, p. 1. He was found guilty of disorderly conduct in July. *Milwaukee Journal*, July 21, 1973, Part 2, p 13.

65. Seaver.

66. Henry J. Schmandt, John C. Goldbach, and Donald B. Vogel, *Milwaukee, A Contemporary Profile* (Praeger Publications, Inc., New York, 1971), 171, 172.

67. Dick Jones, "Odyssey of an Idealist, Activist Ted Seaver sails a rough course toward the common good," *Milwaukee Journal Magazine WISCONSIN,* July 12, 1987, p. 15.

68. Shebesta.

69. Transcript of telephone interview with Goetsch, June 30,1998, confirmed by Goetsch in writing. Goetsch served on the staff of the expressway commission between periods of serving the City of Milwaukee. A discreet and sensible man, he, out of loyalty to Mayor Maier, largely suppressed his private opinion concerning the merits of freeway segments opposed by Maier.

70. Shebesta.

71. Goetsch.

72. *1969 Annual Report*, Milwaukee County Expressway and Transportation Commission, p 1.

73. Shebesta disagreed but said their argument was effective. "A freeway occupies an area the width of at least one city block. Rather than divide neighbors, it displaces some neighbors. In my experience, people living on one street don't know or associate with people on the next street. The Sherman Park 'neighborhood' people successfully used this argument...to derail the Stadium Freeway-North." Letter to author from Harvey Shebesta, June 30, 1998. Kurt Bauer defines neighborhoods differently. "In city planning practice, a medium-density neighborhood occupies about a square mile." Letter to author from Bauer, September 22, 1998.

74. Seaver.

75. Transcript of telephone interview with Cukor (now Mrs. William Broydrick), May 20, 1998, confirmed by her in writing.

76. A substantial majority of Milwaukee County residents voted in favor of completing five freeway segments in the fall of 1974. See page 87. It was the only freeway referendum other than the one in 1967 restricted to the City of Milwaukee. It favored constructing the Downtown Loop freeway through Juneau Park by a two-to-one margin.

77. In the mid-seventies newly elected legislators were often fresh out of college and became full time activist legislators, whereas their predecessors usually had been seasoned by careers in real estate or law before election in their mid-thirties. Some attribute that change to a substantial rise in the salaries of legislators between 1973 ($9,900) and 1975 ($15,906), which had been intended to raise the quality of legislators. On the other hand, Mordecai Lee, elected in 1976, believes many elected then were idealists, like himself, seeking to improve public policy and not attracted by the pay raise. Email letter from Mordecai Lee to author, p 4, August 14,1998.

78. Ernest Norquist survived the Bataan Death March in l941 and four years imprison-
ment by the Japanese. In the l960s he became a civil rights activist in the South.

79. A significant portion of the Bay Freeway in Waukesha County near Oconomowoc
has been completed.

80. *1969 Annual Report,* Milwaukee County Expressway and Transportation
Commission, p. 1.

81. Wisconsin Statutes: 84.295 (3)

82. Prepared statement of Henry A. Reuss at the public hearing on the environmental
impact statement concerning the Park Freeway West, May 13, 1975, pp. 2 and 8.
The statement was initially drafted by Mordecai Lee, Reuss's assistant at the time.

83. *Milwaukee Journal,* June 3, 1972.

84 *Milwaukee Journal*, May 14, 1975.

85. Herbert Goetsch, commissioner of public works of the City of Milwaukee,
journeyed to Washington to lobby successfully, with Reuss's help, for adding the
Hoan Harbor Bridge to the Interstate System as I-794. Interview of Herbert
Goetsch, June 30, l998.

86. The county board, in "approving" the 112 miles, was doing no more than
declaring that they were a desirable planning goal. Only after the elected officials
calculated the cost of the project, weighed it against competing capital expenditures, and began to *budget* their share of the cost could one realistically consider
that the projects would probably go forward. Therefore it may be technically more
accurate to say 78 rather than 112 miles of freeways recommended in 1965 by
SEWRPC were formally approved by the Milwaukee County Board.

Chapter 12

87. Letter to the author from Harvey Shebesta, June 30, 1998.

88. *Milwaukee Journal*, May 9, 1975, p. 1.

89. "Labor Raps Reuss on Parkway Stand," *Milwaukee Journal*, May 14, 1975.

90. Mordecai Lee, "Freeway Update," *The Sherman Park News*, Vol. 6, No. 3, March
1976.

91. The more authentic estimate by SEWRPC was 1,100. "Panel Urges Use of Land,"
Milwaukee Journal, December 17, 1977.

92. Lee, endnote 90.

93. Gary C. Rummler, "US Rejects Impact Study, Throttling Freeway,*" Milwaukee
Journal,* January 18, 1977.

94. The six neutral committee members included two talented civic-minded notables
from the University of Wisconsin Milwaukee (UWM): Economics Professor Eric
Schenker, former chair of the City Harbor Commission; and Evelyn Petshek,
director of UWM Development and former chair of the City Plan Commission.

95. The pro-freeway members were: Orrin J. Bradley, president of the Boston Store;
John S. Randall, former president of Kearney and Trecker, the machine tool
manufacturer; L. William Teweles, former president of the Teweles Seed Co., and
George Watts, who operated a family china shop at Jefferson and Wells Streets
downtown with great skill but whose civic opinions often reflected his lack of governmental experience and factual knowledge.

96. Letter from Mordecai Lee to author, August 5, 1998.

97. *Milwaukee Labor Press*, February 10, 1977.

98. "Expert Prescribes Park Freeway Plan*," Milwaukee Sentinel*, June 17, 1977.

99. Dean Showers, "Freeway Reluctantly Opposed," *Milwaukee Journal*, December 19, 1977. Showers later became one of several chiefs of staff for Mayor John Norquist.

100. Ibid.

101. Ibid.

102. "Planners Delay Freeway Action," Dean Showers, *Milwaukee Sentinel,* December 20, 1977. "Park West raises basic planning questions*," West Side Word*, December 29, 1977.

103. Lawrence Sussman, "Ire Flares over Park West Study," *Milwaukee Journal*, December 20, 1977.

104. Dean Showers, "Planners Delay Freeway Actions," *Milwaukee Sentinel*, December 20, 1977.

105. Lawance Sussman, "Schreiber influences Park West decision," *Milwaukee Journal,* December 29, 1977, pt. 2, p 1.

106. Mileage figures provided by Kurt Bauer, retired executive director of SEWRPC, October 1988.

107. Figures computed by Harvey Shebesta, retired director of the Milwaukee District of the Wisconsin Transportation Department, May 8, 2000, based on annual reports of the Milwaukee County Expressway Commission.

108. Lee and Seaver considered Maier anti-freeway. Bauer thought him to be neutral, favoring some, opposing others. I believed Maier to have favored some, like the Hoan Bridge (it would increase cargo at the city-owned port), but on the whole to have opposed the later freeways. He urged voters to vote against five of them in the 1974 referendum. Thereafter Maier remained silent while rising opposition hammered them to a halt.

Chapter 13

109. John O. Norquist, *The Wealth of Cities - Revitalizing the Centers of American Life,* (Addison-Wesley, Reading, Mass., 1998).

110. *Milwaukee Journal Sentinel*, December 6, 1998.

111. *Freeway System Hours of Congestion - 90-95-99*, WISDOT, July 31, 2000, 10 pp.

112. Letter to author from Kurt W. Bauer, December 1998.

113. The decision to widen I-94 in 1971 had a profound impact on urban growth patterns in the Racine and Kenosha area, attracting development which could have been located close to the cities of Racine and Kenosha if the Lake Freeway had been built. The development along I-94 required the extension of sewer, water, and transit service from Racine and Kenosha systems west to I-94 at enormous cost.

114. In short order the affected local municipalities, Milwaukee County, and the Wisconsin Legislature all adopted resolutions opposing the Bay Freeway. *1969 Annual Report,* Milwaukee County Expressway and Transportation Commission, p 1.

273

Chapter 14

115. 1979 Assembly Bill 563, 1981 Assembly Bill 311, and 1983 Senate Bill 106.

116. Milwaukee County's population was 960,993; the region's, 1,770,492. Wisconsin Legislative Reference fiscal note to 1979 Assembly Bill 563.

117. Senate Amendment No. 1 to 1983 Senate Bill 106, introduced September 28, 1983.

118. Interview with Mordecai Lee, January 4, 2000.

119. Ironically, Norquist in 1990 requested SEWRPC to champion (with partial success) the creation of a regional transportation authority and in 1992 collaborated in its effort to lessen exurban sprawl. For the sprawl study, see Chapter 24.

120. Letter of John O. Norquist to Federal Highway Administration, Washington, August 4, 1995.

121. Letter from U.S. Department of Transportation to David Falstad, Chairman, SEWRPC, December 6, 1995.

122. Chapter 84.03 (7) (repealed around 1990).

123. Recollection of his 1983 warning by Donald L. Stitt, during an interview with author, January 6, 2000.

124. Highway planning has become so controversial that as soon as a legal block is removed, another unrelated one seems to take its place. For example, about 1991, Lee's amendment restricting I-43's width was repealed and the State Department of Transportation briefly considered widening I-43 from Bender Road in Glendale to Brown Deer Road in northern Fox Point. However, Congress in 1991 effectively froze all interstate highway funds. That freeze expired in 1998 but consideration of widening I-43 currently must await SEWRPC's completing a transportation study for the U.S. Department of Transportation on July 1, 2001. That study will estimate the future traffic and needs of the regional freeway system. In effect, SEWRPC is to advise which freeway segments most need repair and which, if any, need additional capacity.

125. The construction of the Airport Freeway Spur in 1978 was no exception, having been agreed to in the final freeway decisions in late 1977, no doubt because of the broad community conviction that quick access to the airport was very much needed for regional passengers and business cargo.

126. Recollection of Kurt Bauer of a statement made to him by Mayor John Norquist shortly after his election in 1988 as mayor of the City of Milwaukee.

127. *Milwaukee East-West Corridor Transportation Study, Major Investment Study/ Draft Environmental Impact Statement*, Wisconsin Department of Transportation, Federal Highway Administration, etc., Dec. 1996, p. S-6.

128. Ibid., S-7.

129. By correcting dangerous freeway design deficiencies as judged from a current state-of-the-art perspective.

130. Later, in 1998, Bloomberg demonstrated that a veteran politician could accept that traffic congestion cannot, politically speaking, be corrected by more lanes or new freeways. She demonstrated her political realism when she became alarmed by a SEWRPC projection that traffic on Capitol Drive in Brookfield would reach 50,000 vehicles a day. She told WISDOT and SEWRPC in 1998 that such traffic

would overload Capitol Drive but declared she would fight any effort to enlarge Capitol Drive beyond its present six-lane capacity. She noted that much of the through traffic would be better accommodated if the abandoned Bay Freeway between western Milwaukee County and Oconomowoc were in existence, but acknowledged that lack of political support made construction of the Bay Freeway impossible. Instead, she said, WISDOT and Waukesha County would have to widen other arterial roads to help carry the increased traffic. This option, however, becomes increasingly more difficult as Waukesha County becomes more urbanized. Source: Philip Evenson, executive director of SEWRPC, who was present at numerous meetings where Bloomberg spoke. Interview with Evenson July 14, 2000.

131. Daniel M. Finley in telephone interview, February 5, 2001.

132. Interstate Surface Transportation Efficiency Act (ISTEA). The funds were allocated to Wisconsin because federal transportation authorities discovered that SEWRPC's 1965 land use transportation plan recommended a transit way along the East-West corridor. ISTEA provided that the secretary of transportation, upon the governor's request after consultation with appropriate local government officials, "may approve substitute bus transit, and light rail projects, in lieu of construction of the I-94 East-West transit way project in Milwaukee and Waukesha counties as identified in the East-West Cost Estimate."

133. The extreme height of the High Rise Bridge part of the interchange was dictated in the 1960s by the Corps of Engineers to assure clearance for ships' masts as they passed up the Menomonee River. They no longer do. Further, many ramps in the "spaghetti interchange" are one-lane wide, causing congestion for many hours each day. Other obsolete design features include substandard horizontal vertical curvature, movements across traffic to ramps on the left, and lane drops. Creative design may not be able to provide dual lanes within the present limited footprint for the interchange. At inter-agency meetings discussing redesign in 2000, Mayor Norquist's engineers opposed enlarging the footprint. Other veteran political leaders believed interchange safety might require enlarging the footprint.

134. "Boulevard of Dreams," *Milwaukee Journal Sentinel,* September 14, 1998.

135. Mayor Zeidler in 1959 vetoed a common council resolution favoring an elevated freeway instead of a boulevard. The council overrode the veto, *Milwaukee Journal Sentinel*, September 14, 1998.

136. *Business Journal,* December 24, 1999.

137. Karl Pierce, WISDOT project manager for the Parkway, *Business Journal*, ibid.

138. SEWRPC staff memorandum "Analysis of Existing and Year 2020 Traffic Impacts on the Termination of the Park East Freeway at N. 4th Street," July 1998.

139. *New York Times*, July 14, 1999.

Chapter 15

140. The legislature on October 27, 1999, inserted a provision in an annual budget bill that no funds could be spent on a light rail system. (1999 Wisconsin Act 9.) However, light rail supporters assert there are loopholes in the provision. *Milwaukee Journal Sentinel*, January 14, 2000.

141. Also, SEWRPC freeways were intended to shape land use consistently with the recommended regional land use plan. Deviations from the plan proved expensive. The not-recommended expansion of the I-94 Freeway in Racine and Kenosha

275

Counties provides an example. Development sprouted along expanded I-94 instead of along the abandoned Lake Freeway next to the cities of Racine and Kenosha with their existing sewer and water services. Later development along I-94 required hundreds of millions of dollars worth of sewer and water extensions.

142. Fortunately, the emission of volatile organic compounds (VOC), the cause of harmful ground level ozone, is decreasing in the six-county non-attainment area, primarily owing to improvements in automotive technology. The figures are: in 1990: 361.1 tons of VOC emitted per day of which 41 percent came from automobiles; 1999: 231.4 tons per day of which 21 percent came from automobiles. SEWRPC and Wisconsin Department of Natural Resources....These figures disprove a widely circulated "myth" that automotive emissions cause most air pollution.

143. *A Regional Transportation System Plan for Southeastern Wisconsin: 2020*, SEWRPC Planning Report No. 46, December 1997, p 12.

144. Transcript of telephone interview with Ted Seaver, May 16, 1998, later confirmed by Seaver.

145. E-mail of Mordecai Lee to author, November 16, l998.

146. Eight SEWRPC advisory committees, arranged by field of expertise, reviewed staff recommendations on transportation plans and level of service. They included public officials with general responsibilities, such as Doyne, Goetsch, and Carl N. Quast, director of planning for the City of Milwaukee; transportation specialists such as Professor Eric Shencker, UWM; Henry M. Mayer, manager of the local transport company; and Harry C. Brockl, City of Milwaukee Port Director; the informed analyst, Norman N. Gill, the executive director of the Citizens' Governmental Research Bureau (now Public Policy Forum); plus a host of suburban municipal planners, engineers, and directors of public works.

147. Norquist, p 54, endnote 109.

148. Letter from J. Michael Mooney, December 18, 1998. Mooney is the foremost developer and manager of industrial parks in the greater Milwaukee area. He was an outstandingly productive member of a SEWRPC advisory committee on urban sprawl in the l990s, which I chaired.

149. *New York Times*, November 24, 1999. This article further states: "Propelled by the 'just in time' method of inventory control ... the number of big trucks has risen l8 percent" in the 1990s according to the American Trucking Association.

150. Many factors spurred an exodus from central cities after World War II: inexpensive land, lower taxes, low gasoline rates, and concern over poor schools and rising crime. See SEWRPC Memorandum Report No. 68, *Regional Land Use Implementation in Southeastern Wisconsin: Status and Needs*, May 1993. See also *Chicago Metropolis 2020,* published in 1999 by the Chicago Commercial Club in association with the American Academy of Arts and Sciences.

151. Mooney, endnote 148.

152. Norquist, p 109.

153. Ibid., 161.

154. Ibid., 164.

155. Ibid., 162.

156. Ibid., 163.

157. The number of motor vehicles registered in the City of Milwaukee increased from 131,967 in 1945 to 208,857 in 1952 or 58.3 percent. Wisconsin Motor Vehicle Department.

158. *Preliminary Plan for a Comprehensive Expressway System for the City of Milwaukee*, Amman and Whitney, 1952, p. 11.

159. In 1952 registrations in the county were 281,358; the city, 208,857. By 1998, they were 603,375 and 366,197 respectively. Wisconsin Department of Motor Vehicles.

160. Bureau of Traffic Engineering and Electrical Services, City of Milwaukee.

161. Southeastern Wisconsin Regional Planning Commission.

162. Southeastern Wisconsin Regional Planning Commission.

163. Norquist, p. 74.

164. SEWRPC Planning Report No. 46, *A Regional Transportation System Plan for Southeastern Wisconsin: 2020*, December 1997, p. 162.

165. Ibid., 163.

166. Doubling the price of gasoline, in contrast, would increase mass transit ridership from 187,000 passengers daily to 272,000, an increase of only 14 percent. See SEWRPC Planning Report No. 41, *A Regional Transportation System Plan for Southeastern Wisconsin: 2010*, December 1994, pp. 434 and 453.

167. Ibid., Table 244, 479.

Chapter 16

168. Flooding, pollution, and preservation of the environmental corridors (woodlands and wetlands).

169. John J. Justen, president of Pfister & Vogel Tanning Company, and Darrell M. Martin, resident manager of the St. Regis Paper Company (formerly Cornell Wood Products).

170. *Milwaukee Journal Sentinel,* August 14, 1998.

171. *Milwaukee Journal Sentinel*, August 9, 1998.

172. *Milwaukee Journal Sentinel*, August 9, 1998. On October 7, 1998, the City of Milwaukee decided to purchase sixteen flooded houses along Lincoln Creek. *Milwaukee Journal Sentinel*, October 8, 1998.

Chapter 17

173. *1958 Annual Report*, Metropolitan Study Commission, p. 23.

174. For example, the EPA regulations required the elimination by treatment of all but 30 parts per million gallons of biological oxygen demand (BOD), (excessive amounts of which kill fish by depriving them of oxygen), suspended solids, which can grow algae and endanger public health in several ways, and 400 parts per million of disease-causing fecal coliform.

175. *USEPA Program Guidance Analysis 61*, by Stevens, Thompson, & Runyon, 1976, its conclusion being later confirmed in 1983 by CH2MHill analysis, and in 1987 by *The Water Resource Management Plan for the Milwaukee Harbor Estuary, SEWRPC Planning Report No 37*.

176. Freeways cost $412 million of which the local share totaled $110 million or 27 percent. See Chapter 12, p. 94, 95.

177. Scott defeated his Democratic opponent, in his heyday, by over one million votes, a margin larger than that separating the Republican Illinois governor from his opponent.

178. Such untreated wastes during a 1885 storm drifted out to Chicago's Lake Michigan drinking water intake pipe, causing an epidemic of cholera, typhoid, and dysentery, which killed many. That calamity caused the civic decision to reverse the Chicago River.

179. The Chicago Sanitary and Ship Canal was known, near the Chicago stockyards, as "Bubbly Creek," and was said to have had in places a scum so thick people could walk on it. *Encyclopedia Britannica* (1985 edition).

180. *How To Bottle Rains*, a pamphlet prepared by Metropolitan Water Reclamation District for Greater Chicago to explain the need for a solution to both pollution and flooding and to help acquire substantial federal funds.

181. By 1999 Chicago had completed 93.4 miles of deep tunnel-reservoirs out of a projected 109, the largest such public works project in the world, costing 3.7 billion dollars by 1996. They stopped overflows from 51 communities in Cook County into the lake except for possibly every 3 to 5 years. Brochures of Metropolitan Water Reclamation District for Greater Chicago, supplied by Margaret Bradley, Information Officer, May 7, 1999.

182. Missouri v. Illinois, 200 U.S. 230 (1906). Illinois claimed its wastes were so diluted by the time they reached St. Louis that they posed no health hazard. The Supreme Court agreed, citing the fact that St. Louis reported no epidemics.

183. Fax from Gene Lukasik, Manager of Government Affairs, North Shore Sanitary District, Gurnee, Ill., May 24, 1999

184. The expert witnesses were specialists in many fields, ranging from aquatic biology to limnology (the science of the movement of lake waters from one level or location to another).

185. To comply with Judge Grady's order would require Milwaukee to excavate deep tunnels capable of holding 2,605 acre-feet of run-off compared with the 1,207 acre-feet required to comply with the Wisconsin state court order. (An acre foot is an acre to the depth of one foot.) Fax to author from Michael McCabe, Director of Legal Operations, MMSD, May 21, 1999.

186. EPA also hoped that higher charges for treating difficult pollutants, like metals, would induce customers to reduce discharges or undertake their own in-house treatment.

187. Herbert A. Goetsch, Commissioner of Public Works for Milwaukee, and Vinton Bacon, former Executive Director for the Chicago Sewerage District, then teaching at UWM, both of whom had worked closely with me as chairman of the SEWRPC Milwaukee River Watershed Committee.

188. Mayor Maier had appointed Williams to the commission upon the recommendation of Norman N. Gill, Milwaukee's highly respected civic watchdog. Gill had been impressed by Williams' chairing a committee of volunteer CPA's which recommended multiple improvements in the City Comptroller's procedures, all of which were accepted.

189. By further coincidences, my son Alexander (Sandy), twenty-six, worked for Williams, who in turn reported up the line to the president, my brother-in-law, Edmund B. Fitzgerald, the same person who had played an essential role in

helping Selig bring the Milwaukee Brewers to Milwaukee seven years earlier. (See chapter 2.) Fitzgerald, who could be as blunt as smart, later told me that he had assigned his nephew Sandy to work for Williams for two reasons: Williams was an outstanding accountant and excellent teacher but so tough that employees would never consider assigning Sandy to Williams as favoritism. Williams taught well but today happily admits he had good material with which to work; Sandy within eighteen years became president of Cutler-Hammer's acquirer, the Eaton Corp. of Cleveland. Five years later in 2000, he became chairman and CEO.

190. The mayor felt that much river pollution originated upstream outside his city but ultimately concluded – after Bauer briefed him privately – that the committee would help reduce that pollution. He then strongly supported the committee's work, even persuading a prominent Milwaukee legislator, behind the scenes, to switch his prior opposition to active support.

Chapter 18

191. The federal common law was a bundle of equitable principles developed in the United States Supreme Court to do justice in inter-state disputes over water pollution (Mo v. Ill, NJ v. NY), water allocation (Cal v. Arizona) (how much water could each draw from the Colorado river) and air pollution. (noxious gases destroying forests and crops (Tennessee v. Copper, 206 U.S. 230).

192. Congress in 1972, to help all cities finance the clean water construction program, authorized the EPA to reimburse up to 75 percent of the cost of local sewage improvement programs complying with federal standards. Congress substantially, but never fully, funded the program.

193. The EPA cited a Congressional mandate in the 1977 Clean Water Act that federal funding of sewerage system improvements be limited to those that were cost-effective. By this time the Comptroller General had specifically questioned the wisdom of advanced waste water treatment. *Comptroller General of the United States: Report to Congress: Better Data on Collection and Planning is Needed to Justify Advanced Waste Treatment* (1976).

194. See Missouri v. Illinois, endnote 182.

195. The court lengthened the usual interval between trial judgment and appellate decision to eighteen months by asking, after six months, for a second round of briefs on three technical questions.

196. 406 U.S. 91, 107 (1972)

197. A petition for a *writ of certiorari* asks the court in its discretion to review a decision below. In contrast, an appeal from an unfavorable decision is based on a statutory or constitutional right of appeal.

198. Barnes and Baxter had worked many late nights on the briefs. In appreciation, Zarwell and I paid their way to Washington so they could witness the Supreme Court argument without charge to the client.

199. Milwaukee v. Illinois, 451 U.S. 304 (1981).

200. Illinois v. Milwaukee, 731 F.2d 403, (7th Cir. Ill., 1984).

201. Appendix D summarizes, in chronological order, the six decisions ruling on which federal law (statutory or common law) and which state law (Wisconsin or Illinois) applied in this case.

202. Raymond Kipp, Dean of Engineering at Marquette University and Chairman of the Metropolitan Sewerage Commission of Milwaukee County; Harry Williams, member (and later chairman) of the City of Milwaukee Sewerage Commission; Vinton Bacon, Professor at UWM and former executive director of the Chicago Sanitary District; Paul Guthrie, supervisor of grants for the DNR; Gerald Schwerm, Village Manager of Brown Deer; and Herbert Goetsch, Commissioner of Public Works of the City of Milwaukee.

203. Harza Engineering of Chicago, designer of the big tunnel in Chicago; Stevens, Thompson, and Runyon of Portland, Oregon, then engaged by the MMSD to recommend a solution to overflows from the combined sewers; and CH2MHill for whom the presenter was Charles (Tom) Gibbs.

204. Donahue & Associates; Howard, Needles, Tammen & Bergendorff; Graef, Anhalt, & Schoemer Associates, Inc.; Polytech, Inc.; J. C. Zimmerman Engineering Corp.; Klug and Smith Co.; Camp, Dresser & McKee; and STRAAM, Inc.

205. In 1979 MMSD adopted a plan to subsidize plumbing repair work on private property in all MMSD communities, up to the extent of $160 million. See p. 161. Later eleven suburban litigants on February 12, 1982 settled their subsequent litigation against MMSD, ironically, by requiring MMSD to abandon its subsidy plan.

206. Much earlier, Ray Leary, the long-time famed chief engineer for both sewerage commissions, provoked by leaky laterals, proposed a law to require that laterals be made of more durable but expensive cast-iron. He lost.

207. To reduce the rivers' foul odor, by diluting their pollution, Milwaukee built two "flushing tunnels" to pump Lake Michigan water from the harbor into the rivers. A common saying among environmental engineers is: "A partial solution to pollution is dilution."

208. 1980 MMSD *Master Facilities Plan*, p. 27.

209. 1980 *CSO Facilities Plan*, Chapter 1, p. 11

210. Yet, eight years were to pass before Judge Grady dismissed his court order. First, the Court of Appeals consumed three years before deciding by a 2 to 1 vote the meaning of the 1981 Supreme Court decision. Then, Judge Grady took five years to determine that a reluctant Illinois owed interest on Milwaukee's costs, to establish the rate of interest, and finally to dismiss the case – in November 1989.

211. *A Water Resource Management Plan for the Milwaukee Harbor Estuary, SEWRPC Planning Report, No. 37*, March and December 1987 (two volumes). The DNR continues twelve years later to assess the water quality impacts of MMSD overflows. Jay Hochmuth in telephone interview, November 12, 1999.

212. MMSD 1980 *Master Facilities Plan*, p. 57

213. Kurt W. Bauer, "Deep Tunnel is effective, efficient," Letter to Editor, *Milwaukee Sentinel*, April 14, 1989. Bauer wrote to protest articles in the newspaper quoting "erroneous" facts and arguments against the deep tunnel by critics who favored separating the combined sewers. Some suburban officials revised those arguments in the fall of 2000 after some sewers, swollen with rain water, backed up into basements or by-passed into ditches and rivers.

214. Letter to author from Harry Williams, July 20, 1999, p. 3.

215. Form letter of Associated Public Contractors of Greater Milwaukee to influential Milwaukeeans, July 15, 1980, criticizing the deep tunnel proposal and strangely written almost six weeks *after* the commissions' decision choosing deep tunnels over sewer separation. Probably the opponents hoped that decision might still be reversed.

216. The form letter in the prior endnote cited the opinion of the U.S. Comptroller General. The opinion, incidentally, had been requested by U.S. Senator Percy of Illinois, a strong opponent of the Chicago deep tunnel. He who pays calls the tune.

217. Plaintiffs included within Milwaukee County: Brown Deer, Cudahy, Franklin, Hales Corners, Glendale, Greendale, Greenfield, Oak Creek, St. Francis, West Allis, and West Milwaukee; but not Bayside, Fox Point, River Hills, Wauwatosa, nor Whitefish Bay. Plaintiffs from Waukesha County: Brookfield, Butler, New Berlin, and Muskego. Plaintiffs= attorneys: George Schmus and Harold H. Fuhrman, long-time attorneys for Brookfield (Schmus succeeded the author at Brookfield in 1960) and Brown Deer, respectively. Complaint, Franklin v. Metropolitan Sewerage Commission, et al., Case No. 531-895, Par. 36.

218. Henry Maier fueled suburban distrust by career-long, bellicose attacks on suburbs and his disdainful refusal to meet with their leaders.

219. Harold H. Furhman, one of the suburbs' attorneys, told the press (incorrectly, as it turned out), "the suburbs did not believe the tunnels would ever be completed.... and the tunnels would probably be abandoned after the hazards predicted will be incurred." *Milwaukee Journal*, November 29, 1981.

220. Par. 36, *Franklin* Complaint, endnote 217.

221. Report of Chandler L. McKelvey, Secretary of Development, to Gov. Lee Sherman Dreyfus, April 1, 1980, pp. 26, 29.

222. *Milwaukee Journal Sentinel,* December 25, 1998.

223. MMSD "Comments on 'Sewer overflows in Wisconsin – A Report of the Natural Resources Board,'" March 15, 2001, p. 1, attached to letter of Anne Spray Kinney, Executive Director of MMSD, to Darrell Bazzell, Secretary of the Department of Natural Resources, March 15, 2001.

224. Letter from James Petersen, Senior MMSD staff attorney to author, July 15, 2000.

225. Interview with Kurt W. Bauer, August 4, 2000. Bauer additionally said: "Further, laterals are more poorly constructed and maintained than public mains. The installation of laterals is not supervised by the municipality. Finally, there are many more miles of private laterals than public mains." [Note Norquist's hasty retreat from trying to force owners to repair faulty laterals...]

226. Telephone interview with Jay Hochmuth, May 23, 2000.

227. "Sewer Overflows in Wisconsin – A Report to the Natural Resources Board," Wisconsin Department of Natural Resources, March 15, 2001.

228. Ibid., 38.

229. Ibid., 22.

230. Ibid., 40, 41.

Chapter 20

231. State ex rel. La Folletee v. County Board of Supervisors, 109 Wis. 2nd 621.

232. Section 20, Chapter 282 Laws of 1981.

233. The suburbs' complaint threatened to invalidate any bonds sold for sewer construction. Bond counsel would not approve the sale of bonds unless the suing suburbs agreed the sale was exempt from this threat.

234. The full task force included: Senator Lynn Adelmann (New Berlin), Representative William Broydick (Milwaukee), Mayor John Barlich (West Allis), Village President Henry Mixter (Whitefish Bay), Alderman John Kalwitz (Milwaukee), Alderman Richard Spaulding (Milwaukee) and Milwaukee County Supervisors Paul Henningsen and Paul Matthews. Milwaukee County Resolution 80.564.

235. See Thielen v. Metropolitan Sewerage Commission. 178 Wis. 34 (1922).

236. Ibid.

237. Wayne Caskey, a Universal Foods Vice President, John Gazierowski, a high-ranking Allen-Bradley Engineer, and Francis Wasielewski, son of a congressman and a politically sophisticated attorney. Wasielewski later became a well-regarded circuit court judge.

238. Letter from C. D. Besadny, Secretary, DNR, to Ed Jackamonis, Speaker of the Wisconsin Assembly, March 18, 1982.

239. Meissner explained to Rader that "our proposal attempts to defuse city-suburban distrust by inserting a gubernatorial buffer between the two sides. Dick Cutler had suggested this before." Letter, Meissner to Rader, December 3, 1981.

240. Broydrick had resigned from the Assembly on October 21, 1981 to become a lobbyist and obtained the district as his first client.

241. Letter of James Ryan, William Broydrick, and David Meissner to Milwaukee area legislators, December 10, 1981.

242. State Senator Gerald D. Kleczka, representing the South Side of Milwaukee; Senator Chester Gerlach, representing suburbs on the South Side of Milwaukee; Representative Mordecai Lee, representing the North Side of Milwaukee; Representative Betty Jo Nelson, representing the northern Milwaukee suburbs; Representative John Young of Brookfield, representing the "contract" municipalities outside Milwaukee County which contracted for service from the District but did not wish to come under its jurisdiction; and Representative Donald L. Stitt, representing Mequon, a contract community, and part of northern Milwaukee County. Meissner and Jim Ryan, whose task force had authored the basic elements of S 501, were also present.

243. Letter from Wisconsin Senator Jim Moody to Greater Milwaukee Committee, April 12, 1982.

244. Telephone interview with James Ryan, January 1999. Ryan was present in 1982 when Maier assailed the governor and many others.

245. Ibid.

246. O.J. White, a flamboyant, mercurial radio celebrity in the inner city, Kristine Martinsek, a capable city administrator, and Charles E. Gillette.

247. Wisconsin State Senator, Margaret Farrow, in telephone interview, January 1999.

Chapter 21

248. See Ch 5, p. 39, and Appendix E, Recommendations B-1 (b) and 6.

249. *Report of Metropolitan Milwaukee Sewerage District's Uniform Capital Recovery Committee*, October 10, 1986, p. 31.

250. *Report on Revenue Requirements of Contract Communities,* PMO, August 28, 1980.

251. Further, the PMO report, written in a period of maximum inflation (the prime interest rate reached 21% in 1980) noted that the 50-year repayment under the contract formula favored the contract communities. "If strong inflationary trends persist, the dollars repaid under today's contract between year 20, when Milwaukee County debt service has stopped, and year 50, when...capital recovery from the contract formula stops, will be all but worthless." In other words, the contract communities would be repaying the district for its borrowed funds in dollars worth a small fraction of what was borrowed.

252. PMO report, endnote 251. The DNR took comparative costs into account in determining whether a community could be best served by its own treatment plant or by a larger regional plant serving the entire watershed, such as the District's. The report suggested one or two municipalities might have lower costs in their own plants. However, the DNR would probably not have permitted separate small treatment plants. Reason: the DNR concluded large regional sewage plants with 24-hour staff and better equipment were more likely to avoid Clean Water Act violations.

253. Memorandum of David Meissner, executive director of the Greater Milwaukee Committee, to its Sewerage Task Force, December 15, 1983.

254. MMSD 1980 Master Facilities Plan, Vol 1-D, Ch 13, citing 1980 data and a $3.75 per $1,000 charge, later revised by 1983 to $3.50 per $1,000. The charge later dropped to $3.

255. March 1983 FLOW packet distributed to municipalities during FLOW's presentations in 1983.

256. Author's letter to Henry Mixter, president of the Village of Whitefish Bay, August 10, 1983.

257. Author's memorandum to the files, October 26, 1983.

258. Memorandum of David G. Meissner to GMC Sewerage Task Force, December 15, 1983.

259. Letter to author from William Mielke, January 25, 2000.

260. James Petersen, senior staff attorney, MMSD, in a note answering author=s question, December 6, 1999.

261. City of Brookfield v. MMSD, 141 Wis. 2d 10 (Ct. App., 1987)

262. Brookfield v. Milwaukee Metropolitan Sewerage District, 144 Wis. 2d 896 (1988).

263. In March 1989.

264. In legal jargon, the judge ruled that MMSD's presentation in its Facilities Plan of revenues through 2005 from the contract communities, based on their contract formula, "estopped" (prevented) MMSD from denying what they implied – a continuance of the contract formula even after the contracts were terminated in 1984. In addition, the court found that MMSD staff had told or written to some contract communities that the contract formula would continue – that status being the official policy at that time (but, unknown to them, shortly to be reversed).

265. Veto Message to Wisconsin Senate, Governor Tommy G. Thompson, December 8, 1989.

266. Not surprisingly, the adversaries in 2000 explained FLOW's refusal to sign

differently. Mielke, FLOW's representative then, states that he discovered errors in the District's predicted peak flow data, which the District refused to correct before the parties were to sign. Letter to author from William Mielke, January 25, 2000. Mielke wrote the errors were confirmed in a later analysis by MMSD around 1998. James Petersen, senior staff attorney for MMSD, who negotiated with the FLOW communities then, said the flow communities did not sign because the agreement forbade development in drainage basins within a municipality where peak flow data showed sewers to be overloaded. New development's additional sewer connections would lead, during heavy rains, to sewage either backing up into basements or being bypassed by the local municipality to streams or ditches, in violation of the district's discharge permits from the DNR.

The district believed it would be blamed by the DNR for the municipalities' bypasses. The municipalities suggested they be allowed development to the extent that unused capacity in their drainage basins mathematically offset the excess flow in their overloaded basins. The district, with implicit DNR support, said "No."

The communities said what they did within their boundaries was not the business of the district; their capacity for further development should be judged solely by the flow they delivered to the district trunk mains at their borders. Interview with James Petersen, January 28, 2000.

267. Brookfield v. Public Service Commission, 186 Wis. 2d 129, June 2, 1994.
268. The contract municipalities paid the District $106,833,603 in unpaid charges plus $23,166,398 for interest over nine years. Written response to author's question by James Petersen, senior attorney, MMSD, December 6, 1999.
269. Handwritten note to author from James Petersen, senior staff attorney, MMSD, January 16, 2000, revised February 3, 2000.

Chapter 22

270. Kurt W. Bauer interview, May 19, 2000.
271. Brady Corporation, Briggs Stratton, Delphi Automotive, Eaton Corporation, Emmpak Foods, Harley Davidson, Johnson Controls, Journal Communications, Miller Brewing, Patrick Cudahy, Rexnord, Rockwell Automation, and Tower Automotive. Recently, Falk, Harnischfeger, Ladish, and Master Lock have fallen below 1,000 employees. Waukesha County contained Cooper Power, GE Medical Systems, and Quad/Graphics, with over 1,000 employees as did Washington County with Serigraph and West Bend Company. Source: Bret Mayborne, Economic Research Director, Metropolitan Milwaukee Association of Commerce, June 18, 2000.
272. The Center for Urban Research at Rutgers University in 1992 estimated that sprawl consumed 59.7 percent more land than compact, managed-growth development. *The Costs of Sprawl Revisited, Tarp Report No. 39, (Costs)* National Academy Press, Washington, DC, 1998, pp. 18-19.
273. *Regional Land Use Plan Implementation in Southeastern Wisconsin; Status and Needs*, Memorandum Report No. 68, Southeastern Wisconsin Regional Planning Commission, 1993, p. 134.

274. SEWRPC, 1991 attitudinal survey. Table 10 (unpublished). A survey by Fannie Mae in 1994 found 80 percent of national households preferred single family homes. *Costs* 24, endnote 272.

275. In 1991, 20 percent of Milwaukee residents disliked the quality of schools in their neighborhood compared with 9 percent in 1972. SEWRPC 1991 attitudinal survey, Table 10 (unpublished). However, the Milwaukee Public School system never declined to the level reached in Detroit, Cleveland, and even Chicago. David Meissner, president, Public Policy Forum, in interview, July 25, 2000.

276. In 1991, 23.8 percent of Milwaukee residents disliked the level of personal safety in their neighborhoods compared with 8.8 percent in 1972. SEWRPC attitudinal survey, Table 10 (unpublished).

277. The percent of white enrollment in the Milwaukee Public School system dropped from 33.5 in 1989 to 20.2 in 1999. Public Policy Forum, *Public Schools in the Milwaukee Metropolitan Area*, 1999. Elected officials avoided mentioning race. It was politically incorrect to do so. Mayor Norquist in his 1998 book, *The Wealth of Cities,* sidesteps the race issue. But George Watts, a determined political novice, by clear implication brought racial fears into his opposition to a proposed light rail system. He stated that light rail would bring crime to suburban rail stations. The public knew what he implied, though he denied any such intention.

278. Robert Bruegemann, an urban historian at the University of Illinois, argues that sprawl started in nineteenth century Europe when horse and buggy and trolley cars linked "suburban neighborhoods" with the older centers of cities. *Costs* 35.

279. Milwaukee's bedroom communities may have resembled Westport, Connecticut. By 1945, Westport, with 5,000 residents including several hundred New York City commuters, boasted a town center including a library, half-timber English Tudor YMCA, a graceful colonial red brick two-story bank (designed by my architect father, whose zealous chairing of Westport's planning commission fostered my lifelong interest in land use planning), a motion picture theater, and twenty-five stores selling almost anything needed. Many homes were within walking distance of shops, schools, and jobs. I traveled by trolley car to a nearby city only to visit the dentist and take dancing lessons.

280. Or Westport, Connecticut, the town where I grew up, but whose subsequent five fold increase in population has changed it for the worse. Westport, between 1945 and 2000, had been transformed. Overpopulation, traffic congestion (three changes of traffic lights required to pass through an intersection), and overcommercialization drove Martha Stewart, one of its more famous residents, back to New York. City. *New York Times Magazine Section,* April 6, 2000, n.p.

281. SEWRPC, Regional Traffic Survey, 1991 (unpublished, the most recent such survey).

Chapter 23

282. *Costs,* endnote 272.

283. Ibid., ii. *Costs'* added: "In addition, buried down deep is a recognition that Americans are wasteful in their consumption of man-made (infrastructure) and natural (land) resources, and that their development choices are selfish in terms of impacts on central cities and the population within them."

284. Ibid., 2.

285. April 2000 update of a 1999 bulletin of the American Trucking Association. *The New York Times*, on June 7, 2000, n.p., after presumably researching several sources, wrote that trucks carried over 80 percent of cargo measured by value.

286. "Urban Sprawl: Not quite the monster they call it," *Economist*, August 21, 1999, p. 24.

287. City of Milwaukee Department of Development, (Mary Stott) April 2000.

288. *Regional Land Use Plan Implementation*, endnote 273.

289. "Economic Status of Milwaukee County Children, 2000," by the Employment and Training Institute of UWM, *Milwaukee Journal Sentinel*, May 29, 2000.

290. "2000 Spending and Taxing Report," Research Brief, Vol 88, Number 7, p. 3, Public Policy Forum, June 5, 2000. The five counties are: Milwaukee, Waukesha, Ozaukee, Washington, and Racine.

291. Ibid., citing Wisconsin Department of Revenue.

292. A Public Policy Report later predicted Waukesha County's tax base would reach $42.5 billion in 2005, passing Milwaukee County's $41 billion forecast for that year. *Milwaukee Journal Sentinel*, November 4, 2000.

293. *Milwaukee Journal Sentinel*, June 8, 2000.

294. *Public Policy Forum, Research Report*, June 5, 2000, p. 5. Milwaukee's rate was $26.52 per $1,000 equalized assessed valuation.

295. Wisconsin Statutes, 87.30.

296. *Regional Land Use Plan Implementation*, p. 121, endnote 273.

297. Ibid., Table 24, p. 67.

Chapter 24

298. "Urban Sprawl: Aren't city centres great?" *Economist*, August 14, 1999, p. 23.

299. Homicides (the most accurately recorded crime statistic) have dropped far more in some cities than in others. No one is sure why. Between 1991 and 1999 homicides per 100,000 inhabitants dropped in Milwaukee from 25.6 to 18.2. By 1999, other cities achieved puzzlingly disparate numbers: St. Louis, 30.7; Chicago, 28.4; Los Angeles, 11.8; New York, 10.5; Boston, 5. John M. Hagedorn, "Murder in Milwaukee," *Wisconsin Interest*, Summer 2000, 17-25, published by Wisconsin Policy Research Institute, Inc., Charles J. Sykes, editor. Hagedorn is Associate Professor of Criminal Justice at the University of Illinois/Chicago. Some experts believe tough, smarter policing (such as practiced by Mayor Rudolph Guiliani in New York) led to lower crime rates.

Others cite mandatory longer prison sentences or the decrease in both in the number of teenagers and crack cocaine users. Hagedorn hypothesizes that cities with lower homicide rates are those like Boston, New York, and Los Angeles which have transformed from manufacturing to the new economy and avoided a high concentration of its black population in segregated high poverty neighborhoods.

Hagedorn writes that Milwaukee scores poorly on these two counts. It has the nation's second highest percent of its workforce in manufacturing at 20.5 percent (second to Detroit at 27.8 percent). Milwaukee's percent of its black population in high poverty segregated areas is the highest in the Midwest at 46.7, more than double the rate in Chicago, Minneapolis, and Cleveland, all just over 21 percent.

300. Whitney Gould, "Make way for Downtown Housing," *Milwaukee Journal Sentinel*, April 7, 2000.

301. Ibid., citing The Brookings Institution Center for Urban and Metropolitan Policy and the Fannie Mae Foundation.

302. Many Milwaukeeans today wish the Brewers' baseball stadium had been located downtown but some concede that may not have been possible. A highly informed civic leader, Robert Milbourne, president of the Greater Milwaukee Committee, told me in April 2000: "The answer depends on whom you talk to and when you talk to them. Mayor Norquist did want it downtown and tried hard to accomplish it during the [1995] legislative debate on [Brewer] financing. Some will say that the Brewers opposed downtown and were afraid to move it for reasons that include parking, money, maybe even fear of downtown crime. Bud Selig recently said he would have considered moving downtown but there was no adequate site and the push for downtown came too late. There was not the leadership that should have pushed a good downtown location if there was one. If a downtown site had been identified and presented to the Brewers in 1990 rather than 1995, things might have been different."

303. Letter to author from Kenneth J. Warren, deputy director, Milwaukee County Transit System, July 20, 2000.

304. David Kuemmel, Adjunct Professor of Civil and Environmental Engineering, Marquette University, interview, July 11, 2000.

305. See also Map 12 for red line showing outer desirable growth boundary.

306. The Farmland Preservation Program enacted earlier by the legislature sought to preserve prime farmland. If a county certified that a farmer's land was prime farmland and he volunteered not to sell it during his lifetime, the farmer received credits against state income taxes. The credits proved to be too small to accomplish their purpose, being limited to 10 percent of the income taxes but no more than $600. *Regional Land Use Plan Implementation*, p. 114, endnote 273.

307. Ibid., p. 144.

308. "Farmland value skyrockets, Strong economy, development credited with 24% rise over one year," *Milwaukee Journal Sentinel,* June 17, 2000.

309. Joseph Laux, Mayor of Neenah, *Milwaukee Journal Sentinel*, June 6, 2000.

310. Author's recollection of what James Klauser said at their conference in Madison, April 1993. Mr. Klauser's written response to the SEWRPC committee's proposals repeated his views. It was contained in a letter on May 13, 1993 from the Secretary of Wisconsin Department of Transportation, Charles H. Thompson, to the author as chairman of the committee. It quoted the Department of Administration's response: "the Department...questions the existence of a widespread consensus that a problem exists in this area. We feel that a common understanding of the problem and its dimensions must precede the solutions offered by the SEWRPC committee....We recommend that SEWRPC take steps to create an intensified awareness of the problem and develop grass roots support for state-level action. Such a process will begin with town officials and the towns associations within each county and eventually develop regional consensus. At that time it may be more appropriate to discuss state involvement." SEWRPC, Memorandum Report No. 68, May 1993, Appendix A, at p. 150.

311. Letters from Senator Fred Risser to author, February 1999 and March 16, 2000 asking for comment on evolving drafts of his bill.

312. Andres Duany and Elizabeth Plater-Zybeck, a husband-wife architectural team who co-authored *Suburban Nation: The Rise of Sprawl and the Decline of the American Dream,* North Point, 2000. She is Dean of the University of Miami School of Architecture.

313. *New Urban News*, Vol 4., No. 5, p. 8, Sept-Oct. 1999.

314. Paul Goldberger, "It Takes a Village: The anti-sprawl doctors make a manifesto," *The New Yorker*, March 27, 2000, p. 129.

315. *Picture Windows: How The Suburbs Happened*, p. 253 by Rosalyn Baxandall and Elizabeth Ewen, Basic Books, New York, 2000. The above quotation appears in *Economist*, May 13, 2000, p. 9.

316. Goldberger, endnote 314.

317. "Town of Cedarburg acclaimed for its careful development," *Milwaukee Journal Sentinel*, November 7, 1999.

318. Michael Ruzicka, executive vice president, Metropolitan Association of Realtors of Milwaukee and Waukesha Counties, Inc., Wauwatosa, interview, July 11, 2000.

319. *Wisconsin Landscapes*, Newsletter of 1000 Friends of Wisconsin & 1,000 Friends of Wisconsin Land Use Institute, June 2000.

320. Kathryn Hayes Tucker, "Saying Goodbye to the 'Burbs'," *New York Times*, March 5, 2000, BU 1, 15.

321. Whitney Gould, "Cherokee Point's close-knit style recalls subdivisions of yester-year," *Milwaukee Journal Sentinel*, April 4, 2000.

322. *New York Times*, June 9, 1998, A-1. See also "Reforming Land Planning Legislation at the Dawn of the 21st Century: The Emerging Influence of Smart Growth and Livable Communities," Brian W. Ohm, Assistant Professor at UW-Madison, *The Urban Lawyer,* Spring 2000, p. 181, 193 (published by the American Bar Association's Section on State and Local Government Law).

323. *Wall Street Journal*, January 4, 2000.

324. Richard A. Lehmann's featured address at a SEWRPC conference in Milwaukee, April 17, 2000, entitled: "Working with the State=s New Smart Growth Law in Southeastern Wisconsin." Lehmann is a scholarly Madison land use attorney.

325. Ibid.

326. Wisconsin Statutes: 66:0295 (2).

327. Wisconsin Statutes: 66.0295 (2)(c).

328. Wisconsin Statutes: 66.0295 (2)(g).

329. David Cieslewicz, executive director of 1,000 Friends of Wisconsin, and one of the four prime lobbyists for the Act. Interview June 30, 2000. Cieslewiz knows Wisconsin well. He grew up in West Allis, graduated from UW-Madison, and served as Government Relations Director for the Wisconsin Chapter of Nature Conservancy. Cieslewicz explained, secondarily, that regional planning was no force whatsoever in the long negotiations over the Act. He cited an example. He suggested to legislators that an error-correcting technical amendment to the Act harmlessly required the newly drawn local comprehensive plans be filed with regional planning commissions as well as neighboring and overlapping jurisdictions and the state. The otherwise very helpful Chairman of the Assembly

Committee on Land Use, Michael Powers, said "No," pointing out that the lobbyist for CORPO, a council of regional planning commissions, had not appeared before his committee to make the request.

330. Wisconsin Statutes: 66.034 (2).

331. Wisconsin Statutes: 66.034 (1).

332. Section 1820, Wisconsin Act 9, 1999 Budget Bill.

333. Harland Kiesow, Executive Director, East Central Wisconsin Regional Planning Commission (ten counties surrounding Menasha), interview, July 5, 2000. Kiesow was an active member of an informal group drafting the definition of comprehensive planning, which communities are required to undertake.

334. *Milwaukee Journal Sentinel*, January 3, 2000.

Chapter 25

335. Brian Ohm and Erich Schmidke, *An Inventory of Land Use Plans in Wisconsin,* Department of Urban and Regional Planning, University of Wisconsin-Madison, Extension Rep. Series, No. 98-3 (1998).

336. "Urban Sprawl in the Governor's Back Yard," *Economist*, July 13, 1999, p. 27.

337. "Georgia Setting Up Tough Anti-Sprawl Agency," *New York Times*, March 24, 1999.

338. Alan Ehrenhalt, executive editor of *Governing Magazine*, New York Times, April 13, 1999, Op. Ed. However antisprawl measures often generate protracted fights between pro-development forces and environmentalists. See what happened in Atlanta two years later: "Collapse of Atlanta Talks Keep Road Builders Idle – Governor Breaks with Environmentalists," *New York Times,* January 4, 2001.

339. "The New Politics of Sprawl," *New York Times*, November 15, 1997.

340. "Battling Sprawl, States Buy Land for Open Space," *New York Times*, June 9, 1998.

341. *Regional Land Use Plan Implementation,* p. 145, endnote 273.

342. From 1.525 million persons in 1960 to 2.544 million in 1998.

343. "Georgia Setting Up Tough Anti-Sprawl Agency," *New York Times*, March 25, 1999.

344. Guy Burgel, head of the Urban Geography Laboratory at the University of Paris, quoted in "The Global Perspective: Fighting Urban Sprawl...Chicago, Paris Population Densities," *USA Today*, January 5, 2000.

345. David Shaw, senior lecturer at the University of Liverpool. *USA Today*, January 5, 2000.

346. Americans cherish the partly mythological legal right of a citizen to do with his land as he chooses. Or did. In the U.S. land use control is largely in the hands of the fragmented local governments, which are, unfortunately, often unconcerned or not guided by any rational area-wide concepts. Our states' decentralization of the power to control land use to local governments facilitates sprawl. Too often developers can obtain what they propose. They know local officials want added tax base. Often the officials do not measure, or are not professionally equipped to measure, the full economic cost of new development. Nor do local officials have a self-interest in considering the impact on neighboring communities. State legislatures by ceding so much power to hundreds of local authorities in metropolitan

regions balkanize land use policy there. Until now, Americans have wanted it that way, as the local government lobby consistently contends without contradiction.

347. *USA Today*, January 5, 2000.

348. Ibid.

349. *New York Times*, July 6, 2000.

350. "Urban Sprawl: not quite the monster they call it," *Economist*, August 21, 1999, p. 24.

351. Pietro Nivola, Senior fellow, Brookings Institution, Washington, D.C., cited in *USA Today*, January 5, 2000.

352. "Urban Sprawl," p. 24, endnote 350.

353. *Costs*, p. 21.

354. Romell, Rick, "Portland Keeps a Firm Grip on Growth," *Milwaukee Journal Sentinel,* October 26, 1999, p. 1.

355. Ibid.

356. *Washington Post,* September 27, 1997.

357. "Urban Sprawl," p. 24, endnote 350.

358. "Tri-Met's Strategic Direction," *Tri-Met Station,* a 1993 bulletin of the Tri-Met transit agency.

359. Genevieve Guiliano, University of Southern California, *Costs*, p. 22.

360. 1995 Wisconsin Act 27. The legislature planned to phase in the new method for assessing prime farmland by 2007. However, in 1999 the Department of Administration by administrative order accelerated the calculating of assessments to 100 percent on the new basis. Senate Democrats sponsored litigation challenging the action as not authorized by the legislature. The Dane County Circuit Court upheld the Department's action on October 31, 2000, saying a legislative committee assigned to review the Department's ruling had "taken no action to block it." *Milwaukee Journal Sentinel,* November 1, 2000.

361. COM 88.33.

362. Don Behm, "Before the Bulldozers Come," *Milwaukee Journal Sentinel,* November 7, 2000, 2-6. The approximate proposed heritage area was recommended earlier for preservation by two SEWRPC studies: the 1971 Milwaukee River Watershed Plan (designating environmental corridors and prime agricultural lands) and the 1997 Regional Natural Areas Management Plan (recommending over 400 specific sites in the seven county region for preservation, including 13 in the proposed heritage area).

363. A Dane County Circuit Court upheld Comm 83 in February 2001 but the plaintiffs appealed in April 2001. *Milwaukee Journal Sentinel*, April 21, 2001.

364. Another geographically smaller effort to establish a growth boundary of sorts occurred in 2000. The Milwaukee Metropolitan Sewerage District took steps to limit possible future extensions of its service area within five large outer suburbs. Only a portion of them are served currently. They are Mequon, Germantown, New Berlin, Muskego, and Franklin. MMSD's guidelines prioritize extensions to areas zoned for compact development (one quarter acre lots). MMSD said more compact development would lessen the length of sewer mains and laterals per homesite, thereby decreasing the amount of rainwater that gets into the sewer system. Franklin and other outer suburbs protested that MMSD sought to become a regional government and control their development. Inner suburbs' leaders, like

the Mayor of Oak Creek, and the Sierra Club agree with the evolving policy. The Metropolitan Association of Realtors warned MMSD that rigid restrictions might backfire by encouraging development to move further away from urban service areas (and use septic tanks. *Milwaukee Journal Sentinel,* September 26, 2000; *Milwaukee Journal Sentinel*, November 14, 2000.

365. Final Report of Metropolitan Study Commission, 1961, p. 21.

366. Ibid.

367. *Milwaukee Journal Sentinel*, September 22, 1997.

368. Robert D. Yaro, Executive Director of the (New York) Regional Planning Association, "Cities and Suburbs Work," *Harvard Magazine,* Jan-Feb 2000, p. 54, 107.

369. Information collated, courtesy of Milwaukee County Historical Society.

370. The Village of Brown Deer was incorporated in 1955 with an area of 1.8 square miles. Subsequent annexations increased this to 18.3 square miles in 1956 but the 1960 census cites 8.8 square miles in 1960. Further annexations and detachments made as a result of litigation reduced the incorporated area to 4.4 square miles in 1960.

371. Appendix B presents the statistics by individual towns and municipalities.

Bibliography

Books

Baxendale, Rosalyn and Ewen, Elizabeth, *Picture Windows: How the Suburbs Happened*. New York: Basic Books, 2000.

Maier, Henry A., *The Mayor Who Made Milwaukee Famous*. Boston Way, Md.: Madison Books, 1992.

Norquist, John O., *The Wealth of Cities, Revitalizing the Centers of American Life*. Reading, Mass.: Addison-Wesley, 1998.

Schmandt, Henry J. and Standing, William H. *The Milwaukee Metropolitan Study Commission*. Indiana University Press, 1965.

Schmandt, Henry J. , Goldbach, John C., and Vogel, David B., *Milwaukee, a Contemporary Profile*. New York: Praeger Publications, 1971.

Strauss, William and House, Neil, *The Fourth Turning*. New York: Broadway Books, 1997.

Transportation Research Board - National Research Council - *The Cost of Sprawl Revisited*, Tarp Report No. 39, Washington, D.C.: National Academy Press, 1998

Documents

Amman & Whitney, *Preliminary Plan for a Comprehensive Expressway System for the City of Milwaukee,* September 1952.

Metropolitan Study Commission

Municipal Boundary Problems - Report of Land Use and Zoning Committee - Feb. 23, 1959.

Annual Report to the Governor, October 15, 1958.

Final Report, 1961.

Major Recommendations of, October 1957 - June 1961.

Milwaukee Metropolitan Sewerage District

> *1980 Master Facilities Plan.*

> *1980 CSO Plan.*

> *Report on Revenue Requirements of Contract Municipalities*, PMO, August 28, 1980.

> *Report of Uniform Capital Recovery Committee*, October 10, 1986.

Milwaukee County Expressway and Transportation Commission

> *1968 Annual Report.*

> *1969 Annual Report.*

Public Policy Forum

> *Public Schools in the Milwaukee Metropolitan Area, 1999.*

> *2000 Spending and Taxing Report, Research Brief, Vol. 88, No. 7,* June 5, 2000.

Southeastern Wisconsin Regional Planning Commission, Waukesha, WI:

> *Recommended Regional Land Use and Transportation Plans: 1990,* SEWRPC Report No. 7, Vol. 3, March 1966.

> *A Regional Transportation System Plan for Southeastern Wisconsin: 2010,* SEWRPC Planning Report No. 41, December 1994.

> *A Regional Transportation System Plan for Southeastern Wisconsin: 2020*, SEWRPC Planning Report No. 46, December 1997.

> *A Water Resources Management Plan for the Milwaukee Harbor Estuary, Alternative and Recommended Plans, SEWRPC* Planning Report No. 37, Vol. 1, December 1987.

> *1991 Attitudinal Survey* (unpublished).

> *Regional Land Use Plan Implementation in Southeastern Wisconsin: Status and Needs*, SEWRPC Memorandum Report, No. 68, May 1993.

(Tarr) Task Force on Local Government Finance and Organization in Wisconsin

> *Report of,* January 1969.

Wisconsin Department of Natural Resources

"Sewer Overflows in Wisconsin," by Jay Hochmuth, March 15, 2001.

Wisconsin Department of Transportation

Milwaukee East-West Transportation Study, December 1996.

Major Articles

Cutler, Richard W., "Characteristics of Land Required for Incorporation or Expansion of a Municipality," *Wisconsin Law Review* (1958) 7.

Economist

"Urban Sprawl: To traffic hell and back." (May 9, 1999): 23.

"Urban Sprawl: Right in the Governor's Back Yard," (July 13, 1999): 26.

"Urban Sprawl: Aren't city centres great?" (August 14, 1999): 23.

"Urban Sprawl: Not quite the monster they call it," (August 21, 1999): 24.

Ehrenhalt, Alan, "New Recruits in the War on Sprawl." *New York Times* (April 13, 1999): Op. Ed.

Firestone, David, "Georgia Setting Up Transportation Anti-Sprawl Agency." *New York Times* (March 25, 1999).

El Nasser, Haya, "The Global Perspective: Fighting Urban Sprawl…. Chicago, Paris Population Densities." *USA Today* (January 5, 2000).

Goldberger, Paul, "It Takes a Village: the anti sprawl doctors make a manifesto." *New Yorker* (March 27, 2000): 128.

Gould, Whitney, "Cherokee Pointe: close-knit style recalls subdivisions of yesteryear." *Milwaukee Journal Sentinel* (April 4, 2000).

"Make Way for Downtown Housing." *Milwaukee Journal Sentinel,* (April 9, 2000).

Hagedorn, John M. "Murder in Milwaukee." *Wisconsin Public Interest* (Summer 2000).

Jones, Dick, "Odyssey of an Idealist, Activist; Ted Seaver sails a rough course toward the common good." *Milwaukee Journal Magazine WISCONSIN* (July 12, 1987).

Johnson, William A., Jr, "Smart Growth and Regional Cooperation: A Tale of a City and County." *State and Local News*, State and Local Government Section of the American Bar Association (Winter 2000).

Murphy, Bruce, "Selig's Secrets." *Milwaukee Magazine* (April 1994): 16.

Ohm, Brian W. "Reforming Land Planning Legislation at the Dawn of the Twenty First Century: The Emerging Influence of Smart Growth and Livable Communities." *The Urban Lawyer.* American Bar Association's Section on State and Local Government Law (Spring 2000).

Romell, Rick, "Portland Keeps a Firm Grip on Growth – Urban Boundary Forces Compact Development." *Milwaukee Journal Sentinel* (October 26, 1999).

Yaro, Robert D., "Cities and Suburbs Work." *Harvard Magazine* (January-February, 2000): 54.

Index of Names

A. O. Smith, 3, 4, 7, 242

Allis-Chalmers, 7, 36, 67, 244

Allis, John, 26

Ament, F. Thomas, 105, 106, 108, 110, 118, 224, 238

Amman & Whitney, 66, endnote 47

Bartholomay, William C. 10, 12, 13, 18

Bauer, Kurt W.
prods author to write book, vii; executive director, SEWRPC, 35 years, 63; highly respected, 63; says most planners favored freeways bypassing cities, 68, endnote 49; defines medium density neighbor-hood as one square mile, 81, end-note 73; suggests 6-6-6 Committee to break freeway dead-lock, 89, 90; reports 61 of 112 miles of approved freeways in Milwaukee County were built, 94, endnote 106; unlike, author thought Henry Maier was neutral on free-ways, 95, endnote 108; concedes government gave inadequate compensation and assistance to those losing homes to freeway construction, 96; ranked comparative present need for proposed freeways abandoned in 1977, 97-100; taught Sanasarian how transportation planning could solve community traffic problems, 103; heard Norquist admit Sanasarian was only person to beat him on a freeway issue, 104; conceptualized Milwaukee River Watershed Study, 123,124, endnote 190; briefed Henry Maier on Milwaukee River Watershed Plan,

137, endnote 190; Regional Water Quality Management Plan, 157; defends deep tunnel against critics favoring sewer separation for combined sewers, 162, endnote 213; warns MMSD against overestimating quantity of clear water municipalities would eliminate from their sewer systems, 167; explains why, 169; defines urban sprawl, 195; explains methodology for designing freeway capacity, 111, Appendix F. 257, 258

Berteau, George 61, 63, 89, 90, 92, 93, 124

Beuscher, Jacob, 49, 51, 52, 58

Bloomberg, Kathryn, 105, endnote 130, 232

Borchert Field, 9

Brannan, Robert W., 77

Braves, (See Milwaukee Braves)

Brennan, James, 197

Brewers, see Milwaukee Brewers

Brookfield, town residents ask author to incorporate as city, v; incorporated in 1954, 27, 31, 53, 235; author serves as Brookfield city attorney, v, 34, 36, 62; legislature authorizes to receive sewer service from MMSD, 39, 255; by 1999 had second highest assessed valuation in metropolitan area, 53; residence of early freeway opponent, 81; twenty minutes commute to downtown Milwaukee, 96; mayor of Brookfield says city suffers from lack of traffic capacity, 105, endnote 130; hit by 1997 flooding, 127; sues MMSD to block its financing solution to combined sewer overflows in Milwaukee, 163, endnote 217; legislative representative among warring factions invited by GMC to resolve deadlock on reforming MMSD governance, 177, endnote 242; unsuccessfully sued MMSD over rate base, 189, endnote 261; loses challenge before PSC against MMSD charging for capital improvements according to assessed valuation rather than sewer use, 192, endnote 267; an early railroad commuter stop, 198; median tax base four times that of Milwaukee, 202, endnote 290; tax base second to Milwaukee, 203; reduces large lot size requirement in old central business district, 215; Mayor Kathryn Bloomberg could conceivably join Mayor John Norquist in proposing growth boundaries on sprawl farther out from Milwaukee, 235; in 1992 loses two major sewer wars case in Wisconsin Supreme Court, 262, 264.

Brown Deer less than 2 square miles when incorporated in 1954, 24; grew to 4.4 square miles in 1960 after litigation shrunk a larger expansion, 251, endnote 370; original incorporation would have been forbidden by 1959 reform of incorporation statutes, 50; Town of Granville residents ask Brown Deer to annex 16 square miles, 29, 51; annexations over one square mile would have required court approval under 1959 (later voided) reform legislation, 51; 16 square mile annexation invalidated by Wisconsin Supreme Court, 29, 57,

85; served by North Shore Fire Department, 46; ignores SEWRPC 1971 advice to purchase flood zone homes near Milwaukee River, 127; after 1997 and 1998 floods, buys them, 127; advises MMSD that municipalities and homeowners should bear the cost of reducing overflows from combined sewers in Milwaukee and Shorewood, 159; joins suburban suit to stop MMSD from defraying such cost, 163, endnote 217.

Broydrick, William 150, 173, 177, 179, 187

Broydrick, Mrs. William (see Cindi Cukor)

Cahill, Harold , 154, 156, 187

Carley, David, 60, 62, 90, 93

CH2MHill, 135, 136, 140, 153, 165, 177

Columbia Hospital, 73, 74

Cukor, Cindi, 81, 82 endnote 75, 86, 87, 90, 96

Cupertino, Dan, 81, 86, 89, 104

Cutler, Richard W.
Raised, Westport, Conn., 3, 5
Civic positions: Fox Point Plan Commission (1952-1993), v; Metropolitan Study Commission (1957-1961,vi; Southeastern Wis. Reg. Planning Comm. (1960-1984), vi; chaired committees on: Milwaukee River Watershed (1965-1971), 123, vii; Freeway deadlock ("6-6-6") (1976-1977), vii; Regional Transportation Authority (1990) vii, 105, Urban sprawl (1992-1993), vii, 209; Wisconsin Legislative Council: Urban Problems Committee: Co-Drafted reform of municipal incorporation and regional planning commission

Fitzgerald, Edmund B., 11-14, 16, 19, 136, endnote 189

Foote, Robert, 35, 44, 45, 253

Fox Point, 5, 26, 34, 35, 38, 46, 103, endnote 124, 163, endnote 217, 186, 198, 249, Appendix B

Geilfuss, John C., 12, endnote 5, 83

Gibbs, Charles V. ("Tom"), 135, 136, 140, 153, 154

Gill, Norman N., 37, 46, 111, endnote 188, 160, 160, 174

Glendale incorporated in 1950 with less than 2 square miles, 24; such a small incorporation would have been prohibited by 1959 reform legislation, 50; grew to 5.7 square miles by 1960, 251 (Appendix B); sought to annex remainder of Town of Milwaukee in 1953, 25; encountered opposition of Fox Point, River Hills, and Bayside which hired author to help, 26, 27; obtained Lake Michigan water through jointly owned utility, 38; member of North Shore Fire Department, 46; legislation prohibited widening I-43 to six lanes north of Bender Road in Glendale, 102; many Glendale homes damaged in 1960 flood, 120; reservoir proposed at Waubeka to relieve that flooding, 124; did not purchase flood-prone homes as suggested by SEWRPC, 127; one of 15 suburbs suing MMSD to block its financing the solution of combined sewer overflows in Milwaukee, 163, endnote 217.

GMC, organization of 150 Milwaukee civic leaders, 33; disturbed by city-suburban fighting, 33; proposed Dineen committee to recommend solutions, 33; lobbied for creation of Metropolitan Study Commission, 33, which would have 15 members from private sector, 35; recommended all GMC commissioners except the author, 35; would be well qualified to have recommended several public officials to serve as commissioners, 47; appoints Sewerage Task Force to break legislative deadlock over reforming governance of MMSD, 176; which, when blocked by Henry Maier, successfully lobbied around him, 176, 177; wins credit from a legislator for its crucial role, 178, but condemnation by Maier, 179; GMC's executive director reports contract municipalities (FLOW) out-argued MMSD on how sewer modernization capital costs should be shared by municipalities served by MMSD, 187, endnote 258.

Goetsch, Herbert A., observes homeowners early welcomed the purchase of their homes for freeways, 79, 80; later hardship of losing homes was principal cause of early opposition to freeways, 80; lobbied Congress for funds for Hoan harbor bridge, 84, endnote 85; believes some abandoned freeways should have been built, 97-100; on SEWRPC panel advising level of service appropriate for freeways. 111, 257, Appendix F; on Milwaukee River Watershed Committee, 123; recommended author as attorney for CH2MHill, 135, endnote 187; recommended author to MMSD for defense in Illinois v. Milwaukee, 136; on panel selecting CH2MHill as

project manager of MMSD Water
Pollution Abatement Program, 153,
endnote 203; on SEWRPC
anti-sprawl committee, 209.

Grady, John T., 134-136, 139-149,
161, 165, 259, Appendix G

Granville, Town of, 22, 23, 25, 27-
31, 34, 235, 250, Appendix B

Greater Milwaukee Committee (see
GMC)

Griffin, Edward J., 73-75

Grossman, LeRoy M., 120-122

Harza Engineering, 123, 153, endnote
203

Hochmuth, Jay G., 155, 161, 170

Houghton, Albert, Jr., 45

Jensen, Robert E., 35, 37, 253

Kamps, Charles O., 76

Karaganis, Joseph V., idealistic
environmental attorney, 132, who
defeated Chicago-area air and
water polluters, 133, before being
hired by Illinois to sue MMSD for
polluting Lake Michigan, 133, and
mercilessly cross-examining
MMSD staff, 136, and negotiating
with author's team over standards
MMSD would be required by court
to achieve, 140; loses bet that U. S.
Supreme Court would not stay
lower court order against
Milwaukee until it decided on
Milwaukee's appeal, 145;
interrupted by Justice White in mid
argument, 146; misinterprets
Milwaukee victory in Supreme
Court, 147; more qualified to
handle Illinois case than others
even though 32 years old, 155;
inquisitorial, 156.

Kasten, George, 12

Katz, William, 135, 136, 154

Kipp, Raymond Dr., 153, endnote
202, 160

Klauser, James, 191, 213, 217, 263

Klotsche, J. Martin, 45, 46

Knowles, Warren, 72, 121

Kohler, Walter A., 33

Leary, Ray, 122, 123, 135, 157, endnote 206

Lee, Mordecai
elected at 28 to legislature, 82, 83;
believes sharp increase in young
legislators in 1970s attributable to
idealism rather than 60 percent
increase in legislative
compensation, 120, endnote 82;
assistant to Congressman Henry
Reuss, an opponent of proposed
Park Freeway West, 83, endnote
82; not persuaded by 1974
pro-freeway referendum to
moderate his opposition to
freeways, 87; attacks proposal of
County Executive John Doyne for
"gap closure" linking already built
Stadium North and Fond du Lac
freeways, 88; one of 18 legislators
campaigning to stop further
freeways, 90, endnote 96; member
of task force to recommend
alternative land use for abandoned
Park Freeway West, 90; works with
UWM planners to propose a
moratorium on further freeway
construction, 91, 92; threatens to
strip SEWRPC of its power to
"veto" federal grants inconsistent
with its planning recommendations,
93; says author "Saved my
District" by voting as SEWRPC
commissioner against Park Freeway West, 94; in 1988 defends his
opposition to freeways in 1970s,
96; with John Norquist led
post-1977 attack on freeways in
legislature, 101; chaired legislative
committee

considering Norquist's bills to emasculate SEWRPC, 102; in 1983 authored legislation to forbid widening I-43 north of Bender Road in Glendale, 102; in 1998 recounts why he opposed freeways in the 1970s and 1980s, 110; contends speed as a freeway purpose was not justified, 110, 111, Appendix F; on committee of warring factions in legislature which GMC Sewer Task Force urged to end deadlock over reforming MMSD governance, 177, endnote 242.

192, 202, 215, 231, endnote 364, 235, 255, Appendix E

Mielke, William, 183, 186, 187, endnote 259, 189, 191, endnote 266, 263

Milwaukee Braves, 9-12, 14, 235

Milwaukee Brewers, vii, 9, 12-14, 16-19, 207, endnote 302, 236

Milwaukee Journal, 7, 8, 26, 64, 86, 178, 196

Mixter, Henry, 47, 173, 187

Moody, James, 91, 94, 178

Moynihan, Daniel Patrick, 69

National Environmental Policy Act ("NEPA"), 80, 83

Nelson, Gaylord, vi, 40, 41, 44, 45, 60, 61, 90, 235

Norquist, John, attacks SEWRPC for violating one-man-one-vote court requirement, 40; but ignores opinion of attorney general to the contrary, 40; joins Seaver coalition fighting construction of more freeways, 81; elected to legislature at 25 in 1974, 82, 236; fails in 1975 to defeat county advisory referendum for freeway in his neighborhood, 87; but drafts letter successfully petitioning Governor Lucey to forbid construction of the Stadium Freeway South, 90; threatens to obtain legislation stripping SEWRPC of its power to "veto" federal grants for projects conflicting with SEWRPC advisory plans, 93; unsuccessfully asks Governor Schreiber not to renew author's appointment as SEWRPC commissioner, which Maier lobbied for, 94; in 1998 writes book, *The Wealth of Cities*, which demonstrates his ideological opposition to freeways, 96; unsuccessfully seeks legislation eliminating pro-freeway majority of commissioners on SEWRPC, 101, 102; unsuccessfully in 1995 asks U.S. government to decertify SEWRPC as the metropolitan transportation planning organization, 102; admits Sanasarian was only person to defeat him on a freeway issue, 104; champions light rail as alternative to more freeway capacity, 105; in 1998 advocates demolishing two elevated freeways downtown, I-794 and Park Freeway East, 106-108; obtains agreement of Governor Thompson and County Executive Ament to demolish Park Freeway East, 108, 238; attacks freeways for enticing industry and people to leave city, 112; while overlooking more fundamental causes, 112; presents many arguments in his book against freeways which are recited together with often contrary facts, 112-118; sponsors River Walk along Milwaukee River, 166; suggests city homeowners be required to repair leaky sewer lateral mains, then withdraws suggestion, 170; sidesteps the race issue in his book, endnote 277; member of New Urbanists devoted to designing mixed-use subdivisions conserving land and less dependent on auto use, 199, 214; seeks to reduce primary factors driving people out of Milwaukee, crime and poor schools, 206; helps launch school choice program in Milwaukee, 206; supported substantial increase in residential units in downtown, 206; works toward making downtown

Milwaukee more attractive to residents and visitors, 207, 208; could only dream of mass transit throughout the metropolitan region, as in Paris, 226; could logically ally with inner suburbs, like Brookfield, in favor of growth boundaries farther out, 232; could conceivably join with Waukesha county executive in proposing Milwaukee and Waukesha counties merge, 233; leadership potential declines in 2000, 234

Northwestern Mutual, 4, 7, 12, 16, 18, 33, 176, 201

Nowakowski, Richard, 124

Oak Creek, incorporated near airport, 25; Oak Creek Law drafted to enable incorporation, 30, 31; incorporation possibly would not have complied with standards of 1959 reform legislation, 50; obtained water from Lake Michigan, 38; proposed Belt Freeway would pass through, 84; development within proposed Belt Freeway route makes its construction prohibitively expensive today, 100; opposed demolition of I-794 in downtown Milwaukee, 107; one MMSD treatment plant located within, 187; opposed MMSD defraying cost of solving combined sewer overflows in Milwaukee, 130; one of 15 suburbs suing MMSD to block such action, 163, endnote 217; mayor of supports MMSD policy in 2000 of encouraging compact development in future outlying MMSD service areas, 231, endnote 364.

O'Donnell, William F., 152, 153, 163, 164, 172-174, 176, 178

Parkinson, George A., 37, 43-45,

254, Appendix D

Paulson, Norman, 156

Quarles & Brady, 12, endnote 5, 136

Rader, I. Andrew ("Tiny"), 176, 177

Recht, Samuel J., 137, 138, 141, 145

Rehnquist, William, 146, 147

Reuss, Henry, 83, 86, 88, 91, 120-122

Reynolds, John W., 17, endnote 13, 83

Ryan, James R., 173-179

Ryan Task Force, (see James Ryan)

Sachse, Earl, 48

Sanasarian, Harout, 103, 104, 160

Schlitz Brewery Co., 6, 18, 108

Schmandt, Henry J., 37, endnote 23, 43-45, endnotes 33-35, 62, 79

Seaver, Theodore ("Ted"), calls himself an "urban guerrilla" in fighting Columbia Hospital expansion, 75; early activist career, 77, 111; combatitive anti-freeway tactics baffle Expressway Commission but are admired by Henry Maier, 77-79; forges alliance to oppose six proposed freeways, 81, 236; wins John Norquist as ally, 82; Supervisor Dan Cupertino as ally, 86; four members of Seaver coalition join SEWRPC 6-6-6 committee which searches for end to freeway deadlock, 90; defends in 1998 his opposition to freeways in 1970s, 96; argues freeways designed to save 5 to 10 minutes commuting time do not justify the costs, 110; an amateur activist for the City of Milwaukee, not the region, 111

Selig, Allan H. ("Bud"), vii, 11-17, 136, endnote 189, 207, endnote 302

Shea, Edmund B., 5

Shebesta, Harvey, 77, 78, endnote 62,

304

Subject Matter Index

—